WORLD WAR II STORIES

THE BANZAI HUNTERS

THE FORGOTTEN ARMADA OF LITTLE SHIPS
THAT DEFEATED THE JAPANESE, 1944–45

PETER HAINING

CONWAY

In memory of Les Gunn, who led me into the Arakan.

Copyright © 2006 Peter Haining

First published in Great Britain in 2006 by Robson Books,
an imprint of Anova Books Company Ltd.

This paperback edition first published in Great Britain in 2007 by
Conway
an imprint of Anova Books Company Ltd
10 Southcombe Street
London W14 0RA

www.anovabooks.com

The author has made every reasonable effort to contact all copyright holders.
Any errors that may have occurred are inadvertent and anyone who for any
reason has not been contacted is invited to write to the publishers so that
a full acknowledgement may be made in subsequent editions of this work.

British Library Cataloguing in Publication Data
A catalogue record for this title is available from the British Library

ISBN 9781844860524

Typeset by SX Composing DTP, Rayleigh, Essex

Printed by Creative Print & Design, Ebbw Vale, Wales

Cover design by Lee-May Lim

The Banzai Hunters

PETER HAINING is a former newspaper reporter, magazine editor and publishing executive who now writes extensively on British history.

He is the author of *The Jail That Went to Sea*, *The Mystery of Rommel's Gold* and *Where the Eagle Landed* in the *World War II Stories* series, as well as other studies of the Second World War, including the highly praised trilogy, *The Day War Broke Out*, *The Spitfire Summer and The Flying Bomb War*. Married with three children and three grandchildren, he lives in Suffolk.

CONTENTS

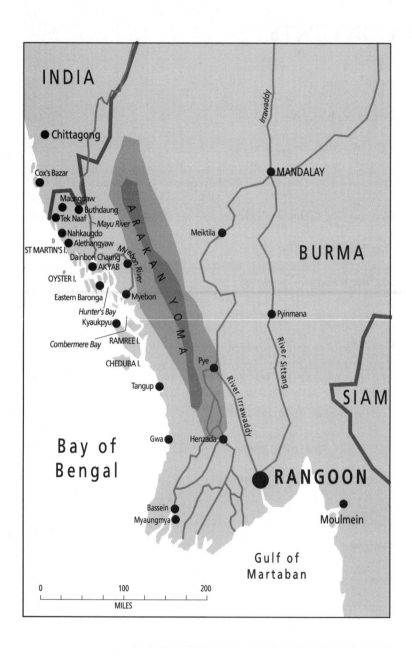

INDIA

Chittagong

Cox's Bazar

Maungdaw
Buthdaung
Tek Naaf
Mayu River
Nahkaugdo
Alethangyaw
ST MARTIN'S I.
Dainbon Chaung
AKYAB
Myebon River
OYSTER I.
Eastern Baronga
Myebon
Hunter's Bay
Kyaukpyu
RAMREE I.
Combermere Bay
CHEDUBA I.
Tangup

Gwa
Henzada

Bassein
Myaungmya

Bay of
Bengal

A R A K A N   Y O M A

Irrawaddy

MANDALAY

Meiktila

BURMA

Pyinmana

River Sittang

River Irrawaddy

Pye

SIAM

RANGOON

Moulmein

Gulf of
Martaban

0   100   200
MILES

Now we are going into battle you will conquer and overrun the British as you have always done. You will smash them and drive them into the sea. Now the sea will run red with your blood as well as theirs and you must take pride in it.

Colonel Tanahashi
CO Japanese 55th Division
Burma, 1944

ORDER OF THE DAY

Having been appointed Supreme Commander of the Allied Command for South East Asia, I address the following Order of the Day to all Forces under my command :

The formation of this Allied Command marks the turn of the tide. No longer do we stand on the defensive, we are passing to the offensive.

This has been made possible by the defeat of Italy, the staggering blows against Germany delivered by the Russian Army and the Allied Air Forces and the failure of the U-Boat campaign.

For a long time the Japanese claimed they were invincible. They based this claim on the victories they gained at a time when we were fighting for our very existence in other theatres, and when reinforcements to meet this new threat in the East could not be made available.

This Japanese claim no longer holds good. In the Solomons and New Guinea, in the Aleutians and in Burma, and at sea in the Pacific and everywhere in the air, the Japanese have received ample proof that they are not invincible. The Germans made the same claim and that has also been completely disproved.

Man for man, aircraft for aircraft, ship for ship, we have beaten the Japanese and we will continue to beat them.

The defeat of Germany is not enough. World peace can never be established until our lives and those of our families are no longer blighted by the constant threat of tyranny and oppression. This will only come about when Japan, the last of the Axis partners, has been forced to surrender. We can then look forward to the day when every man, woman and child, whatever their nationality, race, colour or creed can enjoy that freedom from fear and want which is their right.

The Japanese are determined fanatics who fight to the last man. We must be prepared for this. We shall not go into action until we are fully trained, fully equipped and in every respect ready for the task before us. Our weapons are already superior in quantity and quality, and will become more so.

Under these conditions, however determined and however fanatical the enemy may be, it will avail them nothing because we shall go into action confident of victory. We shall be confident because we know what we are fighting for and we shall know how to fight for it.

This Command combines British, American, Indian, African, Dutch and Chinese troops. Although we are of many races and of many tongues we must fight as one family with confidence not only in ourselves, but each other.

As the Nazi fortress in Europe crumbles, so will further reinforcements for sea, land and air forces become available on a vast scale. With Right and Might both on our side, final victory is assured.

Louis Mountbatten

SUPREME ALLIED COMMANDER

PREFACE

Although the time was not yet 10 a.m. the heat of the sun from the cloudless blue sky was already oppressive, burning the mangrove trees pressed together like so many sentinels on the grey mud banks of the narrow inland river. The only sound to break the stillness was the occasional anguished 'eek-awk' of a sampan bird high in the trees, or a sudden outbreak of childlike chattering from some monkeys in the lower branches. The intermittent noise of splashing might have been the sound of a crocodile sliding into the water – or perhaps just the quiet rumble of the boat in which the group of eight young men were travelling, their eyes scanning the hostile and alien terrain surrounding them.

The vessel – a Mark 3 Landing Craft Support (Medium), its initials LCSM and number 87 painted in black across its camouflaged blue bows – was moving at a few knots up one of the notorious *chaungs** along the Arakan coast of Burma, known today as Myanmar. The vessel had started a reconnaissance patrol at dawn and the tension had barely eased ever since the crew had entered the estuary, which each man knew could turn into a kind of living hell in a split second. At the wheel, the officer in charge, a Second Lieutenant, scanned the waterlogged banks for any sign of the Japanese troops he knew might be only yards away behind the foliage of the trees.

In the craft's conning tower, a tin-helmeted gunner methodically swivelled a .50 Vickers machine gun from one side of the narrow passageway to the other, constantly alert for a target. Beneath him, crouched just below the iron-plated sides of the boat, the remaining crewmembers fingered their weapons and kept watch: listening for any unusual sound or movement. Although this was not their first operation in the Arakan, the group of men, all in their early twenties, had heard enough tales during their time in Burma about the fanatical enemy they were up against to be constantly on their guard. The lingering death that awaited anyone taken prisoner by the Japanese, who were said to bayonet and behead prisoners, was just too horrible to contemplate.

As the landing craft neared a bend, the Second Lieutenant eased back on the two Ford V.8 Scripps 65 hp engines throbbing beneath his feet. He never

---

* *Chaung* A tidal inlet on the Burmese coast. These muddy watercourses vary from the width of a ditch to a river wide enough to carry small boats, particularly near the coast.

liked going around a blind corner too quickly because the maps on which he relied could never be assumed completely accurate. Certainly they were the best available: the carefully drawn blue lines indicating the courses of the rivers and *chaungs* were as up-to-date as the most recent reports by the covert small boat units operating on the Arakan could provide. But the LCSM was just over forty feet long and not easy to turn in a hurry when danger materialised – as it had a habit of doing in these days when, everyone sensed, an invasion was imminent.

The man at the wheel was just edging the boat around the bend when his radio – silent for so long that the sudden blast of static startled him – burst into life. The call was from Command HQ and the words were terse and to the point. A Japanese company had been reported in the vicinity of the *chaung* they were about to pass through and LCSM 87 was in danger of being cornered. There was no need for quiet now if the report was true.

'We've got to turn back *now!*' he barked to his sergeant standing by one of the bulkheads. 'We're surrounded by Japs!'

The officer's voice had barely time to reach the other men on the landing craft before the crackle of gunfire and a whoosh of shells broke out from the dense jungle. In that same instant, a terrible shriek rose from the undergrowth. It was not an animal noise, but it was full of wildness. The words would echo through the minds of the men on the boat long after the noise of the gunfire had ceased. It was a voice full of fury and deadly intent that had become increasingly familiar to those serving on the Arakan.

'*Banzai!*' it screamed, '*Banzai! Banzai!*'*

The Second Lieutenant hauled the wheel over violently and revved the engine to make a turn as the first bullets struck the hull of his boat. Even in those first frenzied moments of the attack, he did not allow himself to forget his training. The best way to get one of these babies around, he knew, was to drive the bows into the mangrove and use the yielding undergrowth as a pivot. As he did so, the boat began to swing sideways and he knew the hours of practise he had put in on training exercises undertaking this manoeuvre had not been wasted.

But the mere act of turning presented the unseen enemy with a better target. As the side of the boat became exposed to the further bank, a shell struck it and slammed one man against the bulkhead. A piece of shrapnel nicked the knee of a gunner crouching in the belly of the craft, his life almost miraculously saved by a tobacco tin which had caused the piece of flying metal to ricochet away from his

---

* The Japanese word 'Banzai' means literally, 'a thousand lives for the emperor'.

head and chest. Bullets also whipped around the heads of the other men as they tried to return the fire from the banks of the *chaung*.

Just as it seemed as if the boat might escape further damage, a direct shot hit the bows, splitting them open, sending a cascade of supplies and armaments into the churning waters. As the shell exploded, a terrible scream was heard above the crackle of gunfire and the vessel's racing engine. One of the crewmen just behind the bows had been hit and was slumped back onto the deck. His body jack-knifed on contact with the hot metal, accentuating the agony of his pain. When he rolled over, his torn shirt revealed a terribly lacerated back from which blood was now streaming.

The lieutenant completed his turn and urged every ounce of power out of the V8 engines. 'Now let's see if the bloody maker's claim of a top speed of 9 knots is worth the paper it's written on', he thought. The screw churned the normally tranquil waters into white foam and, moments later, the landing craft was around the river bend and beyond direct fire.

But escape from the shooting was only the start of the Second Lieutenant's problems as he got his first chance to look at the carnage that had only minutes before been his well-ordered and proficiently run boat. Three of his men were clearly injured – the gunner spread-eagled near the bow, obviously far worse than the others – and the shattered bow was shipping in water by the gallon with every yard he moved. He shouted at two of the crew to help their wounded colleagues and ordered another pair near the bow to begin bailing.

'Get shifting that fucking water,' he yelled. 'I don't fancy our chances if the Japs catch us'.

The next hour would be one that those on board landing craft 87 that January day in 1945 would never forget. Forty miles of river had never seemed so long. But thanks to the skipper's seamanship and a lucky encounter with another landing craft, returning to base through the maze of waterways, that offered the crippled boat a tow, the crew were able to reach the coast and the safety of Akyab harbour.

There was, however, no time for anyone to dwell on the events in the *chaung* until later that day. After the men had their wounds dressed and could begin to organise their thoughts, one fact was very clear. If they had not fully appreciated before that they were dealing with a well-entrenched and efficient enemy determined to hold onto the Arakan – and probably the whole of Burma for that matter – they knew now.

In fact, the message to everyone that month was clear. If the men of the Arakan Coastal Forces, as they were known, were going to defeat the 'Invincible Sons of

Heaven' as the enemy believed themselves to be, secure in the coastal waterways and jungles of the area – the Allied forces would have to show the same kind of expertise and courage as their colleagues who had triumphed the previous June on the shores of France. Although their mission to recapture Burma was as important in its own way as the bridging of the English Channel on D-Day, the environment and climate in which they would have to fight was infinitely worse, while the forces ranged against them were arguably better prepared and certainly better located to prevent an invasion.

It is these men, and others like them whose story is told in this book. Men who fought for every inch of the Arakan Coast in amphibious operations in small boats, as well as in covert attacks on land, to engage the Japanese on a second front while the troops of the Allied 14th Army in India struck south to retake Burma. Like the exploits of the soldiers of the 'Forgotten Army' – as the troops in the Far East war were labelled because their story has always taken second place to the achievements in Europe – it is also a little known episode and has been compiled from a mixture of official documents, contemporary reports and the recollections of those who were there. They were a dedicated band of individuals of all ranks, abilities and nationalities who launched a series of crucial operations to gain a beachhead against the Japanese. Their ultimate victory would inspire Winston Churchill to send a typically Churchillian message of congratulation: 'The Japanese have been challenged and beaten in jungle warfare; their boastfulness has received a salutary exposure'.

Together these men from all over the British Commonwealth wrote a remarkable story of subterfuge, audacity and courage in the dangerous waterways, hostile stretches of swamp and jungle and all along the coast of the Arakan that has earned them the enduring epithet of *The Banzai Hunters*.

1
MAJOR BINKS' NAVY

The man standing on the sun-drenched jetty looked like a figure from an adventure novel or from the pages of a boy's comic. Tall, bare-chested with a pair of shorts tied up around his waist with a length of rope, his only other items of clothing were a piratical scarf knotted around his neck and an ancient yachtsman's cap clamped on his head, which bore all the marks of having survived many storms at sea. As he stood looking across the harbour at the motley collection of vessels lying at anchor, the man acknowledged a number of greetings from passing servicemen and several local people. He was evidently a well-known and respected figure – and despite his unlikely appearance was actually the commander of a small naval force doing battle with the Japanese along the Arakan coast of Burma in February 1944.

Major T.L.F. Firbank – 'Binks' Firbank to his friends and those who sailed with him – was officially Commanding Officer of the 290th Special Purposes Company (Inland Water Transport) based at Teknaf. To everyone in the port at the most southerly point of India [now a part of Bangladesh] the flotilla was better known as 'Binks' Navy' and he was the self-appointed 'Admiral of the Fleet'. Together, he and his men, who were ostensibly in the transport business, were busy earning a reputation for their role in covert operations on the enemy shore, rescuing RAF pilots – and where possible salvaging their aircraft – as well as taking part in the occasional reconnaissance mission and lightning raid, most carried out under the cover of darkness.

The reputation of this 'private armada' – as some in authority liked to think rather disparagingly of Firbank's men and boats – was all the more remarkable considering the limited facilities and ragbag nature of the shipping available to them. The one great advantage the Major had, he believed, was that the Japanese had made no real attempt to gain control of the rivers and *chaungs* during their occupation of Burma. It gave him a sneaking feeling of superiority over the 'little yellow bellies' and a chance to pursue his boyhood passion for seamanship as well as an unquenchable desire to master the waves.

Tommy Firbank was a Somerset lad, born in the early years of the century. The son of a soldier in the Somerset Light Infantry, he had nonetheless felt himself drawn to the seas around Weston-Super-Mare and spent many hours as a youngster yachting in the Bristol Channel. Firbank was educated at Cheltenham College and acceded to his father's wishes by entering Sandhurst. In July 1929, he joined Sam Browne's Cavalry and served in various parts of the world. As a young captain, he was transferred to the Indian Army in 1937 and shortly afterwards appointed Adjutant and Quarter Master at Kitchener College at Nowgong.

After the outbreak of war, Firbank's organisational skills coupled with his knowledge of ships and sailing made him an ideal choice to be CO of the 290th Special Purposes Company – which was to include the remnants of the Inland Water Transport service whose crews had fled from Burma when the Japanese invaded – and he was sent to Calcutta in 1943 to reform the organisation as an amphibious military force. He set about his task with a mixture of dedication and undisguised eccentricity, recruiting men wherever he could find them – in particular spare Royal Indian Navy Volunteer Reserve officers – and turning a number of ancient river paddle steamers into sea-going vessels, mainly by installing teak planks around their guardrails to keep the sea out of the open engine room hatches. Plates also had to be added to the paddles to keep them in the water whenever heavy weather caused them to roll. Firbank is said to have issued his officers with a large spanner to tighten the bolts on the paddles twice a day and an axe to keep their crews shovelling coal!

According to an unpublished manuscript that Firbank wrote about his Army career and the war in the Far East which is now held by the NUS Library in Singapore, once he had raised a viable force the ships were sailed from Calcutta in batches of three and four to Teknaf which was to be their operational base. On the way, several ran into storms that threatened to sink them – one even survived a cyclone in the Bay of Bengal – and a U-Boat attacked another batch. A story that Firbank loved to retell maintained that when one of the paddle steamers was shelled and began to sink, the Royal Indian Navy Volunteer Reserve officer in charge hurled his spanner and axe at the submarine before taking to his lifeboat.

Teknaf was situated on a narrow peninsula that stretched like a skeletal finger for 84 kilometres from Cox's Bazaar – a picturesque Indian port with the world's longest unbroken beach and named after a British lieutenant who had created the community as a sanctuary for refugees from the Arakan in 1799 – to Jackson's Jetty where Firbank was now appraising his little empire. The harbour itself lay on the leeward side of the peninsula, facing the estuary of the River Naf with the Arakan coast on the opposite side. Just across the water on the mainland of Burma was the coastal town of Maungdaw and beyond that in the morning haze, the low-lying, serrated Mayu Hills draped by a black curtain of jungle.

For several months, Major Firbank's ramshackle navy had been working with the Allied forces on what were loosely termed 'combined operations'. Yet, despite the fact his organisation had no support staff and only the most makeshift repair and servicing equipment, it was already helping to execute successful strikes against the Japanese across the estuary in the variety of boats that the CO had recruited from all manner of sources, to augment the original bunch of paddle steamers – each mission carried out as quickly as possible and with the maximum economy of force.

The whole Teknaf peninsula was, in fact, garrisoned by British troops to prevent any possibility of an enemy assault. To some of these men the locality had an oriental allure with its low range of forest-covered hills full of red and green parakeets and wandering wild elephants, in addition to the myriad paddy fields and occasional pagoda glinting in the sun. The muddy, oozing, eastern shore of the Naf was less inviting, though, as were the dark, forbidding mangrove swamps: both a foretaste of what lay ahead for the Allies when they crossed to the Arakan.

The bustling community around the harbour consisted of a conglomeration of native *bashas* – native dwellings or huts – interspersed with a number of larger buildings for maritime work and local commerce. The inhabitants, though, were known to be a very mixed bunch indeed. In the words of Firbank's account Teknaf was, 'a nest of spies, rumour-mongers and doubtful characters of all sorts, including a great many Mughs'. The Major had made a point of learning all about the traits of these local people divided into two groups by race and language. They were either Buddhists – like the Mughs – or Muslims, referred to as Chittagongians after the Indian district from which they had originated. Both hated the other, and in Firbank's estimate – like that of many others – were reckoned to possess a mixture of primitive habits, shrewd intelligence and strong passions.

The Mughs, who spoke a dialect of Burmese, were referred to locally as the Arakanese and were said to be lazy, treacherous and pro-Japanese. The men were distinguished by smooth, hairless faces and the women by vivid red lips that were caused by eating betel nut – which they chewed constantly and spat out regularly. They all loved colourful clothes – the men wearing bright *lungyis* and the woman red drapes – and both sexes smoked endless cigars.

The Chittagongians, by contrast, spoke Bengali and Urdu, were thrifty, hard working and loyal to the British. Although they had a reputation for being superstitious, quarrelsome and terrible liars, they were generally peaceful, stoical and, since the start of the war, had frequently risked their lives and liberty in the Allied cause. Grateful for the protection they received from the British against their hereditary enemies, the Chittagongians had proved themselves to be experts at intrigue and deception and made good scouts and spies behind the Japanese lines. Crucially, they were also skilled boatmen, especially in the use of their dugout canoes known as *kistis*.

The uneasy mix of these two tribes in Teknaf existed even before the war had given the place a notorious reputation. It had become known as a centre for drug trafficking, smuggling and similar devious rackets. According to Major Binks' report, quite a number of those who lived in the town were 'known or suspected fifth columnists' – including almost every policeman – and political agitators travelled regularly between Burma and India, 'spreading their malice against the enemies of their paymasters, the Japs'. The resourceful Binks' had, though, been able to capture some of these troublemakers trying to skulk up the River Naf after nightfall in their *kistis*.

It was against this unsettled background that the ebullient Firbank had been building his small armada of river and sea-going vessels – starting with the remnants of the old Burmese Inland Water Transport services that had been in existence for almost a century. Founded by the British Authorities in India in 1852 during the second Anglo-Burmese war, the company had transported troops, stores and mail from Calcutta to Rangoon until the end of the conflict when it was turned over to commercial work and opened up new routes. The three original ships of the IWT, the *Lord William Bentinck, Damoodah* and the *Nerbuddha,* were soon augmented by sailing ships, tugs, cargo flats and paddle steamers. As the service flourished, further vessels were built, including the comically named *Colonel Phayre* and *Colonel Fytche* – after two old colonial veterans – plus various small river craft, launches and motor boats, to ply the rivers and *chaungs* of the Arakan coast. Within a decade, a whole network of routes was in operation – the longest of these by river over 1,000 miles from Mandalay to Rangoon.

The outbreak of the Second World War and the invasion by the Japanese had seen a dramatic change in the fortunes of the Inland Waterway Transport services. In February 1942, the company fleet comprised over 650 vessels of all types from the large *Express Steamer* – 326 feet long – to steamers, paddle boats, ferries, tugs and even miniature pilot launches. A General Evacuation Order was given to the captains and crews of all these boats to 'proceed upcountry and scuttle all units at different places' to prevent them from falling into the hands of the Japanese. Within days, much of the once large fleet was lying on river beds or sunk in the *chaungs* – in one place alone, the market town of Katha, some 75 ships were sunk in as many hours.

Not every captain obeyed the order, however. A number steamed off to Indian ports like Calcutta, while others made for Cox's Bazaar and Teknaf, some even hoping they might be useful when the British began the task of retaking Burma. It was these IWT remnants, supplemented by local craft belonging to the Chittagongians and a few others probably obtained by coercion or threat, that Major Firbank was under orders to turn into a combined operations task force under the banner of the 290th Special Purposes Company. The idea might have been typical of the makeshift expedients that the British Army was forced to employ when situated far from normal supplies, but it still lit the flame for amphibious operations on the Arakan coast. The omens, though, were not good to begin with, as John Ehrman has written in *Grand Strategy* (1956):

> The Navy viewed the rivers and chaungs of the Arakan as arterial roads: but they were roads which were unlit, unsignposted, of uncertain surface, obstructed by hidden traffic bollards and unexpected road-works, where the motorists could be shelled and mortared by hostile pedestrians. Much of the 'domestic' work of transportation was to be done by the Inland Water Transport – an armada of various craft assembled to supply the Army by water – although their 'turnround' times for loading and unloading were to prove twice as long as the Navy's and naval craft shared some of the burden.

Precise details of the make-up of 'Binks' Navy' in its formative months are difficult to trace, but Wilfred Granville and Robin A. Kelly offer a typically colourful resumé in their lively history, *Inshore Heroes* (1961):

> To begin with the 290th Company consisted of eight old, unwieldy, wood-fired river steamers, four motor launches, and about a dozen Fleming lifeboats which were taken on tow and intended to be used as 'assault craft'. All were wholly innocent of navigational gear. They were manned by Bengali civilians, a very windy lot, and commanded by sporting young Indian Army officers whose ignorance of seamanship was total. Their CO, the debonair Major 'Binks' Firbank, found them 'nice chaps but a wildly undisciplined lot, who took a little bringing to heel'.

The few contemporary accounts of Firbank's flotilla refer to the paddle steamers as being armed with anti-tank guns mounted on wheels to move around the decks,

9

with the ubiquitous .303 inch Bren guns capable of firing 500 rounds per minute for anti-aircraft defence. The crews were mostly made up of local fishermen lead by subalterns who to begin with had very little knowledge of the sea. One report says that the navigation of the ships had to be 'seen to be believed' and on a notorious occasion a captain awoke one morning to find a cow looking through his porthole and his vessel stranded several hundred yards from the water! It apparently remained stuck fast in the mud until the next spring tide. As to messages being passed between the crews, it is said that on some vessels this was achieved by the crews lighting fires on the decks!

Notwithstanding how much 'bringing to heel' Firbank had to use on his untrained crews, the boats in his little navy did begin to demonstrate their usefulness in missions on the Arakan as the war in Burma entered its final phase in 1944. One man who could vouch for this was Lieutenant Leo Green of the Royal Indian Navy who worked with Firbank in a number of the Major's more hazardous operations. Green was a young naval officer who had been transferred from England to the RIN in March 1942 and saw out the Burma campaign as a member of the Arakan Coastal Forces which were established two months later.

This group of versatile small boats, crewed by men of the four Allied navies including the 55th and 56th Royal Indian Navy, 49th South African and 59th Burma Motor Launch Flotillas, was commanded by the authoritarian Captain John Ryland RIN, known to his staff and men with mixed feelings as 'Daddy' Ryland. Born in Surbiton in 1900 and educated at King's College School, he had joined the Royal Indian Navy and gained his 'sea legs' on HMS *Conway*. Ryland's naturally steely manner and attention to detail during the war years would later see him become a respected judge in British Columbia from 1969 until his death in 1991.

Lieutenant Green's launch was ML 413, a Fairmile B, attached to the 56th Flotilla of the 13th and 14th Fairmile Flotillas, said to be among the oldest and most experienced of the Coastal Forces. During his service in the Far East, the lieutenant underwent several testing maritime experiences as a result of which he came to share the view of those who described the Fairmile as 'a small warship' and one of the most versatile of all the craft to be used on the Arakan. The gunboat had originally been designed for anti-submarine patrols and rescue duties in British waters, where it quickly built up a reputation for being able to tackle the toughest wartime coastal assignments. These capabilities made it equally well suited for the dangerous waterways and *chaungs* of Burma – it's success a sharp reproof to those in authority whose initial indifference had almost left it stillborn.

The Fairmile had been designed in the early months of the war by the English boat-builder, Noel Macklin, who was convinced of the need for a new type of gunboat to operate in coastal conflicts. Indeed, so sure was he of his concept, that he personally financed the creation of a prototype to convince officials at the Admiralty. With a top speed of 20 knots, the launch could carry a crew of 16 – including a helmsman, two lookouts, a main gunner, two Anti-Aircraft (AA) gunners and a port and starboard machine gun – and was deliberately heavily armed to protect coastal shipping from marauding submarines. The 'small warship' proved itself very efficient at patrolling the approaches to ports, escorting convoys, chasing sea born raiders and operating in the harshest weather conditions.

Perhaps, though, the Fairmile B's greatest attribute in wartime was that it was prefabricated. It could be put together from a wooden kit and electrical and mechanical components manufactured at the Fairmile factory near London and shipped anywhere in the world for assembly. ML 413 had, though, been built in Bombay with a teak hull and was 112 feet long, with a bream of 18 feet and a draft of 3.6 feet. Powered by two American 650hp V12 Hall-Scott 'Defender' petrol engines, it weighed in at 65 tons and had a range of 840 miles at 12 knots.

The armament on Lieutenant Green's boat was similar to that of the other Fairmiles operating from India, consisting of a standard Bofors 40 mm AA gun on the fo'castle, two 20mm Oerlikons as secondary weapons, and a pair of .303 Lewis MG guns on the quarterdeck. The boat could also carry up to 16 depth charges when required. Apart from its crew, the vessel had enough room to effectively double its complement of passengers when it began taking part in recce operations and dropping off squads of intelligence gatherers and marines on the coast of Burma.

The skipper of ML 413 has been described by those who knew him as 'probably the most unflappable officer on the Arakan'. A conscientious and committed navy man, Green possessed a quiet nature that belied his earlier prowess as a boxer at Christ's Hospital School. After being commissioned, he had joined the 13th Fairmile Flotilla at Lowestoft where his desire for action – not to mention his sense of humour – was soon made evident when he was ordered to plot a course from the East Anglian coast to Weymouth. After wrestling for some time with a mass of charts, data and information, he noticed a slip of paper pinned to a notice board, 'Volunteers for India'. As soon as he had finished his task, it is said, he turned to his CO and informed the somewhat startled man, 'Cheerio – I'm off to India!'

On the sub-continent, Leo Green undoubtedly discovered his forte and began building a happy team on ML 413 with his 'No.1', Lieutenant W.R. 'Dixie' Dean and Midshipman, Paul Usher. Like all crews at the time, the men were thrown together in very close proximity to share in the tedium of patrol duties that could so suddenly be interrupted by intense bursts of action. Green was a great believer in 'democratic' discipline, allowing his men time to get to know each other's little ways and generating a kind of 'family' atmosphere that enhanced the effectiveness of the launch in action. Indeed, this sense of camaraderie was very much in evidence when the gunboat sailed out with the 'piratical' Major Binks on several missions.

These operations included looking out for RAF pilots believed to have crashed on offshore islands, spying on enemy positions and even one or two small assaults. On some of these missions, Firbank would do no more than supply a couple of river steamers and their crews or alternatively six *kistis* for more urgent assignments. Usually when it was planned to raid enemy positions, Firbank would insist on going along to personally command his ships. After one operation at the helm of the steamer *Torotua,* to gather information about troop movements on the coast near Indin, the Major returned with invaluable pay books, letters and an enemy flag found in a deserted Japanese encampment. The documents were, of course, quickly handed over to the Army's Intelligence Service for study, but the flag was presented to the delighted 'Admiral' to hang in his wardroom.

A typical mission for Green and Firbank occurred on 12 February 1944 when they were sent to investigate reports that the Japanese had mounted a gun on the banks of a *chaung* near the town of Alethangyaw. It was believed to be the latest in a complex of coast-watching detachments that were being set up along the Arakan. The outcome of their foray is described in Green's log with his characteristic straightforward attention to detail:

At 16.45, ML 413 contacted Major Firbanks in steam launch, Damoodah, *and received instructions to rendezvous at Narik Eldia Point at 18.00. At 19.46, the second ship, steam launch* Kamakyi *had not arrived and MI 413 undertook her duties, embarking a raiding party and Captain Maurice Budd. Thereafter the two vessels proceeded in company to a point three miles south of Sitaparokia. The whole of this area was strongly held by the Japanese and the raiding force therefore approached with caution. At 23.22, the raiding party embarked in one Fleming lifeboat and proceeded ashore, ML 413 anchoring 7 cables off the beach. At 1.05, bursts of light automatic fire indicated that the raiding party was in contact with the enemy and the Fleming lifeboat was seen to be returning at 1.45. They were embarked by ML 413 at 2.10 and, with the lifeboat in tow, contact was established with the* Damoodah *and the party transferred to this vessel.*

These plain facts give little clue to the dangers faced by the landing party or that Firbank's ancient steamer was within Japanese range. Records of the time indicate that a number of similar land and sea operations were carried out during the rest of February, March and early April, along with some sporadic raids by RAF fighter bombers stationed in India that were parried by Japanese fighters based on the coast. At this point, the monsoon season finally broke across Burma and both forces had little option but to settle down as best they could under the torrential rainstorms and wait for them to end in October.

Unknown to both the Allied and Japanese forces, however, the winter of 1944 would see the start of the crucial conflict that has become known in the history of the war in the Far East as the 'Third Arakan'. It would also see the arrival of a number of small boat units that had been trained and equipped in a manner that 'Binks' Firbank could only have dreamed about. Together these brave and resourceful men would launch a series of amphibious operations that would help to change the course of the war in Burma after three merciless years of Japanese occupation.

*   *   *

The story of the coastal war on the Arakan begins in the immediate aftermath of the infamous bombing raid by 360 Japanese warplanes on Pearl Harbour on 7 December 1941, which killed over 3,000 American servicemen, badly damaged the US Pacific fleet and brought the nation into the Second World War. Within days, Japanese forces had made equally unprovoked invasions against ten other Asian countries, of which Burma was one. On Christmas Day, Hong Kong fell to the Japanese when an enemy force of over 40,000 men overwhelmed 6,000 British and Commonwealth troops. A similar lightning strike against British-held Malaya was followed by the surrender of the great naval base and fortress of Singapore on 15 February 1942. A grim-faced Winston Churchill described this seizure as a 'heavy and far-reaching military defeat' which demanded of everyone the Battle of Britain spirit: 'That calm and poise, combined with grim determination, which not so long ago brought us out of the very jaws of death'.

The same sad tale was repeated in Burma, where 100,000 Japanese troops of the four divisions of 15th Army commanded by Lieutenant General Shojiro Iida stormed the country and occupied Rangoon on 8 March. Then, while orders were frantically being given for the destruction of all the country's main oilfields so that they did not fall into the hands of the invaders, the British Army began one of the longest retreats in military history under the most testing conditions –

outnumbered, lacking air superiority and with the majority of soldiers completely unprepared for jungle warfare. The men did, though, learn about the enemy – and learn fast.

The 1st Battalion Gloucestershire Regiment and 2nd Battalion King's Own Yorkshire Light Infantry under the command of General Sir Harold Alexander – with a certain Lieutenant General William Slim, as Corps Commander – withdrew in four months over 1,100 miles to India. By 2 May, the Japanese had taken the fabled city of Mandalay and forced the last of the sodden, ragged and malaria-ridden British, Indian, Burmese and American-led Chinese troops back over the Himalayan foothills into a kind of safety, albeit one reached with a sense of defeat and heartbreak. At the end of March and having reached the border, the Japanese offensive halted. Here the Imperial Army waited for the monsoon season to pass and what would surely be the next step in their apparently inexorable progress – the invasion of India.

As history now shows, starting from their land and sea bases in India, the Allies would require three attempts to take back what had been so brutally torn from them. The 'First Arakan' – as it has become known – was invoked in September 1942: a diversionary land advance down the Mayu Peninsula by the 14th Indian Division mounted by General Sir Archibald Wavell, the C-in-C Indian, and intended to be followed by a major seaborne assault on the island of Akyab to capture its vital airfield. But as John Winton, a former Navy Lieutenant Commander turned historian, has written in his excellent book, *The Forgotten Fleet* (1969), a plan that began hopefully ended in near-disaster:

The campaign was conducted with a disastrous mixture of delaying caution – so as not to prejudice this first British offensive against the Japanese – and (for some reason) a reckless determination to continue long after all hope had gone. The enemy was allowed time to reinforce positions which could have been captured easily earlier in the campaign. By March 1943, the army was bogged down in a bitter struggle at Donbaik and Rathebaung, which the Japanese had made into formidable defensive positions. When the Japanese launched a series of out-flanking hooks through supposedly impenetrable jungle and across 'impassable' mountain ranges, the check became a stalemate, the stalemate a withdrawal, which quickly became a full-scale retreat to avert catastrophe. By May, the army was back where they had started eight months before and profoundly depressed. It really did appear that the Japanese were invincible in the jungle.

It was evident, too, that the number of vessels available at the time for the amphibious operation was insufficient for the size of the task. All that could be mustered of the efficient Fairmile B gunboats were six from the Royal Indian Navy and five in service with the Burma Royal Navy Volunteer Reserve, plus under one hundred other various ships whose numbers included just 46 landing craft. Although the plan came to nothing, it is worth taking a look at the four types of these craft that were to take part because they will all feature repeatedly in our story.

The largest convoy consisted of 24 Landing Craft, Assault (LCAs), the first British standard assault type vessel that was carried on davits (a small crane for lowering boats) on transport ships and used primarily for raiding operations or large-scale landings of troops. Just over 40 feet long and propelled by two 65hp Ford V-8 engines with twin screws, the LCA could carry 35 troops and 800lbs of equipment. With a range of up to 80 miles at 6 knots when fully loaded, it was armed with a Bren gun in the port cockpit, two .303 Lewis guns and two 2 inch mortars aft.

Next in terms of numbers were the nine Landing Craft, Mechanised (LCMs) – hefty, 45-foot long vessels crewed by six men and purpose built to land a single tank or miscellaneous vehicles on a beach. With an endurance of 56 miles, the LCM was driven by two 60hp Thornycroft petrol engines and could achieve a maximum speed of just over 7 knots. Seven wooden Landing Craft, Personnel (LCP) were added to the roster, each specifically designed for beach landings on difficult coasts. They were capable of carrying 25 fully equipped soldiers for 120 miles at speeds of up to 11 knots. Just less than 37 feet long, the LCP was powered by a Hall-Scott 250 hp petrol engine and crewed by an officer and three men. It had an enclosed cockpit for the gunner armed with a .303 Lewis gun.

The last batch of small vessels, Landing Craft, Support (LCS), had the same hull design as the LCA and were transported to the landing area on davits in order to provide support for assault troops with a battery of machine guns and smoke mortars. Also built of wood but largely encased in 10lb plating, they were 41 feet long, powered by two Ford V-8 65hp engines, had a top speed of 10 knots and a range of 60 miles when fully loaded. One officer, three men and the seven-strong gun crew operated two .50 calibre machine guns, two .303 Lewis guns and one 4 inch smoke mortar. The formidable LCS could also be beached.

Lined up to support these 46 vessels were a number from Firbank's resources including four river steamers, the *Torotua, Athitaka, Surmai* and *Yengua;* three paddle steamers *Aimak, Kadari* and *Uzbek* plus 30 Fleming lifeboats. The headquarters ship was to be the *Barracuda* – a former Danish vessel named the *Heinrich Jensen* – plus two petrol tankers to supply the invasion fleet. However, when the

15

warships and air support that had been earmarked for the assault at Akyab and which might just have made all the difference became 'unavailable', the landing had to be cancelled. The *London Gazette* would later explain the sorry reason for this:

The capture of Akyab had been originally planned as a sea borne expedition, for which the 6th British Brigade of the 2nd Division had been specially trained and was to form a landing force with the 29th British Brigade which had taken part in the Madagascar operations. Unfortunately, the 29th Brigade and their landing crews suffered from Malaria in Madagascar and had to be sent to South Africa to recuperate. It became apparent that neither naval escorts, transports, landing craft, nor air forces to cover the landing would be available in sufficient numbers to undertake the expedition which had every prospect of success if it could have been carried out at the end of 1942 or beginning of 1943, since the Japanese garrison on Akyab was small and there were few defences on the island.

In hindsight, it would appear that the only positive move towards the ultimate goal from this period was the establishment of the naval base at Teknaf and the first combined amphibious operations carried out against the enemy on the Arakan by the army and navy – not forgetting the intrepid 'Major Binks' Navy.

* * *

General Katakura Tadashi, the Burma Area Army's Chief of Staff was, however, in no way complacent about his situation. Indeed, he had become convinced that when the Allied forces began an offensive – as he was sure they would do – the waters of the Arakan on the western flank of his 15th Imperial Army would very likely feature in any incursion plans. With this in mind, in February 1943 he instituted a series of moves to counter any such assault: in particular sending his 55th Division from its headquarters at Mandalay to the coastal strip. The task of keeping this jungle-choked region secure was given to the battle-hardened Major General Tokutaro Sakurai whose men were already familiar with jungle terrain, mangrove swamps and meandering *chaungs*. They were also buoyed by their recent part in driving the British out of Burma.

On the other side of the world, the failure of the 'First Arakan' had been a big disappointment to Winston Churchill and changes were inevitably made. General Wavell was moved to become Viceroy of India and a new supremo appointed to take command of all Allied land, sea and air forces involved in the war against

Japan. The man chosen on 25 August 1943 to fill the role of 'Supreme Allied Commander South-East Asia', was the charismatic Admiral Lord Louis Mountbatten, a man beloved by his staff and men, but resented by some of the more old-fashioned fellow officers who found his colourful background as a destroyer commander and combined operations executive, as well as his fame in the media, not to their liking. Mountbatten's appointment was, though, the best news heard in a long time for many of the troops in the Far East who were already beginning to think of themselves as 'forgotten'.

Mountbatten's directive from the Prime Minister was unequivocal: he was to engage the Japanese 'closely and continuously' and force them to divert resources of men and weaponry from the Pacific. Two months after his appointment, the old Eastern Army in India was disbanded and reformed as the 14th Army. It was to prove one of the most multinational armies in history with men from many of the Commonwealth countries as well as every caste and race from Sikhs to the Naga headhunters. Mountbatten also put a new man in command, Lieutenant General William Slim, a veteran of the First World War in Gallipoli and Mesopotamia where he had been awarded the Military Cross (MC).

Slim had, of course, survived the humiliation of the retreat from Burma and seethed with a desire for revenge. Known to his men as 'Uncle Bill', and described by George Macdonald Fraser in *Quartered Safe Out Here: A Recollection of the War in Burma* (1992) as having 'a robber-baron face under his Gurka hat', he was a burly figure with a great strength of personality and a blunt and matter-of-fact approach to soldiering, and was usually seen carrying his carbine slung over his shoulder, 'like a scruffy private with general's tabs'. Mountbatten knew that Slim was motivated by the single thought that the possession of territory was meaningless – what really mattered was the slaughtering of Japanese. Indeed, he had already introduced a dehumanising metaphor into his conversations about the enemy. In order to understand the Japanese, he said, it was important not to think of them as men or even as animals, but as 'soldier ants' like those to be found in India. He did not think they anticipated fear before the event – and would not admit it if they did. Slim believed the Japanese accepted every order unquestioningly, their discipline was rigid and they would attack even if doing so meant certain annihilation. He had heard that in the Arakan the troops were told that if they died their bodies would be left rotting in the sand, but they would turn to grass, which would wave in the breezes blowing from Japan.

Fuelled by this conviction and his bitter experiences in 1942, Slim instituted new training methods and tactics for his soldiers to make them more adept at jungle fighting. He also recruited the assistance of the RAF to supply his troops and provide aerial cover where possible in the jungle. He looked to the navy, too, for help with the amphibious operations that would inevitably occur. While all this was going on, he also set in motion arrangements for the 'Second Arakan' to begin in the New Year.

Initially, Slim's plans went well. On 9 January 1944, the town of Maungdaw, just across the Indian border and near the River Naf, was taken. A month later Buthidaung, 20 miles to the east, was seized. The men of the 5th and 7th Divisions of the 14th Army were in good heart when Sakurai's troops retaliated in early February, evidently confident of their ability to overcome the Allied defences. However, despite fanatical bravery in the face of withering fire, the Japanese column could not penetrate the defence and were themselves forced to retreat on 26 February. General Slim allowed himself a little smile of satisfaction and wrote in his *Diary:* 'For the first time a British force has met, held and decisively defeated a major Japanese attack'.

Along the Arakan coastline, Captain John Ryland's Coastal Forces played their allotted part in securing the 5th Division's seaward flank, bringing in supplies, landing agents and reconnaissance parties, and carrying out the occasional bombardment. Just before the end of the month they even carried out a diversionary attack on the enemy stronghold at Ramree Island. Although no attempt was made to seize the island, it was the first real foray against the garrison and its vital airfield and procured information that would later prove invaluable.

Major General Sakurai may have been stopped in his tracks for the first time since he entered Burma, but he was far from beaten and retrenched his forces along a line between Maungdaw and Buthidaung. There he was able to hold firm against a series of attacks by the 14th Army's 25th, 26th and 36th Indian Divisions, until the advent of the monsoon season once more interrupted the ebb and flow of war and brought to a close the 'Second Arakan'. A new situation had now arisen, though, as Arthur Swinson, one of the most distinguished historians of the Burma campaign, has explained in his article 'Success in the Arakan' for *Purnell's History of the Second World War* (1966):

> *By the summer of 1944, a stalemate was developing in the Arakan. On the Japanese side, Sakurai had received orders that the coastal strip, the Irrawaddy delta to the east of the Arakan Yomas, and the islands of Ramree and Cheduba should be held at all costs, to protect the rear of the 15th Army. On the British side, a defensive policy had been adopted in the Arakan: any troops still uncommitted there were to be employed on the Central Front in Burma. In short, both sides had settled temporarily for inaction. By late September 1944,*

*however, it had been recognised that the two key objectives for the Allies must
be the islands of Akyab and Ramree.*

In October, as the end of the monsoon season neared, thoughts turned to a
third offensive against the Arakan. Three new facts were evident to Mountbatten
and his officers in the South East Asia Command (SEAC). One, the Japanese
were clearly *not* invincible. Secondly, the entrance to the River Naf on the
Burmese border with India was now secure in Allied hands, enabling the Teknaf
peninsula to be used as a base for combined operations onto the mainland. But
third – and perhaps the most daunting of these facts – was that the enemy was
entrenched in some of the most hostile and difficult territory anywhere in the
world. Not without good reason was the Arakan referred to as 'The Worst Place
on Earth'.

2

'THE WORST PLACE ON EARTH'

The conflict fought by the Allied forces on the Arakan coast has been described by a number of Second World War historians as 'one of the weirdest battles of the war fought on water'. The location itself has earned similar approbation as having probably the world's worst climate and some of the most forbidding terrain on earth in its complex of dense jungles, glutinous swamps, dangerous rivers and innumerable, treacherous *chaungs*. In these serpentine tidal watercourses, which fill with water when the sea is in flood and become beds of parched mud when the tide ebbs, was waged what the Allies came to refer to as the 'Chaung War'. It was to prove a strength-sapping and nerve-testing conflict, not only against the Japanese and the hostile environment, but also its vicious animal, marine and – especially – insect life. As a report in the *London Gazette* explained with matter-of-fact bluntness in January 1945, 'The Arakan is one of the most difficult places on earth to fight in with its thick jungles, razorback mountains, steep, wide valleys, myriad waterways and plethora of debilitating and deadly tropical diseases'.

The savage and largely untameable nature of much of this strip of land is, in fact, reflected in both its geography and history. Today absorbed into Burma's Rakhine State, it stretches for 400 miles along the eastern coast of the Bay of the Bengal from the Naf River to Cape Negrais. The Arakan once covered 20,000 square miles, but after the recent partition of the country has been reduced to 14,200 square miles. The Naf separates it from the Chittagong province that is now Bangladesh, while it is isolated from the rest of Burma by a mountain limb that runs just a few miles inland called the Arakan Yomas. These mountains are classified as 'near impassable' – indeed, they have frequently proved an obstacle against conquest – and also feed the rivers and waterways on the coastal plain, particularly during the monsoon season. Dominating the lowland area – which varies between thirty miles wide just south of Chittagong to a few hundred yards at the aptly named Foul Point – is the Mayu Range of sheer, rocky hills. Their name translates sinisterly as 'Mad Woman Range' and they are largely covered by thick, impenetrable jungle. All along the coast are numerous islands, of which the most important in our story are Akyab, Ramree, Cheduba and the intriguingly named 'Diamond Island'.

The very word Arakan is the subject of a great deal of controversy with claims that it is either Arabic or Persian. Popular legend believes it to be a corruption of the Sanscrit word *Rakshasa* meaning 'monster' or 'demon'. It is said that the name was first applied by the early Buddhists to the unconverted tribes they found living on the wild plain. Certainly, the very earliest inhabitants belonged to the Negrito group and are mentioned in the *Arkanese Chronicles* as *bilus* meaning 'cannibals'.*

According to another local tradition, the Buddha himself visited the Arakan and was greeted by King Canrasuriya who asked to make a colossal image of the holy man. The resulting mahamuni statue is believed to be the only true and contemporary likeness and is generally regarded as one of the most sacred objects in the Buddhist world. In 1784, it was seized from its resting place in the Arakan and taken away by King Bodawpaya to Mandalay where it is now covered in so much gold that the original form can hardly be discerned.

A succession of over 200 native princesses are said to have ruled the Arakan as a sovereign, independent kingdom right down to modern times and local history claims they once possessed an empire that stretched over parts of Bengal and even a portion of China. For a time the roving Portuguese ruled the province – helping to create a naval force and encouraging trade with other countries – until it was seceded to the British in 1826 under the treaty of Yandaboo. The old city of Arakan on the Koladaign River, which was for years the capital, finally had to give up its status because of its remoteness from the ports and harbours on the coast and the unhealthiness of its climate. Akyab on the Bay of Bengal, which is today known as Sittwe, replaced it.

The unhealthiness of the region was, indeed, one of the first battles any newcomers to the Arakan had to come to terms with, as it is home to virtually every tropical disease. The fact that in the first Burmese war a British expedition had been almost entirely wiped out by disease was not a very encouraging statistic, even for those Allied troops who arrived with doctors in attendance and first aid kits full of the latest medicines including iodine, calamine and field dressings.

By far the most common and deadliest sickness was malaria, which is caused by a single-cell organism, *Plasmodium,* and is transmitted by mosquitoes, the bite of some strains producing huge septic sores. The disease results in fevers, chills,

---

*The cannibal tradition of the Arakan was revived by a Japanese historian, Tamura Yoshio in *Hiroku Dai Toa Senshi: Biruma Hen* (Secret History of the War in East Asia: Burma, 1953) which claimed that some Japanese soldiers serving on the Arakan had been 'offered women in marriage by a strange, cannibalistic tribe'. The story is, though, believed to be pure fiction.

sweats and swelling of the liver and spleen that leaves those who survive prostrate for weeks on end. Scrub typhus – a tick-born variant of the typhus carried by lice – was also prevalent. It could occur in epidemic numbers, causing a fever that might last for fourteen debilitating days *unless* supplies of DDT – a now-banned pesticide used to treat it – were to hand.

Those Allied troops pursuing their missions on land through the 'hellish jungle mountains', as Slim called them, as well as those moving by water, had to deal with strength-sapping heat and humidity. Temperatures on the Arakan might reach 130°F and 15 inches of water could fall in a single day. Equally, the men might fall victim to foot rot, dengue fever, cholera, scabies, yaws, sprue and a foul smelling mould that developed in the areas of the armpits or the crotch. Even more unpleasant was the ailment named 'Naga Sores', a stinking, five-inch-long blister, which eats away flesh to the bone and can be fatal. Chafed, blistered or bloodied flesh was constantly at risk of contamination from jungle filth and would rapidly turn septic if not treated. Gut-wrenching dysentery, too, was rife among those who served on the Arakan and stories are told of some acute cases where the victims cut holes in their shorts so that they were able to instantly relieve themselves when the need arose.

Probably, though, the most loathed 'enemy' of all were the red, black or brown blood-sucking leeches that lived in vast numbers in the beds of sticky black mud in swamps, streams and *chaungs* and attached themselves by a front sucker armed with concealed fangs to any unsuspecting passer-by. There were few certain ways of preventing their attacks beyond keeping the whole body covered – and at night plugging the ears with cotton wool to prevent an unwelcome intruder up to eight inches in length that could gorge itself with blood. Michael Lowry who experienced the deprivations of leeches has written in *Fighting Through To Kohima: A Memoir of War in India and Burma* (2003):

> It was during the monsoon periods when we were in and out of water-filled paddy-fields and chaungs that we suffered the explorations of leeches around our bodies; new British blood was apparently nectar to them. The leeches would usually get their sustenance by entering our boots through the lace-holes. They got so bloated by this apparent bottomless pit of blood that they would never have seen daylight again had it not been for the pain the men felt as the swollen leeches tried to share a boot which only just fitted a swollen foot. Some leeches were doubtless old soldiers at the game and raced up the inside of a man's clothing and took more juicy blood from around the crutch. They were devils to extract as their strong suckers at the mouth and the rear appeared to be glued

to the human skin; just trying to pull them off was usually unsuccessful, whereas touching them with salt or a burning cigarette end usually did the trick, but doing it in some sensitive places was an art. You can't always light a cigarette and salt isn't always to hand.

Add to all this horror swarms of huge, persistent black flies and various other vicious, biting, stinging, rapacious insects attacking anyone on an operation in the region and the story is still not even half told. There was also the matter of the monsoon and the jungle with its fearsome wildlife that constantly encroached around the waterways where the battle for the Arakan was fought. Lastly, and most dangerous of all, lurked the fanatical Japanese fighters who – it was well known among the Allied forces – preferred death to capture.

* * *

The Burmese monsoon season – the word is derived from the Dutch *monssoen* meaning a fierce wind and rainstorm – sweeps in from the southwest in late April and from then until October precipitates one of the highest incidences of rainfall in the world. In that six months, as much as 375 inches of rain can fall, surging against the mountains and pouring down through the rivers and *chaungs* to the coast. The season begins in April with occasional short, violent bursts that last for a few hours and are known as the 'Mango Showers' because they cause the fruits on the mango trees to drop. In the following month, the rain is continuous and beats on the Arakan in particular with terrifying violence. The sheer volume of water that falls can turn valleys into lakes, cause rivers to rise 30 feet in a single night, and leave paths ankle deep in mud and quite indistinguishable from the *chaungs*. These downpours continue until mid-October when the high temperatures over the land and sea create the dry northeast monsoon that provides little respite for men and their animals until March when the cycle begins all over again.

The effect of the elements on Allied and Japanese operations during these seasons was far reaching – in many instances causing postponements or cancellation. No one who served on the Arakan ever forgot their time there, especially the unpleasantness of waiting in sodden tents through days and weeks of inactivity, nor the moments of pure horror when the bodies of colleagues who had died from disease or enemy action and been buried, began rising up through the mud to the surface.

The combination of temperature and humidity sapped the men's energy and willpower almost beyond endurance. The rain fell so hard at times that visibility was virtually down to zero and it was impossible for anyone to see a hand in front of their face. Some of the hardier troops joked that it was possible to take a shower in the monsoon rainstorm – as long as your body was strong enough to withstand the force of the raindrops! An often-repeated account claimed that a certain British officer was forced to borrow a raft on 5 November 1943 in order to get to his mess hall when 13 inches of rain fell in just 24 hours!

Another story is told of Mountbatten: not long after he had taken up his position as Supreme Allied Commander he asked to be flown over the Arakan coast. Looking out of the aircraft's window, he turned to the pilot and enquired the name of the river passing below. He is said to have been somewhat taken aback by the man's reply: 'That's not a river, sir – it *was* a road!' It was in that moment, Mountbatten explained later, he realised how reading local maps would become very difficult – if not impossible – and on-the-spot reconnaissance would be essential to the success of any covert mission or landing. Despite such problems, though, he was determined that operations would go on despite the weather and informed his officers in characteristic manner, 'There will be no drawing stumps this year – we will march on, fight on and fly on!'

The first Allied operations into the Arakan coastal waterways made it clear to everyone that they were facing an environment that could make their lives a living nightmare. A man did not need long in these hazardous places to realise why they were considered so difficult to fight in and demanded every ounce of strength, patience and particularly bravery, in order to stay alive when dealing with the climate, the wildlife and the largely unseen enemy.

The muddy waters of the estuaries and the larger rivers were perhaps marginally less upsetting with their hordes of slithering jellyfish, water snakes, roaming mahseers and, at night, weird flashes of phosphorescent light. But there were even more unnerving moments awaiting those who suddenly caught sight of a shark's fin gliding through the water. These were a species of river shark, the *Glyphis siamensis,* referred to locally as the 'Irrawaddy River Shark' – for years thought to be extinct, but now, it seemed, making a re-appearance. Despite its small size, the shark had a reputation as a man-eater among the Burmese because of its arrow-like head and serrated and flared teeth in both the upper and lower jaws. The creature's notoriety had, though, most probably been earned because of its similarity to the ferocious *Glyphis gangeticus* of India, known to have attacked people swimming far up rivers in West Bengal.

River sharks aside, entering the dripping wet foliage of the Arakan jungle – where some of the trees towered up as high as 80 feet and were so densely packed together it was as dark as night all day long – was also enough to upset anybody, particularly any man who suffered from claustrophobia. All around, the vegetation varied from thickets of bamboo and mangroves to towering elephant grass and vast drapes of *lianas* – great creepers that entangled the trees until they reached the canopy high above. Often the only way through this impenetrable vegetation was to hack a path with an axe, machete or the long-bladed *dah* used by the Burmese. The task was made no less arduous and unpleasant by the fact that when the rotting vegetation was chopped down it released a stench that was enough to upset the strongest stomach. Whether travelling by boat or on foot, men were often astonished at how quickly the foliage they cut down grew again. A patrol that had passed through a particular patch of vegetation one day could find within a matter of hours there was no sign of human beings ever having passed that way. A down side of this was that it was virtually impossible to find any enemy tracks to follow.

No member of an Allied unit who entered the Arakan swamps was ever surprised to learn they were uninhabited, although several species of mammals and a number of birds called it home. These included the white-brown nuthatch and the inappropriately named striped laughing thrush. Among the mammals could be found the occasional herd of marauding elephants – indeed, a British soldier on patrol in 1944 was killed by one of these huge creatures that grabbed his rifle with its trunk and beat him to death – as well as tigers, leopards and the voracious sun bear that would eat just about anything it could get its paws on. For good measure, there were also hoolook gibbons, a small ape known for its agility in trees and for its unnerving scream. The shrieks of these creatures joining the cacophony of other animal noises that heralded each dawn and dusk was enough to send a shiver up the spine of any man in the Arakan.

Because of the darkness in the jungle, night-time operations were made even more difficult, with vision down to a few feet and the slightest sound a possible harbinger of danger. The pitch-black conditions also made keeping in the right direction a problem and there was always a danger of attracting sniper fire if any kind of illumination was required to read a map or issue orders. On the other hand, of course, the deep shadows made it easier for men to move unseen and sometimes even get to within a few yards of an unsuspecting enemy. Speaking from the Allied point of view, Charles Ogburn, a lieutenant who served in the Arakan wrote in an article, 'Uncommon Misery: The 1944–45 Burma Campaign' (1959), that it was 'so incomparably the worst experience that I could hardly believe it for the rest of my life'. He continued:

You never knew from one moment to the next when you'd run into the Japanese. Soldiers lived in constant agonising anticipation of a sniper's bullet and were so jittery on occasions an entire battery of artillery might be called in to eliminate a solitary sniper. In fact, the terrors of the jungle left indelible marks on the men in Burma. Many came down with 'Jungle Happiness'. When they returned to civilian life they found themselves ill at ease among crowds and bright lights and sometimes even their family and friends.

* * *

The conditions in which the Allies fought were, of course, exactly the same for the Japanese. But the truth was that as the 'Third Arakan' was about to begin, the occupiers were the more experienced and hardened to fighting in the unforgiving terrain. They suffered the same debilitating illnesses and were very aware of the dangerous insects and animals that could make life such a profound misery. As fighters, though, they were anatomically and psychologically very different: facts pointed out by Captain Malcolm Montieth in the lectures he gave to the troops on their way to Burma. In his opening remarks, Montieth always insisted that 'it might perhaps be fair to say that the Japanese are the first barbarous and primitive enemy, fighting from the motives of purest patriotism, and equipped with modern arms, that the western world has encountered'. After describing the appearance of the men they were about to fight as, 'small with muscular, rather hairless bodies, thick, strong legs and short arms, a peeping look due to the double-fold in the upper lid, but in no sense of the word yellow', Montieth would go on in an echo of Slim word's:

The Japanese have a peculiar animal-like quality. Even their dead look like shot game. Though bodily clean, their living habits are filthy. All their intimate possessions, such as clothing and blankets, have a most distinctive smell, a legacy, presumably from the bodies of their owners. In attack, they scream, thereby producing such a volume and quality of sound that it is difficult to believe that it emerges from human throats. In defence, after being stunned and stupefied by bombardment, they crouch in small niches and holes like trapped beasts, often weeping hysterically, but fighting desperately to the last.

Although Montieth warned his listeners that it was 'impossible to predict the behaviour or reactions of the Japanese', another officer, Captain Anthony Irwin, who fought against them in several campaigns in Burma, was in no doubt about what made them such formidable opponents. In a nutshell, it was their philosophy of life, as the Captain explained in his remarkable personal narrative of the war, *Burmese Outpost* (1945):

The whole training of the individual soldier is different from that of any other soldier in the world. It starts hundreds of years before he is born. The subjugation of the individual to the State, the supremacy of the military over all else, has not, as with the German, arisen within a generation or two, but has been the basis of national behaviour as long as they have had a national religion. In this way it never becomes necessary to tell a Japanese soldier to hold on to the last man and the last round – that is instilled in him from birth. Without doubt the Jap is the finest of all Eastern soldiers. He can fight in the jungle and the heat and the climate are not strange to him. He can go for days in this country with a bag of rice and water from a village pond.

Another soldier, Major Jack Masters, who spent fourteen years on active duty with the Indian Army, also formed a perceptive view of his adversaries. Born in Calcutta, the fifth generation of his family to serve in India, Masters got his intimate knowledge of the Japanese culture first hand while serving as a Brigadier of General Orde Wingate's Chindits and describes his impressions in *The Road Past Mandalay: A Personal Narrative* (1963):*

They believed in something and were willing to die for it, for any smallest detail that would help to achieve it. What else is bravery? They pressed home their attacks when no other troops in the world would have done so, when all hope of success was gone; except that it never really is, for who can know what the enemy has suffered, what is his state of mind? The Japanese simply came on, using all their skill and rage, until they were stopped by death. In defence they held their ground with a furious tenacity that never faltered. They had to be killed, company by company, squad by squad, man by man to the last. Frugal and bestial, barbarous and brave, artistic and brutal, they were the dushman [enemy], and we now set about, in all seriousness, the task of killing every one of them.

Post war Japanese records indicate that the majority of their soldiers in Burma had been largely recruited from the rural population of the country whose tough

* After the war, writing as John Masters, he produced a number of best sellers including *Bugles and a Tiger* (1948) based on his life as a young professional soldier in India and two other novels set on the troubled sub-continent, *Nightrunners of Bengal* (1951) and *Bhowani Junction* (1954).

farmers made excellent soldiers. They had been trained to fight with a .256in calibre rifle to which a 15-inch bayonet was attached 'in order to instil fear into the enemy' – although this did not help their sharp shooting and accuracy. Their machine guns were considered to be no match for the British .303 Lee-Enfield Bren gun, but their grenade discharger could effectively shoot a 1lb 12oz shell up to 700 yards with considerable accuracy.

Apart from the surprise element of the Japanese invasion of Burma, the key to their success was twofold. They undoubtedly had extensive reconnaissance of the country carried out by spies for some years prior to their arrival, in order to provide their troops with information about the terrain and details of what they could expect to find. Secondly, a high standard of training for their infantrymen involving long marches and gruelling field exercises enabled them to cover long distances on foot carrying heavy loads. The men were also taught to live frugally off the land and make the most of any enemy equipment that fell into their hands.

Once the Japanese had occupied the Arakan they created their defensive positions with great care – often using the *chaungs* that were natural obstacles in any circumstances and could be improved by digging a system of pits and bunkers. Julian Thompson, who served as a Royal Marine Commando, rising to the rank of Major General, describes these formidable encampments in his book, *War in Burma 1942–1945* (2002):

> They were well sited, in mutual support so that attackers assaulting one bunker came under flanking fire from at least one other. Roofed with logs and about five feet of earth, they were impervious to field artillery shells and all too often even to medium bombs. Well camouflaged, they were only spotted with difficulty, even from as close as fifty yards or less. Each would be held by five to thirty men manning medium and light machine guns. Attacking troops arriving on top of the bunkers would be treated to a heavy enemy bombardment brought down on themselves by the Japanese, secure in their own inviolability, and in any case not caring overmuch if they inflicted casualties on their own troops. Every single occupant of each bunker had to be killed before the position could be deemed secure.

The Japanese also developed a number of oral deceptions to supplement their defences. These schemes included breaking into radio messages with misleading information. The cajoling contralto tones of 'Tokyo Rose' were frequently heard delivering messages such as, 'New British Fourteenth Army will be destroyed – why not go home? It's all over for you in Burma!' Sometimes hidden Japanese soldiers would call out in perfect English, 'Johnny, I'm wounded, over here', in the hope an unwary soldier might reveal his position; while on other occasions they might shout, 'British soldier why are you here? Your wives are waiting for you!' Cruellest of all, wounded Allied soldiers were used a number of times as 'bait' to lure their colleagues out into the open to be cut down by withering gunfire.

Whatever advantages these tricks might have given the Imperial troops – and initially it seems that the more superstitious of the Allied soldiers were largely ignorant of their enemy's ethos and according to some accounts tended to regard them as almost 'super-bogeymen' – the Japanese had a simple attitude towards any form of surrender, as David W. Tschanz has written in *The Burma War* (1981):

The character of the Japanese enemy greatly compounded the problem for the Allies – these fanatical fighters almost always preferred death to capture. They used hari-kiri, *a ceremonial suicide by ripping open the belly, substituted in battle by clasping a hand grenade to the stomach. They treated all prisoners with scorn and derision, as it was not something they would contemplate. One Japanese sniper, dubbed 'Little Willie' by the British troops he engaged, fired from a hole in a tree for three weeks, picking off eight officers, despite frantic efforts to get him with mortar and small arms fire. He eventually slipped away unscathed. In another documented incident, Japanese infantry attacked British tanks with nothing more than swords.*

If this eccentricity seemed to verge on madness at times, it was somewhat in keeping with the character of the Japanese commander on the Arakan, Major General Tokutaro Sakurai, who had played a major role in driving the British out of Burma to India. An extraordinary figure who attracted a fierce loyalty from his men yet punished any form of insubordination quite ruthlessly, he is described by Louis Allen in *Burma: The Longest War 1941–45* (1984):

'Tokuta', as Sakurai was affectionately nicknamed, was a boisterous personality who had come to 55 Division with a considerable reputation. He was an old China hand and stories of his bravery and dash were common currency in the division. When he was an intelligence major on the staff of the China Expeditionary Force he negotiated a ceasefire with Sung Che-yuan's army in Peking. The negotiations took place on the wall of a fortification, by the Kuang An Gate, and 'Tokuta' spotted the Chinese closing the gate and getting ready to fire on the Japanese party. To stop them, he leaped straight down from the high wall.

According to Allen, Sakurai always lead his men from the front and was a particular specialist in night combat. His eccentric streak had, though, got him into trouble in China when he used a group of unscrupulous Japanese roughnecks – referred to as *Shinagoro* and considered to be virtual gangsters – on one of his intelligence gathering missions. Although they provided valuable information, the men's use of violence upset a number of those in charge of Japanese army public relations and 'Tokuta' was reprimanded by his superiors.

The Major General was sent to the Arakan in command of 55 Division Infantry Group to protect the coastal flank of the 15th Imperial Army. Typically, he also had an audacious plan of his own to take on the British and capture their commander. 'It'll be child's play to smash the enemy in the Mayu Peninsula', he is reported to have informed his closest army confidants. The larger-than-life-commander was also known to his adversaries, including Major John Shipster, the winner of a DSO for bravery in the Arakan campaign. Writing in his enthralling personal memoir, *Mist on the Rice-Fields* (2000), Shipster recalls:

> Major General 'Tokuta' Sukarai arrived in the Arakan wearing a long pearl necklace around his neck. He told surprised officers that they were his 'Buddha's – my lucky charms'. Later, at a regimental officers' mess dinner, 'Tokuta' insisted on doing a Chinese folk dance; he stripped naked, and during his dancing puffed away at lighted cigarettes stuffed up his nose and in the corners of his mouth. When the dance was ended the cigarettes were given to the nearest officers to smoke. 'Tokuta's' striptease act became legendary throughout the entire Burmese Army.

By November 1944, the two adversaries were in position and the third Allied attempt to take Burma was ready to begin. The objective of Mountbatten and Slim was to drive the Japanese army south in pincer movements from the land and sea, seize the enemy airfields to ensure control of the skies and, ultimately, cut off the retreating troops. Now, though, a new element was about to be introduced into the war, as Arthur Swinson explains:

> Fighting in the jungle is like fighting in a fog: it smothers long-range weapons and enables the attacker to come to close quarters with small loss. Heavy bombers and heavy guns are useless if there is no visible target upon which they can be directed, and tanks are reduced to the role of mobile pillboxes, each needing a close escort of infantry to protect it from the enemy who can rise up unseen within a yard of it. At first, the Japanese infantry, tough, resolute,

lightly armed, and trained for these very conditions, had every advantage over an opponent accustomed to rely upon a wide range of supporting weapons. But by 1944, the Allied troops had learned the rules of this highly specialised form of warfare, and were quite as tough and skilful at it as their opponents. As the prospects of a full-scale invasion to throw the Japanese right out of Burma grew, it became more necessary than ever to gain exact information of their positions and strength. Normal patrolling could and did maintain contact with the forward positions, but special arrangements had to be devised to find out what was going on further back.

It was the cue for the group of men known collectively as the Banzai Hunters to begin their operations. The moment had arrived for the combined operations units that had been set up and already undertaken many months, even years, of exhaustive training, to turn the tables on the Japanese in the very environment that had been so firmly in their grasp since the start of the Far East war. It was a challenge that these men of many different skills and from all kinds of backgrounds really relished . . .

3

'SHERLOCK' HOLMES AND THE ADVENTURE AT NAHKAUNGDO

The six men on the darkened beach illuminated only by a canopy of twinkling stars, were all wearing tattered khaki shirts and the traditional Burmese *lungyi,* a calf-length piece of cotton wrapped around their legs and tucked in at the waist. They shifted their bare feet impatiently in the pearl-coloured sand, their eyes never still as they gazed around from the waves that gently lapped the shore to the jungle behind them where fireflies were beginning to dance in the shadows. In the surf, one of the paddle canoes known as a *kisti* rode gently up and down the sand as if anxious – like the group of men – to be off on the mission.

When one of the men carrying a tommy gun under his arm shivered involuntarily as a sharp, damp breeze blew in from the sea, his companion turned and looked around the group. It was time to go he told himself, and he knew that the others were ready, particularly the figure who had shivered. Despite his curious clothes, the man was actually a corporal and the only other Englishman in the party except their leader, also a British officer.

The officer checked the .38 pistol under his *lungyi* and looked at the sea again to satisfy himself that the tide was indeed now on the turn. Without a word, he nodded his head in the direction of the canoe and all six men climbed aboard. One of the figures in an even more ragged *lungyi* than the rest immediately stationed himself in the prow, while the remaining three took up the oars and began to steadily pull away from the beach.

Soon the sound of the waves lapping on the shore faded into the distance and a stillness fell over the ocean, disturbed only by the regular swishing of the oarsmen. To the left of the boat, the coast of the Arakan slipped by until a few tiny glistening lights indicated that the little port known as Maungdaw was coming into view. Just beyond it, all the members of the party knew, lay an extensive *chaung* known locally by the curious name of *Magyi* (Large Woman). It was to be their objective for the night.

When the *kisti* was about half a mile from the coast, the leader of the group spoke for the first time since they had left dry land. His voice was resolute and authoritative: 'Remember, we are not out to kill Japs. This is not a fighting mission. We fight only if attacked. So the first rule is absolute quiet. Until we meet our friends, we must *not* be heard or seen'.

The man's eyes glinted against his blackened features as he studied the five other faces one by one. From each he received a ready nod of acknowledgement. They seemed to share his optimism that on this, the last night of the old year, the new one might bring the break through in the war that they had all been working for. Not another word was spoken as the steady pulling of the oars took them closer to land. It was almost precisely 11 p.m. when the *kisti* bumped against the bank of mangrove trees at the side of the *chaung* and the men knew they were now in enemy occupied territory.

Another mission on the Arakan was about to start for Major Denis Holmes and a small group of men of V (for Victory) Force. Holmes, the 'Quiet Major' to his admirers, 'Sherlock' Holmes to his friends and, quirkily, 'Watson' to the military who had given him his code-name, was ready and prepared, he hoped, for any eventuality. Once again the British soldier who was acknowledged as a master of disguise and an expert at subterfuge was about to put his skills to the test, as one of the leading undercover officers now preparing the way for the Allied invasion of Burma.

* * *

The decision to form the covert organisation known as the 'V Force' to work behind Japanese lines had been made as a direct result of the lack of a spy network in Burma to provide the Allied forces with information about their adversary's movements. The Japanese had, of course, marched into the country complete with a vast amount of information thanks largely to the 30,000 or so of their countrymen living there before the war. 'Nearly all of them spies', one British intelligence officer had remarked bitterly as he set about playing catch-up in the quest for *khubba,* the local word for news or information. According to this man, the Japanese had known virtually every jungle track in the country when they had invaded – and many of these had probably even been marked out for them beforehand by their most active agents, including the anti-British Mughs and the Buddhist monks (*Hpoongyis*). The need for an intelligence-gathering organisation was therefore essential as Major Frank Bullen of the 7th Indian Division who was then serving on the frontier between the two countries, has explained in his *War Diary* (1945):

> *'V Force' was created originally in 1942 when the Japanese successes in Burma*
> *threatened to extend into India itself. So, all along 600 miles of frontier from the*
> *Patkoi Range in the north to the Bay of Bengal in the south, the local tribes were*
> *organised to undertake guerrilla operations against the Japanese lines of*
> *communication, should these pass through their country. After the Japanese*
> *advance was halted, the activities of the 'V Force', whose organisation, arming*
> *and training had meanwhile proceeded slowly but surely, gradually changed in*
> *character from a defensive, post-occupational role to the more aggressive, active*
> *task of patrolling into enemy held territory to get information on which to build the*
> *Allied plans for the future recovery of Burma.*

Major Bullen says that the handful of British officers who were set to lead literally hundreds of Burmese tribesmen in different groups, initially had to make do with the most basic equipment. Armaments were taken from shops, museums and private collections and even single and double-barrelled shotguns had to be called into service until modern rifles and automatics became available. Those who had the toughest time, he explains, included people like Denis Holmes in the Arakan. 'That sector', he wrote, 'experienced the full cycle of defeat, partial recovery, renewed disappointment and decisive victory during which its natives, friendly and hostile, Mussulman and Maugh, played their respective parts'. Bullen believed that in perhaps no other theatre of war did the morale of British and Indian fighting men and their attitude to their conditions and their enemy, 'pass through such depths before reaching the heights'.

This, then, was the cauldron in which Major Denis Holmes had learned his spy-craft and honed his *khubba* gathering skills. It had at last enabled him to get to grips with the enemy and fire some shots in anger after ten years of regular army service and just missing the action because of one chance of fate or another. Born in Burma in 1913, the son of a retired civil servant, Holmes had set his heart on an army career and joined the Indian Army in November 1935. His natural aptitude for military life led to him becoming a Regular Service Officer in the 1st Punjab Regiment and by 1938 he had been promoted to Lieutenant. However, he was seconded to the Assam Rifles, an armed policing unit, and annoyingly missed the fighting his regiment undertook in Abyssinia and the Western Desert. On his return to the 1st Punjab, they were assigned an inactive role and Holmes found himself commanding a light anti-aircraft battery in Central India. When, finally, the opportunity to change all this arose in Burma, the wiry 30-year-old spent the 600-mile journey hoping his long wait to get into the action might at last be over. What he found is described by

C.E. Lucas Phillips in his excellent military history of the Burma war, *The Raiders of the Arakan* (1971):

By any stretch of the imagination, the 'Arakan Zone' of V Force was a very unmilitary affair. It had not been formed until September 1942 in preparation for the 14th Division's offensive, but, being composed of native villagers quite unsuited to the use of arms, had proved futile. The only bright spot in their dismal story had been a fine raid on Taung Bazaar by a hell of a fine guy named Gretton Foster. They had been disbanded in disgust, but Slim – seeing their potential value in a purely intelligence capacity – had stepped in to save them. Apart from two or three British officers they were a civilian show, run by the shrunken remnants of the Burma Civil Service.

Denis Holmes was, of course, at an impasse where his career was concerned at this moment in time. Life at divisional headquarters working on everyday duties was not what stirred the blood of a man who was anxious for the chance of tackling the Japanese at close quarters. He had for years fancied lone missions – especially behind enemy lines. He also believed his organisational skills would help him bring together the right kind of men to succeed in this dangerous area of covert warfare. When Holmes heard that V Force in the Arakan were a man short, Phillips writes, he did not hesitate for a moment to put in an application for an interview.

Holmes arrived at Bawli Bazaar on the Indian border for a meeting with Lieutenant Colonel Archie Donald, the man in charge of the 'Arakan Zone'. Somewhat to his surprise, he found himself confronted by a burly, hard-drinking, foul-mouthed former senior officer of the Burma Police Force. Yet, despite their obviously different temperaments, the quieter junior quickly found himself taking to his superior with a mixture of amusement and admiration.

The Lieutenant Colonel – who Holmes would later discover was nicknamed 'Rockbound' for a reason no one could remember – had lived in the Arakan for many years before the war. It was said that there was little that he did not know about the country and its native population. While the two men sat down to share a meal together, Donald spelled out the realities of what would be Holmes' mission – interspersed with humour and a string of crude jokes. V Force was 'a force of eyes', he said, and Holmes would have to be the brains behind the eyes. The manner of Donald's briefing apparently followed the same course as all those he gave to recruits as another of his protégés, Anthony Irwin, has written in his book. The narrative would have been no different for the reserved major says Irwin, quoting the former policeman verbatim:

I have to be fair and tell you frankly from the start that this is a damned risky game. If you should get caught by those foul Japanese bastards, God help you. If you join us, you will be quite on your own. Some of the chaps you will have to deal with are a pretty rum lot. Jailbirds, smugglers, racketeers and all sorts. But some damned good types, too. They are not soldiers and are not armed. You have to use these chaps to gather in as much as you can about the enemy, his movements, supplies, unit identifications and so on. You will have to assess the validity of the information that you get and pass it back as quickly as possible. You have to learn whom you can trust and who you can't and you have to look out for the double agent. But the chaps we use are nearly all Chittagonians, who loathe the Mughs and the Japs like hell, so are usually to be trusted. A lot also depends on whether they bloody well like you!

Holmes assured his host that after a lifetime spent on the continent he was used to dealing with Burmese and Indian natives and could speak Urdu. Donald nodded and said that Holmes would need to set up a group of 'scouts' or informants behind the enemy lines. These men could either report to him or, ideally, he should try and get to see them in their villages. They should be paid well, 'Rockbound' added with a grin, because they had to be 'bloody careful or the Japs will pin them to the ground with bayonets and skin them alive!' Holmes would also have to deal with every type of informer from patriots to double agents:

You'll find they are odds and sods of all kinds. Most of them pretty decent blokes, friendly and loyal, with plenty of guts. Others have police records and would cut your throat for five bob, but they know we have the edge on them. Most you will have to put through the hoop, like we coppers do, by close questioning.

It was long past midnight when the two men had a final drink and Holmes returned to his tent. His mind was whirling with thoughts about what he had agreed to do – and the dangers it obviously entailed. His mission was going to call for a hell of a lot of trust and a great deal of luck. Lieutenant Colonel Donald's final words were still ringing in his ears when he fell asleep that night:

Just take things easy and you'll find you'll get into it easily enough. We all had to start like this, it being a newish show, and we've got to find our own way around. Oh, by the way, there's a bastard in Maungdaw who's been talking to the locals about 'The New Masters'. That doesn't make sense; there aren't any New Masters; the old ones aren't gone yet. The King's the Master here. Get that cunt for me if you can!

* * *

The words of 'Rockbound' Donald were never far from Holmes' mind when he began to assemble his team to work on undercover operations in the Arakan. He cast his net through the ranks of military personnel and among the local peasants keen to help the British effort to rid their country of the brutal *Japani*. In the end, the group that the Major assembled was as diverse and multi-skilled as his literary namesake in Victorian London might have wished for.

There was obviously a place for his orderly, Khyber Khan, an imposing Hazarawal Pathan (sepoy) from the North West Frontier who had been with Holmes ever since his appointment as a Lieutenant. Tall and intelligent, the Indian was also an excellent shot and Holmes rewarded him for his devoted service by immediately appointing him a Staff NCO or *havildar*. Khyber Khan, for his part, promoted himself as instructor in the use of the Bren-gun, believing that as an Indian hill-tribe warrior he was a superior shot to any plainsman that the Major might recruit.

For his second in command and bodyguard, Holmes chose Corporal Robert Disbury, a Regular soldier and member of the 2nd Battalion of the West Yorkshire Regiment, who was then stationed on garrison duty at Teknaf. A quietly spoken veteran with honours for his service in Africa and a General Services Medal for Palestine, Disbury was a North Countryman, stockily built with a single-minded determination evident in the square set of his jaw. He quickly earned Holmes' confidence and became privy to his leader's plans – indeed, Disbury soon became known, unofficially, as the Major's 'Watson'.

A local Burmese who proved invaluable to Holmes was Muhammad Shaffi, a Chittagong farmer whose life had been ruined by the invasion of the 'yellow dogs' and who was now devoted to bringing about their exit – preferably dead. Despite his past, Shaffi a broad-shouldered young man in his mid-twenties, was forever cheerful and possessed natural leadership qualities. His knowledge of the Arakan jungle, rivers and *chaungs* was second to none, and Holmes came to trust Shaffi's instincts whenever they were deep in enemy territory. The Major saw him as a natural guerrilla fighter, blessed with almost second sight and acute hearing, not to mention a remarkably sensitive nose that enabled him to smell the odour of Japanese soldiers from as far as 25 yards away! Shaffi possessed a natural Muslim fatalism and a deep admiration for the British, demonstrating his affection for the country – and Holmes in particular – on every mission they undertook. So much did the English soldier come to value Shaffi that he eventually gave him the honourable Indian army title of a *Jemadar*.

Although Holmes spoke Urdu, he knew the importance of a good interpreter and picked another man who was also known as Muhammad Shaffi, though a 'little, clerky fellow' (to quote a V Force report) whose deferential manner and small stature made him immediately distinguishable from the burly young farmer. With this man's assistance, Holmes added more scouts and informers to his motley crew. Among the first was Danu Meah, whose name was shorted to 'Danny' and who made a passable cook. A ragged, furtive guide whose Indian name was unpronounceable so he became 'Dick Turpin' followed him. An equally unkempt native who wore a curious conical hat and proved to be an excellent go-between swelled the ranks. He was nicknamed 'Harpo Marx' and followed everywhere by a threatening young man whom Holmes' immediately nicknamed 'Tommy Gun'.

Probably the most impressive member of the 'Arakan Zone' force, however, was the sinister-looking Muhammad Siddiq. With his piercing dark eyes, black beard and white skull-cap which gave him an uncanny likeness to Rasputin, Siddiq was actually a *mulvi* (Muslim religious teacher) and was soon referred to by one and all as 'Sid Dick'. Two brothers, Yakub and Hashim Boli, both enormous men whose surname meant 'wrestler' in Burmese after the popular local sport, also looked like a pair not to be trifled with. They were never seen without their broad-bladed *dahs,* which they used with equal dexterity to cut a way through the jungle or chop off the head of any *Japani* who might have the misfortune to cross their path.

Two more extraordinary characters completed Holmes' team: 'Kaloo the Killer' and Abdul Khalique, known as 'The Inspector'. Kaloo was straight from the pages of a *crime noir* novel: an intimidating villain, a cunning thief and a practised murderer. Among his victims, he claimed to have assassinated the Deputy Commissioner of Akyab and said he had been on the run throughout the war. Although Holmes initially had the greatest reservations about recruiting Kaloo, he soon formed a grudging admiration for the man who proved to be a daring scout and a reliable contact with village people, albeit with his own special method of extracting information from those who might otherwise be reluctant to talk!

'The Inspector' was an entirely different character. An extraordinary-looking man with a long grey goatee beard and an expression of serious contemplation, Khalique wore a large toupee, a *lungyi* or shorts, socks held up by suspenders and brown Japanese boots that he had taken from the corpse of an enemy soldier two or three years before. Around his middle, he wore a brown belt into which were stuffed two pistols. 'The Inspector's' career before joining Holmes' group had, in fact, been as exemplary as Kaloo's had been disreputable. It transpired that his family had been murdered by Mughs, after which he had devoted his energy to touring the villages of the Arakan drumming up support for the British and gathering *bushti* about the Japanese as he moved from one community to the next.

Sensibly, Holmes quickly made himself one with his men. Off came his army uniform – which he knew would make him easy to spot by enemy agents – and on went a *lungyi*. To this he added a green vest and tucked his webbing belt and revolver under the sarong. His white legs soon darkened in the fierce heat and under advice from his *Jemader,* Shaffi, he shaved off his moustache and kept his face smooth as Burmese men naturally went clean-shaven. Holmes knew, though, that he was running a terrible risk if he was caught by the Japanese in native dress. Equally, he was sure that if his undercover operation was to succeed in the Arakan, he needed to merge into the environment as completely as possible. Yet, despite his best endeavours, Holmes *did* become known to the Japanese and was amused to learn later that the enemy Intelligence Service had set a price on his capture – dead or alive. On being given this piece of information by one of his scouts, he is reputed to have joked with Corporal Disbury, 'Makes me feel hellish important – like Robin Hood and the Scarlet Pimpernel!'

Holmes and his 'Baker Street Irregulars' wasted no time in getting busy, moving through the jungles and along the rivers and *chaungs* of the Arakan collecting *khubba*. To begin with, they heard and saw little beyond the sound of their own movement as they forced their way through the dripping foliage or forded the swollen waterways between one community and next. With the monsoon season keeping most Japanese army activities to a minimum, Holmes was able to familiarise himself with the terrain and fine-tune the operations of his men to increase the supply of information. One typical report written during the early days on file in the Cabinet Office Official Histories in the National Archives will demonstrate how the V Force developed its *modus operandi*. The narrator may be Holmes himself, but this is uncertain:

One night 15/16, I was on the east bank opposite the enemy. A large fire was lit and there was much noise of hammering and boats being pushed together.

There was shouting and waving of torches. I was forced to lie up to avoid Jap patrols, but at 0200 hours I went down stream to where the noise came from. It seemed to be a stores area. I lay up all day and in the evening they were taken down to the riverbank. At 1630 hours men were seen going north along the riverbank to collect boats that were spaced at about 20 yard intervals along the bank. After dark, six boats were collected, lashed with bamboos and then lengths of decking placed on top. The collection of boats were lashed together and one end fixed to the bank. The other end was allowed to swing across the river until it hit the opposite bank 300 yards away. Immediately a number of men crossed the bridge with ammunition boxes and these were followed by bullocks, ponies and horses. Some 100 men with green and white boxes followed and each made two journeys. At daylight, a motor boat dragged the far end of the bridge upstream back to the east bank, where it was dismantled and decking removed.

Such evidence of Japanese troop movements, the extent of their ammunition and their methods of travel was invaluable to V Force and pure gold when sent on to Allied intelligence. Success also emboldened Holmes and his team, and the Major looked to go further, as C.E. Lucas Phillips has written:

As he went deeper into the country, the sensation that there was no one in front of him but a dangerous enemy lent excitement to his life. He made special friends with the Naf fishermen and frequently got one of them to paddle him down the enemy-held coast in a kisti, *going as near as he dared to occupied Maungdaw. He quickly got accustomed to these primitive dugout canoes, which he grew to prefer to other craft for his later clandestine trips in hostile waters. He would tie up in some* chaung, *make contact with his scouts there, and return with the tide, watching the fish-hawks wheel overhead and the cormorants dive for their prey.*

Aside from first-hand observation and contact with spies, the members of the 'Arakan Zone' of the V Force also encountered double agents who carried Japanese passports. Holmes soon found they seemed remarkably anxious to betray their paymasters in return for British sugar, tea and cigarettes. The Major did not fool himself about the total loyalty of such spies and suspected that in some cases they sold their booty back to the occupying troops at exorbitant prices.

Documents relating to the V Force also indicate that the curious names of some of the villages that featured in reports were proving to be as tongue twisting as those of their inhabitants. Holmes, it would seem, soon fell into the way of using the slang terms that had been adopted by British troops for towns like Alethangyaw (meaning 'The Middle Crossing') anglicised to 'I'll-thank-you', or Nahkaungdo, ('The Short-Nosed Village') which had become 'No-Can-Do'. It was at the latter, in fact, on New Years Day 1945, that 'Sherlock' Holmes would have one of his most memorable adventures with the Japanese . . .

* * *

In November 1944, as the monsoon season gave way to the drier weather, Denis Holmes set up an operational base at Teknaf. The small port was just across the river from the territory he and his men were scouring for information about Japanese movements and it seemed to the Major an ideal spot from which to launch the reconnaissance trips and armed raids that would soon become a feature of the next stage of the Arakan campaign, for what had previously been mainly overland missions were now to give way to seaborne operations. The concept excited Holmes as he laid his plans in the spacious *basha* he had commandeered close to the jetty. The fun he evidently had with the local argot was also apparent when he hung up a sign above the door of the house that read, 'Dewdrop Inn'.

Holmes had also been assigned a larger craft to add to the little *kistis* that were his main form of transport to the waterways and *chaungs* of the occupied coast. The boat was a large, carvel-built sampan propelled by two oars in the stern. To ensure good luck on their missions, 'Sid Dick', the *mulvi,* had painted an eye on the prow to protect the craft from evil when at sea. As the weeks passed and Holmes spent more time afloat, he found himself becoming 'more of a seafarer than I had imagined possible' for someone who had spent his life in the army. He relished the fresh ozone after all the dust clouds, flies and mosquitoes that plagued life on land. The Major was also encouraged by the news that the Japanese seemed to have an antipathy to the sea and had made no efforts to secure the Bay of Bengal, its estuaries and waterways, as any other occupying force would surely have done.

Night after night, disguised and well armed, Holmes and a team of his men would cross as unobtrusively as possible to the mainland. There they would navigate to a suitable landing point and disperse to gather the latest information and gossip from the villages of the Arakan. On the majority of trips, the *Jemadar,* Muhammed Shaffi, would be at the forefront of the party, unerringly taking the party to and from their destinations.

Shaffi was again at the head of the party of six on 31 December 1944 when Holmes set out to meet an informant named Baba Khan who lived to the south of Maungdaw and was offering the British major what he said would be 'most important *khubba*'. Khan was insistent that he was being watched by the Japanese and could not risk coming to Holmes. The starlit journey from Teknaf to the 'Large Woman' *chaung* passed off without incident – Holmes only speaking once to warn his men tersely, 'Until we meet our friends we must *not* be heard or seen'.

However, just as the *kisti* was about to squelch to a stop against one of the muddy banks, the situation changed dramatically. A vivid flare exploded into the sky, followed by another and then several more. As the landscape was bathed in light, two or three machine guns opened fire. Voices rang out and several bullets splashed into the water. The Japanese had obviously spotted them.

According to Denis Holmes' later account of the incident, it was the ever-resourceful Muhammed Shaffi who reacted first – off his own initiative and without waiting for instructions. The *Jemadar* had seized a paddle from the man beside him, swung the boat into open water, and even as Corporal Disbury was grabbing for his Tommy gun to open fire, started shouting in Bengali at the figures on the shore. Miraculously, the firing ceased almost at once and Shaffi urged the others to row back out to sea. Minutes later, with the coast slipping behind them, the grinning Shaffi explained that the firers had been Japanese sentries and he had implored them not to shoot, as they were fishermen. He shouted that they had been brought back to the wrong place by the tide. They wished no harm and would go away at once. The subterfuge worked.

Half an hour later, a very relieved party with the *Jemadar* still smiling in the bow, made landfall in another *chaung* several miles behind enemy lines. Making certain first that there were no more Japanese in the undergrowth, Holmes, Disbury and Shaffi stepped ashore, leaving Khyber Khan in charge of the two boatmen until their return. Now there was no need for the major to reiterate his demand for silence as the trio squelched off through the mud to their rendezvous.

There was, however, one further incident during the trek. Just as Corporal Disbury was struggling through a particularly glutinous mud patch, his *lungyi* slipped down to his ankles. 'Fucking hell', the soldier hissed through clenched teeth as he tried to wrestle the cloth back up his legs while preventing his Tommy gun from dropping into the mud. The corporal's embarrassment was not helped when Shaffi, grinning even more broadly, came to his assistance and pulled up the dangling cloth as effortlessly as if he was putting a nappy on an overgrown child. The story later became one that 'Watson' did not like to hear repeated in his presence.

Shaffi again led his two companions through dense undergrowth to the meeting with Baba Khan. The Burmese proved to be a rather frightened little man who clasped Holmes' hands and broke into a torrent of words in Arakanese. He was a mine of information about the movement of Japanese troops and supplies and even produced from the folds of his *lungyi,* a map of enemy positions on the coast. Furthermore, the little man had details of the river craft being used to supply the *Japani* and said he had heard they were planning to use sampans to try to set up a civil administration. Baba Khan rounded off his *bushti* by telling Holmes that a Japanese Intelligence Officer, Lieutenant Honu, was travelling through the area trying to recruit local people to the enemy cause. He was apparently due at the village of Lambaguna (The Long Village), an important Japanese supply centre, about 7 miles to the south, the following noon.

Holmes made up his mind in an instant. He had a lot of valuable information and it might be madness not to return immediately to Teknaf, but here was a perfect opportunity to see *and* hear Japanese strategy at work. Thanking the little man for his help and thrusting a wad of notes into his hands, he returned with the other two to the boat, deep in thought. At the beach, he explained he wanted to go further down the coast to Lambaguna. No one said a word and the party quickly sped along until they reached the little village that until now had been merely a slang name, 'No-Can-Do'. Holmes had no time to enjoy the joke, though, and decided that only he and Shaffi should land and go to Lambaguna. The rest – including the reluctant Corporal Disbury – would remain behind.

Holmes was scarcely aware that a new year was dawning as the little boat dropped him and the *Jemadar* at Nahkaungdo. But he was sure now that he and his resourceful companion *could* do what he had in mind. Their landing point proved to be a tiny, elongated stretch of land – an island at high tide and connected to the mainland when the sea ebbed. A small cluster of fisherman's huts was the only sign of human habitation. Holmes at once sensed a greater significance to the place, as he later wrote in his report for Lieutenant Colonel Donald:

> *The beach here is shelving, so that landing is easy with very good cover against enemy observation from the mainland. It would seem to me to be the perfect jumping off point for secret missions.*

Joked about as 'No-Can-Do' might be, it would indeed soon become a regular base for raiding parties – thanks largely to Holmes' perception. But such a proposal was for the future as he and Shaffi struck off through clinging low mist into the hinterland and tramped steadily towards their destination. It might seem like madness what they were doing, but who would suspect that a British soldier disguised in black face-paint and wearing a *lungyi* would venture almost 14 miles inside enemy lines? His only protection – apart from the faithful *Jemadar* – was the .38 pistol that still nestled in the sweaty recess just below his armpit.

The two men reached Lambaguna shortly before noon, at the same time as a jostling throng of locals were also arriving to hear the *Japani* intelligence officer. Keeping their eyes averted, Holmes and Shaffi were able to observe a number of armed Japanese in the market place; the soldiers watching the crowds of natives with barely disguised distaste. The pair hid themselves in a corner of the market place, the air pungent with the smell of vegetables and spices and a hint of the odour of the Japanese standing only yards away. For just a moment Holmes had an urge to drop the secrecy and send a few of the little bastards to hell. But the Major knew he had to control his feelings – and, in any event, the man who was obviously Lieutenant Honu had appeared with an escort of ten soldiers and soon began addressing the fidgeting assembly.

The Japanese spoke in Urdu, using a sharp nasal tone, but one that Holmes could still understand. Honu was promising the local population a golden future if they were loyal to Japan and looked after her soldiers with supplies of rice and general provisions. Together, their two nations would drive the 'white man' from the Arakan and after that all of Burma and the Far East. He promised them the Japanese Army would soon be launching a 'great offensive' that would 'destroy the decadent British Army'.

Though much of what Lieutenant Honu said was clearly bombast, it matched with the information that Baba Khan had given Denis Holmes. The Major looked round at Muhammed Shaffi and indicated he had heard enough and that it was time for them to leave. He was in no doubt that the trip to Nahkaungdo had been worth the risk and he wanted to get his vital intelligence back to base as soon possible.

Now, the man known as 'Sherlock' Holmes told himself as the pair tramped back across the countryside to the sea, the plot was definitely thickening. The case for some serious retaliation against the Japanese could be made, and it was perhaps time for direct action to be taken.

4

INTO THE WHITE MAN'S GRAVE

The rumour spread like wildfire across the Teknaf Peninsula almost as soon as the New Year dawned in 1945. Soldiers and local people alike were told stories that the Japanese were making plans for an attack across the narrow divide of the River Naf to where the Allied forces were assembling for action. While the Indians and Burmese chattered fearfully in their *bashas* and on the streets of Teknaf, the military personnel quizzed one another about the 'flap' that seemed to be going on at various army posts. Anthony Irwin who was in the vicinity has recalled the feeling of apprehension in his book *Burmese Outpost*: 'They were very uncertain times and there was a story a Japanese commando force was reported to be heading upriver for Maungdaw and hundreds of their soldiers were massing at Godusara for a land attack. It was all bloody nonsense, of course'.

The evidence suggests that the Japanese themselves had started the rumour through men like the intelligence officer, Lieutenant Honu. Using the scouts and spies in their pay, they had spread the story that they were about to launch a counter attack against the Allied forces on the coast. It did not take the officers at Teknaf long to assure their own men who had been debating the gossip that it was quite untrue – but the uneasy local population were understandably harder to convince. According to Irwin, the top brass's arguments were not helped that same week in January when a completely spurious report appeared in an Indian newspaper which described how the Royal Indian Navy had not only intercepted a Japanese waterborne assault from Maungdaw, but had sunk or driven back the entire enemy fleet without the loss of a single life!

There was, however, as is so often the case, a small element of truth in the gossip. It was not *Japanese* troops who were threatening an invasion, but British commandoes of Number 3 Commando, who had unobtrusively arrived on the peninsula and would soon become the only Commando Brigade to serve in the Far East in the Second World War. They had been busy for some time making preparations to mount operations against the enemy-held islands along the Arakan coast. Foremost among these was Akyab, a low-lying, triangular-shaped island of approximately five square miles located at the mouth of the Kaladan River. A century before, this inhospitable spot with its myriad *chaungs,* creeks and mangrove swamps had earned the reputation of being 'a white man's grave'.

Akyab was rated a major Allied objective because of its airfield near the main town at the southern-most tip of the island. Ever since the Japanese occupied Burma, all attacking British forces had to be supplied by air from India. But these aircraft could not reach further south than Mandalay and by taking possession of Akyab and its larger neighbour, Ramree, some 50 miles further south, it would be possible to supply the army while it was on the offensive all the way from Mandalay to Taungup. In the Taungup area, there were also some other airfields that would be suitable for supporting an armoured thrust to Rangoon. Akyab was, therefore, the key to unlocking the Arakan coast as Captain Norman Parker – involved in naval strategy in Burma at this time – has written in *The Story of the Arakan Coastal Forces* (1987):

> *The ultimate objective of our planning was for a large-scale amphibious attack on Rangoon to take place before the monsoon and preferably before 15 March 1945. The date was eventually abandoned owing to inadequate resources being available, but it was still aimed to reach Rangoon before the Monsoon, which was due in early May. The capture of this vital town would then release substantial forces for use in other areas against the Japanese.*

The story of the first attempt to capture a Japanese stronghold on the Arakan is, however, as bizarre an episode as anything that occurred in Burma during the entire war . . .

* * *

The men who would initiate the return of Allied Forces to the Arakan were the troops of No 44 Royal Marines and No 5 Commando, collectively referred to throughout the campaign as 3 Commando. This designation remained the same even when their colleagues of No 1 Commando and No 42 Royal Marines – who had been delayed at the port of Trincomalee in Ceylon [now Sri Lanka] by transportation problems – finally arrived in Burma. Details of the operations of 44 Commando – known to its men as 'The Four-Four' – can be found in the unit's authoritative *War Diary* (ADM202 95-97) held in the National Archives at Kew; while for 5 Commando there is no better source than the recollections of Peter

Young, the legendary commando and veteran of D-Day, who was once again at the heart of the action on the other side of the world.

The official records of Royal Marine Commando 44 show they were formed on 1 August 1943 with the purpose of 'continuing the marine tradition of landing operations from the sea'. Lieutenant Colonel F.C. Horton, 'an exceptionally fine and gentlemanly officer' was appointed as CO, charged with creating a fit and highly disciplined unit of just over 400 men in seven Troops. To demonstrate his own commitment to the ideals and purpose of RMC 44, Horton announced he would train alongside the men every step of the way.

With high expectations placed upon them, the recruits were dispatched to arguably the toughest training establishment in the world: the Commando Depot at Achnacarry in the heart of the Western Highlands and some 14 miles from the nearest town, Fort William. The mixture of a punishing Scottish terrain and harsh climate where torrential rain was an almost everyday occurrence proved an ideal test for what lay ahead for the men of 'Four Four' in Burma. Only the awful heat and vicious insect-life were missing.

The gruelling training programme they underwent was reckoned to be harder than anything known in the armed forces. It included swimming, boat work, climbing, unarmed combat, the use of weapons and bayonet drill plus speed marching by day and night. Indeed, some exercises were so realistic that fatalities occurred on a regular basis: as many as 40 men are believed to have died from among the 25,000 who passed through Achnacarry during the war years. The infamous 'Death Ride' on a 50 foot rope over the fast flowing River Arkaig with live ammunition exploding below, alone claimed two lives on one tragic day.

In charge of the Combat Depot was the formidable Lieutenant Colonel Charles Vaughan, a veteran of the Coldstream Guards, who had served in the First World War. He believed that the training should provide the new marine commandos with the opportunity to show 'courage, determination, initiative and spirit'. He also felt that every man who came to Achnacarry should experience a sense of 'real adventure' as he ran, jumped, swam or fired weapons over the remote countryside. Vaughan's mixture of quiet authority and iron will earned him several nick-names from his charges including 'The Laird of Achnacarry', 'The Wolf of Badenoch' and even 'The Rommel of the North'. To ram home the message of the programme, he even had mock graves erected at the entrance to the Depot – the tombstones inscribed with object lessons explaining precisely *what* the 'dead' had failed to do while under training!

The men of 'Four-Four' who later served on the Arakan never forgot the spectacular 'Night Opposed Landing Exercise' in which they took part in

Scotland shortly before their 'passing out' ceremony as marines. Military historian Tony Mackenzie has described this operation in his excellent history, *Achnacarry to the Arakan: A Diary of the Commando at War* (1996):

> *The object was to land raiding troops (the trainees) on to a defended beach, from which they would be faced by a barrage of live ammunition fired by the instructors, who were past masters at 'shooting to miss'. Small arms, machine guns firing on fixed lines, mortars, smoke canisters, stun grenades, thunder-flashes, very lights and parachute flares were all used to simulate the defensive opposition likely to be encountered in battle conditions. As the commandos came ashore from their boats, live grenades would be exploding in the shallow muddy water. After they had placed their demolition charges against the target they would withdraw under fire. Whilst paddling away from the beach in the assault boats, it was quite likely that mortar bombs would drop so close to the boats that the occupants would be soaked in the spray and live rounds fired from Bren guns would hit the hand held paddles of the men who were propelling the retreating craft away from the beach.*

In November 1943, 44 Royal Marine Commando were issued with their first orders. They were instructed to proceed to the Far East where they were to link up with other marines and commandos to go into operation wherever they were needed in the war with the Japanese. Before the men had even set sail, however, it was realised that if the initials for the new brigade were shortened they created an unfortunate association with the Nazi SS storm troopers. The substitution of 3 Commando Brigade was hastily agreed.

A month long sea voyage on the former passenger liner, *Reina del Pacifico,* through the Mediterranean, via the Suez Canal, and across the Indian Ocean to Bombay, helped the men of 44 to adapt to the change of climate from wet and windy Scotland. During the voyage, lectures were given about the Japanese Army and its soldiers, the facts of jungle warfare and especially the problems of coping with the climate of the Arakan and its alternate fetid heat and drenching monsoons. Special acclimatisation courses were also held at Cox's Bazaar before the commandos went to Burma in order to prepare them for action.

It was on 5 March 1944 that 44 set up base at Nhila on the Teknaf Peninsula. The men were told they were ideally placed here to carry out amphibious operations to aid the 14th Army's second attempt to push south from India against the entrenched Japanese. A week later, they took part in the first of two missions, code-named 'Operation Screwdriver'. Both bore the acknowledged hallmarks of the traditional three-part commando operation: a sea landing, sustained harassment of the enemy and then an ordered withdrawal. The first of these, just before midnight on 11 March, was directed against Alethangyaw, with the purpose of neutralising the occupiers and allowing the other units of the brigade to move into the surrounding hills where larger numbers of Japanese were known to have gathered.

However, after landing at Cypress Point, Alethangyaw proved more heavily defended than had been expected – particularly by machine gun emplacements and snipers in treetops – causing a degree of confusion among the men on their first active operation in the dark. Yet despite having to contend with a series of running battles against the well-hidden Japanese, the seven troops of 'Four Four' had a chance to utilise all the skills they had developed in the Highlands. In the next 48 hours they managed to inflict extensive casualties and commence a recce of the surrounding hills. Only one patrol, however, established contact with the enemy and two days later Lieutenant Colonel Horton ordered his men to return to Cypress Point and re-embark for Nhila. A later estimate would claim that between 35 and 50 Japanese had been killed, at the cost of two of 44 officers and two other ranks missing believed dead.

The marines crossed the Naf again in two barges on 21 March with Nahkaungdo, Lambaguna, and another small settlement, Hinthaya, as their objectives. Their previous exploits had obviously come to the attention of the Japanese because the *War Diary* reveals that the following morning an Oriental voice suddenly broke into a radio transmission, boasting: 'We know 44 Commando have returned! This time you will not be so fortunate as we have brought up a large number of guns to blast you out!' The hardened raiders could not restrain a little smile of amusement as they moved into position.

Once again the 'Four Four' reaped the rewards for their dedication. On 30 March, a Japanese patrol was ambushed and five men killed. Two days later, Hinthaya was raided leaving five enemy dead and on 6 April it was the turn of an enemy patrol of sixteen men to be caught unawares near the Ton *chaung*, resulting in eleven Jap fatalities. The Japanese were soon reinforcing their troops in the Arakan, however, and it became evident that the 14th Army would not be able to try another push before the onset of the monsoon. The marines were ordered to return to base and a game of cat and mouse ensued with radio transmissions and carefully placed articles of deception to effect the withdrawal of the 44 before the enemy was aware what was happening and could give chase.

Lieutenant Horton and his men could be reasonably satisfied with what they had achieved in 'Operation Screwdriver'. But when the 'Second Arakan' ended in stalemate and 'Four Four' was moved to a new deployment in Assam, many of the marines who had now tasted conflict on the coast nursed a hope they might come back and get a real chance of turning the screw on the Japanese. They did not have to wait long for the opportunity.

* * *

The marines of 44 were, in fact, ordered back to Teknaf just six months later. They barely had time to make camp before they were joined on the peninsula by another force, No 5 Commando, a unit already held in high regard and also intended for the next stage of the battle. Formed in July 1940 largely from regulars and reservists who had escaped from Dunkirk, the commandos had earned their laurels with raids on St. Nazaire and Antsirane, as well as preventing the French colony of Madagascar from being invaded by the Japanese. No 5 had their first taste of the Indian continent in January 1944 when they were sent to the border to help prevent any Japanese advance from Burma. The end of that year saw them moved to Teknaf and a makeshift camp of tents and bamboo *bashas*. They were just getting used to the area when the sudden appearance of the Deputy Brigade Commander, Colonel Peter Young, made everyone in the ranks suspect that 'something was in the air'.

Young, who was well on the way to ensuring his stature as one of the most colourful, commanding and influential soldiers of his generation, had a reputation for appearing when action was being planned. His visit to Teknaf was therefore monitored with the greatest interest by one and all: for he was a man known to admire 'genuine battle' – to use his own words – although he was well aware of the hardships it engendered and the human lives it could cost.

A bluff, hearty and larger-than-life figure, Young possessed a remarkable sensitivity to the problems of others. Indeed, during his army career he had made a practice of never asking for anything to be done that he could not do himself. He believed that the greatest quality any commander possessed was, 'the gift of making his men feel that if *he* takes them into battle they cannot possibility lose'. He had, in fact, been fascinated by war all his life – in particular the English Civil War and the Cavaliers whom he greatly admired and, some of his fellow officers said, emulated. This interest had been inspired while reading history at Trinity College, Oxford, and his rise from second lieutenant in the Bedfordshire and Hertfordshire Regiment – which he joined in 1939 – to the position of Brigadier in 1945, was to prove nothing short of meteoric.

At the beginning of the war, Young had been sent almost at once to France where nothing would keep him from front line action and he was wounded during the evacuation from Dunkirk. Recovering quickly and anxious to rejoin the conflict, his bravery and evident leadership skills made him a natural for the newly formed No.3 Commando Brigade and with them he took part in raids on Guernsey, Lofoten and Vaago – during the latter winning an MC. One battle achievement followed another, as a tribute to him in *The Daily Telegraph* of 14 September 1988 reports:

After a period on the staff at Combined Operations HQ, Peter Young became second-in-command of 3 Commando and took part in the Dieppe Raid. Here he managed to take his raiding force up the cliffs on a network of barbed wire that, as he put it, an over-conscientious German officer had inadvertently provided for them to walk on. Young was the only Commando officer to reach his objective and bring back all his men. At one point, when they were approaching enemy machine guns through a cornfield, he encouraged his soldiers by telling them 'not to worry about bullets as standing corn made an effective protection'. He was awarded a DSO for his part in this raid.

The year 1943 saw Young leading 3 Commando raids in Italy – winning two Bars to add to his MC – and in 1944 returning to Normandy. Here, he and his men were in the vanguard of the landings, where they secured the bridgehead at Le Plein despite heavy German counter attacks. Young lead the advance on Angoville after which the defeat of the Germans in France became inevitable. It was probably inevitable, too, that such a remarkable man – still only 29 – would be sent to Burma to help in the defeat of the Japanese. Young was, in truth, a living legend when he arrived at Teknaf that November.

The commandos had not, though, been idle since their arrival and had already carried out a number of demanding training exercises by day and night. In particular, they had become proficient at crossing the River Naf under the cover of darkness in Goatley boats to scout enemy positions. These collapsible craft with a wooden bottom and canvas sides weighed just 2 cwt and could be assembled by two men in under a minute. They carried a crew of seven – six men using paddles – and were proficient at calm-water crossings. Apparently, though, they could be a bit of a nightmare if the weather turned stormy.

Shortly after Peter Young's arrival a joint night exercise between 5 Commando and 'Four Four' was arranged. Code-named 'Operation Sarong', it set the marines the task of overcoming their colleagues – a task that the veteran defenders prevented, although one of their number was quite badly burned during the explosions of some phosphorous bombs. Young, who was keen to get the feel of action himself in this new environment, was suddenly presented with the opportunity and decided to take it, as he explains in his gripping narrative, *Storm From The Sea* (1958):

> When I arrived at Teknaf it was to find that the Commanding Officer, Brigadier W.J. Nonweiler, had fallen ill and was in hospital. A week later he was sent home to recover his health, leaving me temporarily in command of the brigade. The men were eager for action, which had long been denied them, and it was only the acute shortage of landing craft that prevented us embarking on a full raiding programme. Instead it was decided to raid Elizabeth Island in Hunter's Bay, forty miles south of Akyab, in order to collect information and, if possible, a prisoner. I decided to accompany this expedition myself.

Young remembers that he and a party of 30 men set out on a lovely day and sailed down the Arakan coast in a motor launch towing one of the Eureka landing craft similar to the type he had used in the Dieppe landings. The journey was 'like a pleasure cruise' and the party reached Hunter's Bay without any difficulty. However, he says, night had already fallen when the group disembarked into the landing-craft: 'Landing near the village of Ondaw, the marines marched two and a half miles across country, harassed by wild boars as they went, and fell upon a Japanese section post guarding another beach. What casualties they inflicted I cannot say'.

During the course of the expedition, Peter Young discovered for himself some of the problems facing troops fighting on the Arakan. One marine in the party lost his way in the dark and was soon surrounded by Japanese soldiers. Although the man, Chappell, shot several of the enemy, he was finally forced to surrender and was taken, bound hand and foot, to Myebon. Amazingly, the tough soldier survived his captivity and was repatriated at the end of the war. For the rest of the men, getting back to base also proved to be no easy matter, as Young recalls:

> There was a good deal of surf around the island and, worse still, the landing craft broke down. We stood on the beach and watched it drift farther and farther away and felt more and more idiotic. A gallant Indian seaman worked in the water for 40 minutes and finally freed the propeller of the weeds that were clogging it. After that the craft came to life again, but even so we had to swim for it. It says much for the discipline of those marines that not one of them lost his weapon.

The mission also failed in its objective of capturing a Japanese prisoner – although two Burmese encountered during the raid volunteered to return to Teknaf as 'captives'. Nevertheless, valuable lessons had been learned and several more night and day exercises were carried out by the marines and the commandos with varying degrees of success in the estuaries, rivers and *chaungs* of the Arakan coast in the weeks up to Christmas.

Then, in the first week of the New Year, the decision was made to try and take the island of Akyab and set about achieving what the eager war correspondents and Allied propagandists would later describe as 'the first move in the reoccupation of Burma'. This, the media hoped, would herald the big push towards Rangoon, almost a thousand miles away. Yet once again in the story of the Banzai Hunters it would prove to be a mission filled with surprises.

* * *

Akyab [the modern Sittwe] is a city, district and island on the Bay of Bengal situated at the confluence of three rivers, the Mayu, the Kaladan and the Lemyu. It is the capital of Rakhine State and regarded as an important port and rice-milling centre – no mean achievement for what had for centuries been a small and isolated fishing community. The harbour that provides the hub around which the prosperity of the island has flourished resembles a huge circular lake about two miles in diameter. Its location, the facilities of its port and an airfield are an obvious indication of the importance placed upon it by Mountbatten and his chiefs of staff when the third Arakan campaign was launched.

It had not been until the first Burmese war of 1825–26 when Akyab and the rest of the Arakan fell into the hands of the British that its fortunes began to change. The cession of the district by the Treaty of Yandaboo enabled the new government to remove the restrictions on trade that had been imposed by the Burmese, enabling it to grow rapidly into an important maritime centre. The port was also selected as the new seat of government, replacing the old capital of Myohaung, and became the northernmost district of lower Burma.

During the first half century of British rule, the population grew to over 15,000 inhabitants. That figure had doubled by the start of the twentieth century making Akyab the third port of Burma. A number of public buildings also replaced the old bamboo *bashas,* and several large rice mills were erected close to the port. The level tracts of well-watered land on the mainland provided the ideal location for growing rice and the network of waterways generated by the three rivers enabled crops to be easily and cheaply transported to the port. The flourishing rice trade was later supplemented by the discovery of oil and Sittwe is today a centre of undersea exploration for this important natural resource.

In January 1945, however, Akyab had been in Japanese hands for over three years and was showing signs of a negligent occupation. The airfield was pockmarked with craters and the control buildings shabby and forlorn. The T-shaped steel jetty in the harbour was a rusting wreck untouched since the Burma RNVR had abandoned it. Two sunken ships lay embedded alongside and the quays were a mass of wrecked structures from which the Japanese and Burmese had systematically removed the roofs and floors – apparently for firewood for use in cooking. Jungle flora and fauna had encroached into many of the buildings and was now growing profusely inside the peeling walls. It was this unprepossessing jumble that the Allies planned to retake on 4 January in 'Operation Lightning' as John Winton explains in *The Forgotten Fleet*:

> A full-scale amphibious assault on Akyab ('Operation Talon') was originally fixed for 18 February, but was cancelled. After some shuffling of alternative plans, the date of the landing, to be carried out without preliminary air or sea bombardment, was hurriedly brought forward to 3 January. In the event, the Akyab landing ('Operation Lightning') was planned, mounted and carried out in six days.

The reason for this hurried revision will become apparent shortly – but there was no lack of careful planning for the armada of ships and troops to carry out the assault. The details of the composition of this assembly make for impressive reading. The naval forces were to be under the command of Rear Admiral B.C.S. Martin with his Chief of Staff, Captain E.W. Bush, as Senior Officer of the Assault Group. No 3 Commando Brigade would embark from Teknaf and be put ashore on Akyab to take the island. The majority of these men were to be transported in two 5-knot convoys. Convoy 'Able' would leave at 4.30 a.m. with Captain Bush in the Headquarters Ship and Commander G.G. Mojer, Senior Officer Convoy, in a Fairmile; with Convoy 'Baker' following 15 minutes later led by Commander H.R.M. Nicholl, Deputy Senior Officer, Assault Group in a Landing Craft Control (LCC), a converted Fairmile packed with navigational aids, echo sounders and ASDIC.*

---

* There is evidence to suggest that the Japanese held the Fairmiles in high regard because their size and speed and the distances over which they operated were seemingly beyond their storage capacity for petrol. The Japs believed they must be powered by an engine superior to anything in their Navy and have incredibly effective armour plating. In January 1945 at least two attempts were made to ambush Fairmiles in the Arakan *chaungs* and there were a number of other instances when Japanese troops tried to shoot and disable one of the motor launches in order to take it away to 'unravel its secrets', according to Coastal Forces officer, Lieutenant Allan Russell.

In fact, Fairmiles played a major role in both convoys. In 'Able', ten of the versatile gun boats towed the same number of LCSs, with twenty LCMs towing twenty LCAs, and a further two Landing Craft Infantry (LCIs) hauling a further pair of LCAs. The wooden hulled LCIs – similar in design to the LCS – were 105 feet sized infantry carriers designed for raider operations, powered by two supercharged 1,500 hp Hall-Scott engines, possessing a top speed of 15 knots and an endurance range of 550 miles. Crewed by two officers and fifteen men, they had a capacity for six officers and 96 fully equipped troops who were embarked over four bow ramps. It was claimed in typically quirky fashion that eighteen bicycles could be stored on deck!

Six British Yard Mine Sweepers (BYMS), home-built versions of the American Yard Class Minesweepers that had been launched in the United States in January 1942, dominated convoy 'Baker'. With 136-feet long wooden hulls and non-ferrous fixings to reduce the magnetic signature, they were powered by 1,200 hp diesel engines, weighed 300 tons and carried a crew of 38. By 1944, the BYMS had a track record of being manned by tumultuous seamen and officers, a fact no doubt attributable to the dangerous nature of their work. The six minesweepers in 'Baker' each towed two LCAs. Another six Landing Craft Tank (LCTs) followed them pulling nine LCPs. The sturdy LCTs with their 500hp Paxman Diesel engines and armour-plated sides were built to carry tanks and heavy weaponry.

A third 12-knot convoy, 'Charlie' with Rear Admiral Martin on board HM *Napier,* accompanied by *Nepal* and *Shoreham,* left after the other two at 6.30 a.m. Its purpose was to carry out a bombardment and land the remaining troops on Akyab. Tony Mackenzie has recorded the story of 'Operation Lightning' in his account of the 'Four Four':

> *The mess decks of all the vessels were crowded with marines and their equipment. Some men resorted to sleeping on deck when the convoy anchored in the River Naf for the night in company with the destroyers* Napier *and* Nepal. *Then, at first light, all the assembled ships moved off, sailing south towards Akyab Island and their appointment with the Japs.*

In terms of numbers, the flotilla amounted to the largest amphibious lift seen so far in Burma during the war. To some observers it was also one of the strangest with the addition of a number of old riverboats, rice barges and rickety sampans – several of which had been seconded from Major Firbanks' fleet – bringing up the rear. John Winton takes up the story again:

The convoys had a passage of some 45 miles to the landing position, which was
about seven miles off the beach. The haste with which 'Lightning' had been
mounted led to a somewhat extempore appearance of equipment on the beach.
Limit signs were made of canvas from the officers' wash-place at Teknaf.
Hurricane lamps, borrowed from the Army, were covered with coloured bunting
from the base decorations. But the landing went off almost without a hitch. H-hour
had been fixed at 12.30 and the first wave touched down half a minute early. By
13.50 the whole commando and a squadron of medium tanks were ashore.

A big surprise awaited the men as they poured into 'the white man's grave',
however. The entire town of Akyab was deserted. The Japanese had vanished
without leaving a single man to hold their former stronghold. Peter Young
remembers the mixture of bewilderment and disappointment among the troops
as they marched ashore:

The Japs had already left – it was rumoured that they had departed as much as
a week beforehand. An RAF officer flying over the place had thought it looked
rather deserted. So we landed unopposed. It was not an absolutely dry landing,
but I was able to sit down on the beach, take off my boots and socks and dry my
feet in peace. A gentlemanly operation!*

To others who had waited impatiently for weeks for this moment, the landing was
a 'crashing anticlimax'. There was no sign of the three battalions of enemy troops
believed to be occupying the island. The beach defences including fortified
bunkers and anti-tank ditches were silent and deserted and two 'tanks' turned out
to be dummies made from bamboo and other jungle vegetation. An untidy sprawl
of Japanese graves and a vast quantity of rubbish and useless material littered the
entire area.

The only sights to be seen by the advancing force was the flight of some seabirds;
while the only sounds were the rumble of Allied tanks as they trundled noisily from
the LCTs onto the grubby harbour. The stone pier, ramshackle iron wharfs and
timber jetties stood gaunt and abandoned under the glare of the morning's sun. As
the minutes turned to hours, however, the civilian population who had fled from the
vicinity as the assault force had loomed into view, began returning in small, anxious

---

* The RAF pilot was, in fact, Group Captain Dennis David, accompanied by an artillery officer, who noticed a complete absence
of Japanese aircraft on the airfield. The pair landed and were told by a native headman that the enemy had left and they had
effectively 'captured Akyab' according to David's obtuary in *The Times* in September 2000.

groups hoping to find they had new and more kindly masters.

Inspection by the marines quickly revealed that the Japanese had left hardly a building undamaged. It was clear that days of gruelling work lay ahead to repair what the enemy had demolished or neglected so that the island could become operational once again. Only by restoring the jetties in the port and reopening the shattered airfield would Akyab be able to provide support for the 14th Army. But just as thoughts were turning to these tasks, there was a sudden shock as Lieutenant General Sir Philip Christison, a member of Mountbatten's staff who flew to the island immediately after the landing, has recorded in a document (82/15/1) on file at the National Archive. It tells the story of an incident that has been overlooked in almost every account of the war in Burma:

But not all the Japs had left. A number remained in the northeast corner waiting for craft to take them over to the mainland. I instructed troops to go in and round them up. At 2200 hours on 9 January, I heard heavy firing from the northeast. The Japs were surely not going to attempt to re-capture Akyab? I though it highly unlikely in the circumstances, though it would have been in accordance with their tactics.

That very night, says Christison, four Japanese armoured landing craft each carrying 50 men with heavy and light machine gun support tried to rescue their stranded colleagues. Close fighting in the dark between the Allied troops and the invaders lasted for over an hour before the Japanese ran for their boats and made off back to the mainland. Two nights later, another group of 40 soldiers also attempted to land, hurling grenades before them as a covering party came ashore further down the beach. The Lieutenant General continues his dramatic account:

Suddenly a large 70-foot armoured motor launch appeared and was thought to be ours. But it put on a searchlight and opened fire on our men with 2-pounder guns and medium machine guns. With it there were three landing craft. This was a brilliant effort by the Japs, a copybook little operation, but it cost them two officers and 22 other ranks killed. Now Akyab really was clear of the enemy.

With this success – albeit an unopposed one with the exception of the bloody skirmish on the beach – the omens now looked much brighter for the future of the 'Third Arakan', as John Winton has commented:

The Allies had gained a most valuable island, with an all-weather airfield and command of the Mayu and Kaladan rivers, estuaries and the entrances to the inland water-ways of the south Arakan. 'Lightning' had been excellent training and had confirmed the Navy's ability to put the Army ashore where and when they were wanted. The crews of the landing craft had both gained and inspired confidence.

Winton's remark about confidence being inspired among the crews of the landing craft is a perceptive and interesting one. For this was indeed what was happening to a group of young men who had not long arrived from England and been quickly plunged into the battle on the Arakan in small boats. These recruits, mostly in their twenties, had joined up from all over the country hoping to help win the war. Many had expected to see action in Europe; few had imagined finding themselves on the other side of the world in a hothouse hell fighting what would become know as 'The Chaung War'. It is the story of one of these unsung Banzai Hunters – typical of many of his colleagues – that comes next. A tale that he is, in fact, only able to tell thanks to an almost miraculous escape from death in LCS 87 when it was ambushed by Japanese snipers in a one-way *chaung* on the Arakan.

5
THE CHAUNG WAR

Several hundred young men in small armoured boats set out daily during the early weeks of 1945 to enter the hinterland of the Arakan and fight what became known as 'The Chaung War'. They were men of varied nationalities – including British, Indian, South African, Australians and New Zealanders – from differing backgrounds and with differing expectations. Some were eager for conflict with the Japanese, some were nervous and a few were scared. They were all reliant on the boats that represented the difference between life and death, their officers who were mostly little older than them and, especially, one another.

According to those who saw action, this 'war' made a deep impression on everyone and, for those who survived, proved to be a mixture of the strange, the stealthy and the secretive. It involved deception and camouflage and often lying in wait *listening* – waiting to pick-up an agent or carry out a brief, deadly ambush on an unsuspecting enemy. Their area of operation covered hundreds of miles along the coast where the sea, the rivers, the tiny islands, the mud banks and jungle all seemed to merge into one. Military documents from the time of 'Third Arakan' indicate the confusion that existed during the early days with some Navy maps showing 'land' where those of the Army designate the area as 'water'. In almost every case, the marking of a particular spot as a 'beach' proved to be a misnomer, for the Arakan *chaungs* offered few recognisable landing places and were often no more than a convenient gap in a mangrove swamp where the tangle of submerged tree roots, rotting foliage and mud still made landing a hazardous operation at either high or low tide. Bernard Fergusson who served in the area has vividly described in his autobiography, *Beyond The Chindwin* (1945), how the water-ways in which the conflict was fought out varied considerably in both width and navigability:

> *Some were 200 yards wide and could be navigated for certain distances by sloops; others were only a few feet across and could be penetrated only by canoe. Even in the widest* chaungs *there were likely to be shoals in mid-channel,*

rocks, jagged tree stumps and hidden snags. In places the Japanese had planted stakes, covered at high water, and stretched trip-wires between the banks, set to detonate concealed mines, or built booms festooned with grenades. At low water, in perpetual dusk, under the overhanging branches, the mangrove roots assumed fantastically tortured shapes and every operation was a test of the stoutest nerves.

The 'Chaung War' also demanded new tactics, new types of disguise and new means of ambush that had to be devised by the men of the Arakan Coastal Forces. Netting and mangrove branches for patrol duties, for example, often camouflaged the LCAs, while on the most dangerous missions soldiers with machine guns and mortars augmented their crews. Fairmiles, by contrast, would lie up inside the smallest *chaungs* with their engines stopped, waiting for an unsuspecting enemy sampan to slip by on the ebb tide. Inevitably, of course, there were occasions when Allied Forces and the Japanese met head-on in the winding creeks – and then it became a case of who first overcame their surprise and acted that survived. G.R. Stevens who has written about this phase of the Burma War in his *History of the 2ⁿᵈ King Edward VII's Own Gurkha Rifles 1921–1948* (1952) says: 'The perversities of weather and terrain imposed even greater strains than the malice of the enemy; life necessitated the transformation of each man from mammal to near-amphibian'.

This is the story of one of these men, how he adapted to the conditions and what happened to him during 'The Chaung War'.

* * *

Marine Les Gunn could sense from the first moment he saw the sweltering jungle foliage and treacherous muddy *chaungs* of the Arakan why it was called, 'the worst place on earth'. From the prow of LCS 87 as it churned the waters of the Bay of Bengal towards the shoreline of Burma, he knew it was a world away from the picturesque rural Suffolk village that had been the only life he had known since his birth in September 1924. Two years ago he had left the little community full of the high spirits and bravado of many young men of his generation going off to fight for their country – and was about to experience the realities of a type of warfare he could scarcely have imagined.

Les, a strong young man almost 6 feet tall with direct blue eyes, an easy smile and a lively sense of humour, was one of three children of Leonard Gunn, a roadman in the village of Groton. Here, in the heart of the East Anglian countryside, Les had grown up as the war clouds gathered over Britain. After the conflict had finally broken out, Les's father had been put to work supervising German Prisoners of War on local farms, while his teenage sons followed the action on the radio and in the pages of newspapers.

Although East Anglia was a potential invasion point for the Germans and its skies the battleground for the RAF and *Luftwaffe* aircraft fighting the Battle of Britain, the normal tranquillity of Groton was rarely broken. Les grew up without any clear idea of a career, although he briefly thought of becoming a parson, he says. Early in 1941, however, with the conflict now being fought on a global scale after Japan had bombed Pearl Harbour and forced the entry of the US into the war, Les saw a newspaper photograph that would have an extraordinary effect on his life:

It was in the Daily Mirror: *a picture of a group of soldiers crawling through some swampy undergrowth in Burma. The report said they were marines fighting in the battle of the Arakan. Although no one knew it then, they were about to be driven out by the Japs and it would be almost four years before they fought their way back. I showed the picture to my dad and said, 'That's where I want to go!' He probably thought I was mad and didn't give it a second thought. But that's how things turned out.*

In May 1942, like a number of his friends, Les volunteered for the Royal Marines. He was too young, though, and it was not until August when he was just a month short of his eighteenth birthday, that he was finally accepted for training as a 'sea going marine'. He was sent to Chatham Barracks on the banks of the Medway and there the young man who had never previously spent any time by the sea and could not even swim, began his initiation into one of the most illustrious of Britain's maritime services. Firstly at Chatham, and later at another base at Gosport on the Solent, he was toughened on assault courses, instructed how to handle weapons and introduced to the skills of Landing Craft Combined Operations that would become his future.

A posting in the summer of 1943 took Les to Hayling Island near the great naval docks at Portsmouth. Here he joined 903 Flotilla and first set his eyes on the boat that would become the centre of his life on the other side of the world. The Landing Craft Support (Medium) – LCS for short – was not the most impressive craft at anchor in the crowded Solent, Les remembers, but he would have cause to thank its speed, manoeuvrability and armament before the war was over. It bore the freshly painted number 87 on both sides of its pointed bow and like the others of its type destined for transportation to the Far East, would prove reliable and very durable under fire.

Riding low in the water, the craft had two decks, a bulkhead and conning tower. It was actually a Mark 3 with several improvements over its two predecessors, although it utilised the same hull. Measuring 41 feet 2 inches long with a beam of 10 feet 1 inches, it was driven by two powerful 64 hp Ford V-8 Scripps engines. When unladen it displaced just over 11 tons and could take 12.8 tons when fully loaded. The LCS had a fuel capacity of 98 gallons of petrol, a maximum speed of 9 knots and a range of 90 miles running at top speed.

Even from a distance, though, the boat's armoured sides and weaponry hinted at an inherent strength. Les and the other crewmembers would discover that it had 10lb heavy-duty plating on the hull sides and decks as well as on the conning tower, ammunition hoist and bulkheads. In the turret were two .50 power-operated Vickers machine guns plus two .303 Lewis guns and a four inch smoke mortar on the forward deck. Completing the weaponry was a supply of 10lb high explosive bombs and 12 Type-18 smoke generators that could be used for creating an escape screen when a hasty exit from enemy fire became necessary. The Mark 3 was built to carry a crew of one officer, three men and six gunners. The units were intended to be almost entirely self-sufficient; carrying their own supplies of ammunition, jerry cans of fuel and maintaining contact with base and other craft by radio or, when required, semaphore signals.

The young men who would make up the crew of number 87 had to wait until the day after their arrival before they were allowed to go on board their vessel. It was immediately apparent to them all that space would be at a premium. They would have to sleep where they could and the cooking facilities were so basic that other than boiling water to make tea or heat up tinned food, they would be dining most of the time on 'compo' rations – biscuits, bully beef, beans and the like. Going to the toilet was apparently very simply just a matter of hanging the appropriate part of the anatomy over the stern of the boat whenever the need arose.

Les and the rest of the crew spent the months of that summer and autumn familiarising themselves with the landing craft on the waters and inlets of the Solent. Their skipper was a man only a couple of years older than most of them – 20-year-old Second Lieutenant Johnnie Lancaster, a Royal Navy officer from London. His second in command was Sergeant Steve Pinnock, and there were two other ranks, Corporals Hutchby and Hallam, who were fated to be involved in a terrible tragedy on the very first day LCS 87 went into action. Just before Christmas 1943, however, as part of the crew's training, they were ordered up to

Invergordan on the windswept Cromarty Firth in Scotland. Les remembers the trip on board the large combat transport ship, HMS *Glenearn,* from Tilbury up the east coast in a very wintry North Sea as something of a nightmare:

It was just like a prison ship. The conditions were appalling and for Christmas Day we only had Irish stew. And not even water to drink! All the time, the tannoy system kept playing 'There's No Place Like Home'. One of the boys in the NAAFI got so desperate that he jumped ship at Invergordon.

The first training exercise that Les went on the following morning – Boxing Day – was an even more unhappy experience. In biting cold winds, with snow sweeping across the Moray Firth and the sea getting rougher by the minute, he was packed in with a couple of dozen other fully equipped men into an LCA. This was one of the original British standard assault type vessels: 41 feet long with two 65 hp Ford V-8 engines and twin screws. It had a Lewis gun cockpit and fortified double doors and had been designed for use in large-scale troop landings. The boat was, in fact, the forerunner of the LCS in which Les had been training – although it had a smaller range, around 60 miles, and a slower speed at 6 knots – and it did not take him long to find that it lacked all its successor's few niceties. The exercise was routed to take the trainee marines around the ominously named Black Isle to Inverness. Les recalls the trip vividly:

As we ploughed through the sea the weather got worse and worse. The well behind the steel doors began to fill up with water. I grabbed a steel helmet and tried to bale out, but the level just kept getting higher. I realised we were sinking. I wrestled with the tags on my duffle coat to get it off and all of a sudden I was head-over-heels in the sea. I couldn't swim and all I could see were these kit bags and weapons going down with me. Then a pair of legs swam by and I just grabbed them. The swimmer somehow got to the surface with me hanging on and I was just in time to see the LCA stern up. At that moment the crew of an LCS who must have seen what happened arrived and I was pulled on board.

Les Gunn is in no doubt as to just how lucky he was to escape with his life that day – and also what he owed to a certain 'Tubby' Hayward from Bristol who pulled him from the stormy waters of the Moray Firth. He was also convinced that the ability of the LCS to withstand the terrible weather was a good omen for the future. Six other men on that Boxing Day exercise were not so lucky, however, and their deaths contributed to one of the worst Second World War maritime training disasters in Scotland.

After his fortunate escape, Les was briefly hospitalised in Inverness and then took part in a number of other landing exercises in and around Burghead Bay near Lossiemouth. He and the other marines were dropped in landing craft from either of two naval cruisers, HMS *Battleaxe* and HMS *Cutlass,* and buffeted their way through the rising waves to the beaches. By and large, the operations went off successfully, although occasionally they were hampered by mist or fog. Sometimes when the water grew really rough, oil would be poured over the sea to help the landing craft get to the shore.

The only time Les says he felt scared during all of these exercises was when the landing craft were being lowered overboard. They were transported to the scene of the operations hanging on davits from the side of the ships and then dropped into the water. When fully loaded with 25 men the little boats sometimes swung precariously while being winched down from the deck or raised again after a sortie had been completed.

> *If your boat happened to be slung from the top deck, it could be one hell of a ride up or down. Of course, none of us knew that these exercises were all part of the preparations for D-Day. But just as they were finally assembling all the craft together for the crossing, some of us were told we were not going. Apparently there were not enough ships to take everybody over. So instead I got leave for the first time in months! I went home to Groton and only read about what happened in France later.*

Les was, of course, disappointed at not being able to put his training to use. He had no way of knowing that he would soon be taking part in another series of vital coastal operations to bring down an enemy – just as D-Day had done. He waited patiently for his next posting, which was not long in arriving. But it was not, as he might have expected, across the English Channel or somewhere similar in Europe. Instead, he was to travel over 3,000 miles to the very place he had set his heart on when reading the *Daily Mirror* two years before . . .

* * *

In June 1944, the members of Second Lieutenant Johnnie Lancaster's LCS No 87 joined the troop ship, HMS *Strathaird,* at Greenock and sailed to Bombay. The men were briefed that they were going to launch a new campaign against the

Japanese in Burma. While their landing craft was transported separately, the men were able to enjoy the voyage as part of a large convoy and made the most of the beautiful weather and the complete absence of U-Boats to spoil the calm as they crossed three oceans. It would be the last time many of them would have the chance for rest and relaxation in the next year.

During the sea journey, Les grew friendly with Ron Haddock, a lad just a month older than himself whom he first met at Gosport. It was there the two men discovered they had grown-up not far from one another – Ron was from the town of Ipswich just 13 miles from Les's village. Les also got on well with two of the other marines, Charlie Green, a signalman, and Jack Garnett, also a gunner. Their mates soon knew this high-spirited trio as 'The Three Gs'. The last member of the nine-man crew was Tommy Driver, designated a 'stoker', although he had trained to be the landing craft's mechanic. The trip to India – Les would recall later – was a time when a mixture of common interests and ribald humour strengthened the camaraderie between the men as they prepared for the dangerous days that lay ahead.

By the time the crew reached India and were reunited with their boat, they were all in the mood for some action. After a brief stop at Bombay, LCS 87 was dispatched south down the coast to the port of Cochin on the Arabian Sea to take part in more exercises. However, Les did not even have a chance to look at the famous old city before he suddenly fell ill. He was diagnosed with dysentery and had to spend the next month in hospital while the other marines trained in and around the inlets of Kerala.

In August, Les was able to rejoin his mates as they were transferred again across the Bay of Bengal to the Indian seaport of Chittagong, today the second largest city of Bangladesh. Built on the banks of the Karnaphuli River, the port had been described by the seventh-century Chinese poet, Huen Tsang, as 'a sleeping beauty emerging from mists and water' and was home to a multi-ethnic community who made their living on the sea or in the harbour's many industries. Here the marines' training began in earnest, although the picturesque Patenga Sea Beach about 14 miles from Chittagong where they often landed was very different from the conditions they would soon face a little more than fifty miles down the coast in Burma. Only the evident anxiety of the population – fearful the Japanese might invade after surviving an air raid and the spread of some insidious rumours – spoiled an otherwise idyllic interval.

In November 1944, LCS 87 was assigned to the assault units of the Arakan Coastal Forces under the command of Captain John Ryland. Ryland had set up his headquarters on HIMS *Cheetah* at Trombay and established operational bases around the Indian coast at Cochin, Mandapam, Madras, Vizagapatam and Chittagong. His senior men consisted of a mixture of Royal Navy officers and members of the Royal Indian Navy Volunteer Reserve – many of them former civil servants and tea planters with a good understanding of the Indian ratings that served under them. Despite their lack of practical experience, the men took part in several naval engagements with the Japanese and helped to repulse enemy submarine attacks on Vizagapatam and Columbo. Even allowing for a constant shortage of materials, Coastal Forces played their part in preventing any Japanese advance into India. The intention that they might actually be able to take the fight to the enemy seemed unlikely, though, as Tony Goulden, who served on the Arakan has written in *From Trombay to Changi* (1987):

> *The omens were not particularly bright that this non-existent force (in May 1942) could be built up to harry the Japanese and in 1944 to range up and down the Burma coast to prevent the use by the Japanese of the coastal route, and indeed chase them up every chaung, inlet and harbour so that even Burmese fishing boats were afraid to go to sea. These achievements with minimal losses were not backed by copious supplies of food, water, weaponry and spares. They were achieved despite a shortage of everything except good humour, good seamanship, good engineering and well-built ships operating under conditions for which they were never designed and equipped.*

According to Goulden, as the force's expertise grew what made the men so determined was the fact that 'every man jack of the British establishment down through the echelons of power to the lowliest soldier and most hairy-arsed stoker in the Navy bitterly hated the Japanese for attacking them when they were down'. The author says they would have 'willingly strangled with their bare hands' any enemy soldier they could catch.

In the months that followed the ranks of the Coastal Forces was swelled by men and boats from the South African Naval Force (SANF), Royal Australian Navy (RAN), and Royal New Zealand Navy (RNZN). The survivors of the Burma Navy who had managed to escape from the country during the invasion and were now determined to recapture their land and their former way of life also joined these units.

The tide of war was in the balance when Les Gunn and the crew of LCS 87 set off from Chittagong to join 'Assault Force Arakan'. They found themselves in good company with the other small landing and assault craft crewed by various nationalities – though contact between them was infrequent as the demands of

their tasks grew in rate and number off the forbidding coast. Although reconnaissance photographs taken by the RAF gave an impression of its vast swathes
of trees, criss-crossed by silver ribbons of water, once they got near to the shore
the reality proved very different. The missions they were assigned largely
consisted of ferrying army officers and agents into the Arakan or alternately
preventing Japanese supplies from reaching their troops on the coast. A surviving
copy of the instructions for a typical operation at this time – marked 'Most Secret'
and available at the National Archives after being declassified – provides a
fascinating insight into the procedures:

> **Object.** *To land agents on the N.W. point of Kaun Taung Island in Hunter's
> Bay. These agents will remain ashore for five days and will endeavour to
> ascertain the routes and times of Japanese country craft convoys along the
> island waterways between Taungup and Akyab. Being in all respects ready for
> sea and having embarked agents and conducting officer, you are to sail
> from Chittagong at 1700 hours. You will enter Hunter's Bay and land agents on
> the N.W. Point of Kaun Taung Island at 2300 hours. Having completed
> the landing, you will leave not later than 2330 hours and proceed
> to Chittagong.*

The document continues with the perhaps even more vital 'Phase 2':

> **Pick Up.** *You will repeat the above operation, leaving the outer examination buoy
> Chittagong at 0430 hours and timing your approach to reach the N.W. tip of
> Kaun Taung Island at 2230 hours. Having reached this position you will embark
> the agents under the direction of the conducting officer. You will leave not later
> than 0000 hours and proceed to Chittagong to arrive P.M. Action with enemy
> forces is to be avoided if possible and the operation is to be discontinued at your
> discretion. On no account are any Naval Personnel to be landed.*

Such precise instructions give no clue, of course, to the dangers and high drama
that might occur on such a mission. However, Johnnie Lancaster and his crew had
the unenviable distinction of experiencing just the kind of risks they could expect
even as they were preparing for their very first assignment on 1 January 1945. It
was another date that has remained in Les Gunn's memory because of the tragedy
it brought upon the group of young men so keen to 'do their duty'. He recalls the
events tersely and not without emotion:

We were anchored off Akyab getting ammunition from this supply ship when a Jap plane suddenly appeared over the shore. He seemed to be heading for HMS Phoebe, which was anchored in the bay. As soon as the alarm went off, Corporal Hutchby jumped onto the deck and grabbed hold of one of the guns and began firing without taking proper aim. I think he just panicked, as it was the first time we had seen any Japs. Anyhow, the bullets went all over the place and one of them killed Corporal Hallam. It was all a terrible accident. Hutchby was absolutely devastated, so they sent him home.

It could not have been a worse introduction to the war for the crew of LCS 87. But they had a mission to fulfil and the following day began the first of numerous journeys into the *chaungs*. With each foray their confidence grew while at the same time helping them to learn the vital art of avoiding being detected by the Japanese. Lieutenant Allan Holme-Russell, the skipper of a Fairmile ML 477, which also survived a close call while operating in the same vicinity attacking Japanese supply launches and sampans, has recalled how this skill was perfected in an article, 'The Story of Arakan Coastal Forces' (1946). Referring to it as an art, 'that called for the patience of Job and a sense of humour to overcome the strain of lying at anchor or moored to a tree, just waiting and waiting', he explained:

Boats often stayed motionless for days, for where visibility was never further than the last and next bends, hearing is by far the most useful sense. Shoes were forbidden and we all got used to giving orders in whispers. The worst fear when lying close under the trees was that a Jap would creep to the mangrove edge at night. It would have been a simple matter for him to toss a grenade on to our bridge or spray the decks with a Tommy gun. After three months of eye and ear straining this fear was the only one that remained – always quicker when a croc splashed, a monkey chattered or a sampan bird began his monotonous impersonation.

The message that Lieutenant Russell passed on to new arrivals on the Arakan was to always be aware of how vulnerable their craft were in the confined waters of the *chaungs*. During daylight they were easy to spot by Japanese hiding in the mangroves and at night the slightest sounds could alert the listening enemy. There was also the little matter of not getting lost in the maze of rivers and tributaries. Johnnie Lancaster and his crew also became aware of the problems of finding their way about, as Les Gunn recalls:

There were no marine charts of the chaungs. *We had to use army maps on which the water had been coloured blue. Every time the reconnaissance people went out they brought back new information about rocks, banks and shoals, but in that climate things could change in a matter of hours. There were lots of stories about boats hitting underwater rocks – and I don't suppose there was a single crew that did not have a nasty moment when they felt the hull of their vessel hitting bottom while they were a long way from the coast!*

Experience taught the men of LSC 87 that it was often best to use the butt end of their weapons to turn the boat around – or else the skipper had to drive the craft into the mangrove banks of the narrower *chaungs* and use the bow as a pivot. It was on one mission in the Arakan that same January which called for a quick about-turn that brought Les and his mates within a heartbeat of death. He still remembers the events as if they happened yesterday:

It was about ten o'clock in the morning and the weather was lovely. We were some way up this chaung *when we suddenly got a call on the radio that Japs surrounded us. As soon as they opened fire from the trees we had to turn round as quickly as possible and fight our way out. I was sitting on the floor passing up ammunition to the gunner in the turret when a piece of shrapnel hit my tobacco tin and ricocheted against my knee. It sliced the tin in half and wounded me, but just missed my head. I was bloody lucky.*

His friend from Ipswich, Ron Haddock, was not so fortunate, however.

One of the Jap shells hit us near the conning tower and trapped Sergeant Pinnock against a bulkhead surrounded by twisted metal. Another struck the bow where Ron was trying to return the Japs' fire. It blew a big hole, pitched all our supplies into the water and seriously injured Ron. The skin on his back was terribly lacerated and the explosion deafened him. I could see he was hurt, but the officer was shouting at us about the water that was pouring in and told us to get on bailing while he got the boat out. If we had jumped overboard the Japs would have captured us.

While Les and Jack Garnett worked frantically to stem the water pouring into the boat, Lancaster manoeuvred the damaged vessel as fast as he could away from the scene of the ambush. Further down the *chaung*, with the gunfire and shelling becoming more sporadic, LCS 87 met another patrol craft. It only took an instant for the officer on the bridge to sum up the state of the boat with its broken bows and offer a tow back to the coast.

As soon as the two boats were attached, Second Lieutenant Lancaster could take stock of his craft and his men. Pinnock, Gunn and a couple of the others were bleeding and shocked, but nowhere near as badly hurt as Ron Haddock. There was nothing that could be done for the young gunner for the moment, except make him as comfortable as possible. Les and Jack Garnett continued bailing for what seemed like an eternity until they reached an estuary and saw the Bay of Bengal just beyond. There were sighs of relief from everyone when the reassuring sight of the cruiser, HMS *Phoebe,* finally came into view. Les takes up the story again:

> As soon as we reached the Phoebe, the wounded were taken off in a launch to get treatment. The rest of us had to stay with the boat while it was repaired. I remember that the seamen on the launch promised to come back the following morning with some breakfast. We had visions of all sorts of treats. But when they turned up we were in for another disappointment. All they had for us were two tins of herrings in tomato sauce! It was one of those moments when we almost wished we were back in the chaungs, because at least there you might find some pink water melons that were absolutely delicious to eat!

The demands of the Arakan campaign were by now gathering momentum and LCS 87 was made seaworthy as quickly as possible. Within a fortnight the vessel was ferrying military personnel into the Arakan once again. The risks continued undiminished for those on board, their number now depleted for a second time by the loss of Ron Haddock who had been sent to the Royal Indian Navy hospital in Chittagong. They were 'nervous times', Les remembers, for this particular band of Banzai Hunters.

The operations continued with military personnel being put ashore on covert operations and the crew always hoping the men would be there when they returned. On some of these journeys there were close calls. Les Gunn says that there was hardly a day when the gunners on the two 'stripped' Lewis .303 guns did not run them hot with rapid fire at an elusive enemy. Indeed, it was not unusual for these men to end a mission with their chests burned from being in close proximity to the heavy, rattling barrels. There were also occasional agonising delays on the landing craft as they waited for the return of a commando or a marine. Again the memories are etched on Les' memory:

There were times when our own people would begin shelling the Arakan while we were still in a chaung. *Whenever we heard them, we prayed they would not accidentally hit us. On one occasion I remember we heard the shells getting closer and closer as we sat waiting for an officer to return. Finally, we had no alternative but to move as they were getting so near we would have been hit. After the shelling was over we did go back for the man, though.*

Sometimes there were rare moments of humour – usually unintentional, according to Les. But a laugh now and then was very welcome, even if it did seem on occasions like the laugh of condemned men who were never in any doubt what might happen to them if they fell into the hands of the Japanese.

One night before we were due to go into the Arakan, Lieutenant Lancaster gave us all a swig of rum. He said we were going on a risky mission into the chaungs *looking for some Japs who were believed to have gone native. The story was they had thrown away their uniforms and were wearing loin clothes and trying to behave like Burmese. Anyhow, the rum made me fall asleep while we were travelling along the coast and I remember absolutely nothing about what happened – or even if anything* did!

The intense heat of January in the Arakan was also an ever-present concern. Les remembers an encounter with a group of Green Howards (light infantry regiment) who were being ferried up one of the *chaungs*. He was busy making a cup of tea on his Dixie. Unable to resist the temptation for a bit of banter, he held up his cup as the soldiers passed and asked if anyone would like a cuppa. 'One of the soldiers turned and grinned at me. He shouted, "It's so bloody hot you could boil that quicker on my shovel!"'

Moments like these were rare, though, as the plans for invading the Arakan took shape. It was evident that thanks to the intelligence gathering of the men fighting 'The Chaung War', invaluable information was being provided for Mountbatten and his staff and bigger landings and assaults could be put on the agenda. Soon men like Les Gunn and his mates on the landing craft would be transferred from just taking solo operators into the Arakan to transporting whole units of soldiers to actually invade the coast:

We never got to know the men we took into the Arakan to operate behind the Japs' lines. They seemed to come in and out of our lives like shadows. Some of them were obviously on missions for the Coastal Forces, while the others we thought had something to do with the amphibious units supposed to be operating in the area. None of us really knew – except they were all brave men going into that terrible place.

This tribute by Les Gunn is still heartfelt many years later. And the truth is that it would be many months before the young man from the little Suffolk village learned the full story of the next stage of the battle for Burma. Even today, with the releasing of wartime records, it is still not possible to discover the names of all the intrepid navy and army officers who carried out secret missions on the Arakan. What *is* known is that a substantial number belonged to four clandestine small boat units that had been brought together under the inspired leadership of one of the finest Royal Marine officers, Lieutenant-Colonel H.G. Hasler, who had earlier in the war led the daring operation immortalised by the tag of the 'Cockleshell Heroes'. The part of 'Blondie' Hasler – as he was familiarly known – in the recapture of Burma is largely unknown and has, until now, been much underrated.

6

'THE KAMIKAZES OF THE SEA'

The spray being kicked up by the little boat as it sped across Mengham Rythe just off the coast of Hayling Island was conspicuous enough to be seen at Eastney from where the craft had just left, as well as by the few people out and about on a clear morning in July 1942. If any of these folk had chosen to look carefully at the boat as it carved through the spume-tipped waves of the Solent, they would probably have been equally surprised at the craft and the man hunched over the controls. Such was the speed, though, that it is doubtful whether anyone caught more than a glimpse of the balding man with a blonde moustache, his face whipped by the wind and spray, and his curious little boat that was being driven in English waters for the very first time. The man was, in fact, Acting Major H.G. 'Blondie' Hasler and his boat was an Italian invention known as a *Motoscafi da Turismo Modificat* or 'Modified Touring Motor Boat'. Since arriving in Britain, though, it had been renamed more accurately as an EMB or 'Explosive Motor Boat'.

The little vessel was categorised as a 'one-man, fast planning dinghy' and had been developed by the *Regia Marina* for use in one-way missions against enemy vessels. When Mussolini had taken Italy into the war in June 1940, his warships were inferior to the Royal Navy in terms of their armour and lack of radar and his naval officers knew – if *Il Duce* did not – they would have to rely on their submarines and torpedo boats for successful attacks. The addition to the assault forces of the MTM loaded with explosives was to prove a lethal boost to Italian maritime power when it was put into service with the 10th Light Flotilla.

The craft was just 19 feet long with a turtle-shaped deck and a shallow draft, six-cylinder engine carrying twin propellers on a single shaft. It had been built to attain the highest speeds – it was said to be able to reach in excess of 27 knots – along with maximum destructive power: a 660lb explosive charge fitted into a compartment in the bow. The boat's sole purpose was to be rammed by its driver at an unsuspecting victim. Once the rudder had been locked in place, the man would free himself and allow the lethal weapon to strike the enemy's keel. He would be kept afloat by a balsa wood backrest – designed to be detachable like a life raft – and then picked up by another Italian vessel; or, more likely, to find his way to shore and into captivity.

The men of the 10th Light Flotilla found the 'explosive' boat very fast but also versatile as well. In order to gain entry to harbours blocked by netting, it was possible for the driver to lift the screw and rudder out of the water to get over, and also be very precise in setting the course to achieve maximum impact. When the boat struck its target, it would often cause a devastating reaction along the hull and tear a huge hole below the water line making sinking inevitable.

Although the British major at the controls of the renamed EMB that summer morning knew all about its fearsome reputation – which had been growing ever since 26 March when six of the boats had first attacked and sunk the British heavy cruiser, HMS *York* and damaged a Norwegian tanker, the *Pericles,* in Suda Bay, Crete – he was merely intent on testing its speed and manoeuvrability. There were no explosives nestling beneath its buffeting little deck. The boat he was testing had been found abandoned and unexploded outside the Grand Harbour in Malta following another Italian attack and shipped to Britain for precise inspection. It was Hasler's first outing at the controls and as a man who had always loved a nautical challenge, he grabbed the opportunity. He was in for a ride he would never forget.

For several minutes, Hasler raced across the choppy waters making sharp turns one way and another. Finally, he decided to shut off the throttle at 27 knots to measure the craft's stopping distance. It turned out to be a very great deal shorter than he had imagined. For in that instant, Hasler's attention had been momentarily distracted to his instrument panel and he did not see the shallow mud bank that brought a shuddering end to his trial run.

Immediately appreciating his mistake, the major knew that he had made another error as the wake from his sudden halt swept across the boat's open stern. That was where the balsa wood life raft, which he had so off-handedly decided to leave behind, *should* have been. Drenched and angry with himself, Hasler knew that he had no alterative but to sit tight and just hope the boat would not sink before a rescuer reached him.

Fortunately for Hasler, Sub Lieutenant Bill Ladbroke, a former powerboat racer who had been in charge of bringing the MTM back from Malta for trials in home waters, grew suspicious when the impetuous pilot did not return after half an hour. He set off in a small powered boat and had to restrain himself from a broad grin when he found the major stuck firmly on the mud bank. Ladbroke suggested as tactfully as he could that it would be as well to refit the life raft if any future tests were carried out – and then pulled the still-annoyed Hasler off the mud bank and towed him back to Eastney.

Despite this indignity, the day was to prove a defining moment for 'Blondie' Hasler. He had discovered – without any lasting damage – why the *Motoscafi da Turismo Modificati* had become known as 'The Kamikaze of the Sea'. He could, though, have no notion how apt the expression would prove as far as his own future was concerned – or where it would take him. Indeed, the term might also be seen as somehow indicative of the courage that would be shown by his amphibious units that took part in missions against the Japanese, though never throwing away their lives like the enemy.*

A few days after the incident, on 6 July, Hasler's 'embryo idea' for a small boat operations group came into being with the formation of the Royal Marines Boom Patrol Detachment, specifically with the purpose of attacking enemy shipping. The RMBPD would be the first small boat unit completely manned by Royal Marines and would take part in one of the most famous naval operations of the Second World War remembered by history as the 'Cockleshell Heroes'. More significantly as far as this narrative is concerned, it represents a crucial moment in the story of the small boats that would play such an important part in the battle for the Arakan. A role that subsequently prompted Lieutenant Commander Lawrence Hornby of the Small Operations Group (SOG) to suggest, ' "Blondie's" contribution to allied victory in the Far East has never been adequately recognised'.

In this chapter – and those that follow – the record will, I hope, be put straight. Hasler was not just a 'Cockleshell Hero' or, after the war, one of the progenitors of single-handed ocean racing. He was also the 'founding father' of the amphibious Special Forces who played a key role in the defeat of the Japanese in Burma.

* * *

Herbert George Hasler who is acknowledged today as a man who had a deep understanding of, and faith in, small boats, was the son of an officer in the Royal

---

*According to Captain Jock Stewart, another member of Hasler's team, a British version of the MTM was constructed complete with a 'raft seat' that dragged off the driver just before the boat hit its target. He says, 'Hasler used this as a chance to develop a canoe, because he felt that the driver of the boat would have a greater chance of escape if there was someone nearby in a canoe who could pick him up. He thought quite rightly that the explosive motorboat would take a very long time to develop. So to keep his unit employed he wanted canoes, but at the back of his mind he always had the idea of attacking enemy ships in harbour by stealth in a canoe.'

Army Medical Corp. Born the second of two sons on 27 February 1914, he lost his father just three years later in May 1917: Lieutenant Hasler was drowned when the troopship SS *Transylvania* bound for the British and French campaign in Salonika was torpedoed by a German submarine in the Gulf of Genoa. Although the Lieutenant had been no lover of ocean travel, his son was caught up in the romance of the sea and while growing up in Southsea spent much of his childhood on the beach there which faces the eastern Solent and the English Channel.

Young Hasler was known as 'Bert' by his mother, 'George' by his family and relatives, but once he reached his twenties earned the soubriquet by which he would forever after be known, 'Blondie', due to his thinning fair hair and luxuriant golden moustache. According to family stories, as a child he would spend hours at Southsea Canoe Lake near his home watching men and boys sailing their model yachts, dreaming of one day having one of his own. He was just twelve when he built his first sea-going craft, a two-seater, canvas-covered canoe, using every school holiday to learn the complexities of sailing and navigation around the waters and mud flats of Langstone Harbour. He also added sails to this boat, as his biographer, Ewen Southby-Tailyour – whose father served in the Royal Marines with Hasler – has written in his excellent book, *Blondie* (1998):

> *Experiments were tried with various rigs, contrived out of any lengths of cloth that could be scrounged, produced some very basic forms of propulsion and, as a contemporary note admits, even that was downwind; nevertheless the die was cast. Just seventeen years later, Lieutenant-Colonel H.G. Hasler was designing similar craft and their sails for less peaceful purposes in the Far East.*

Young Hasler attended Wellington College in Berkshire where he showed himself to have great stamina and endurance, excelling at swimming (he was captain of the college team), boxing and cross-country running. Once again, during the holidays, he built another boat, a ten-foot, dart-shaped punt. This enabled him to sail on and off Southsea beach and around Hayling Island with far greater ease and skill than his earlier canoe. During the second summer he owned this homemade boat he ventured further afield, sometimes for days at a time, and gained his first experience sailing in creeks around the Isle of Wight. He had not the faintest inkling that he would return to the area within a few years to begin a vital wartime commission.

In September 1932, aged eighteen, Hasler applied to join the Royal Marines and after sitting the standard exams and interviews was accepted as a Probationary Second Lieutenant. Two months later he was back in 'home waters' when he was sent with the Plymouth Division to the RM Barracks at Eastney. Legend has it that it was only his passion for sailing a 20-foot, gaff-cutter-rigged fishing smack, *Violet,* which he bought in May 1933 and sailed whenever the opportunity arose, that prevented him from passing out at the top of his group at the end of the three year training period. Sadly, this boat sank in a storm while at anchor in Langstone Harbour – the only boat Blondie was ever to lose.

The years that followed saw Hasler sailing ever longer distances – the Channel Islands were a popular destination – improving his handling of various types of vessels and developing his sea skills to quite extraordinary lengths. While at sea, he would go for long periods without sleep, live in primitive conditions in his boat or on a beach, and willingly put up with cold and wet conditions in leaky and sub-standard boats to improve his endurance. Blondie was clearly pushing his life to extremes and practising a rigorous self-sufficiency that would prove invaluable not only to him, but all those who would serve under his command.

Hasler's training as a Royal Marine involved service at sea with other detachments, landing stores and equipment on beaches under military conditions, and developing the qualities of leadership that would enhance his career. He also revealed a talent for tackling mechanical problems and proposing solutions for military and naval problems. In fact, it became evident that Blondie had something of the inventor about him as well as a consuming desire to improve Royal Marine operations whenever and wherever they might take place.

In 1934, the young officer purchased the *Trivia,* a 12-foot dinghy with 100 square foot of sail, which became a great favourite and is credited with having done most to foster his great seamanship. Although not fast, the boat proved ideal for coastal sailing and one of Hasler's log entries in June 1935 reveals – significantly – that he had discovered one of the prime assets of a small craft like the *Trivia:* 'We see the bottom before we hit it and will always know exactly where we are by day and have a very good working idea at night'.

When sailing, Hasler regularly encountered bad weather and had one memorable experience at the notorious Portland Race where only his skill and some good luck from the 'Deity responsible for nautical fools' – to quote his own words – brought him safely back to land at Lulworth Cove. After returning to Portsmouth in less dramatic circumstances, he knew he had reached another landmark in his life. In future, he decided, he wanted sailing in small boats to take precedence in his life over purely military assignments.

Later that year, Hasler was made a Probationary Lieutenant and at Christmas received his first operational posting to the battleship, HMS *Queen Elizabeth.* Despite his attachment to small boats, he apparently spent the next two years serving contentedly on the flagship of the Mediterranean Fleet as it patrolled the trouble spots following the Italian threat to invade Abyssinia that would move the world inexorably towards war. For a time the young Marine officer was stationed at Alexandria where he once again had the opportunity to exercise his passion for sailing, this time with the Royal Yacht Club of Egypt and took part in races with fellow officers. He also went on excursions with native guides for duck shooting along the coast. Hasler's ability to relate to the locals would stand him in good stead when the needs of war later required him to recruit guides on more hostile shores.

In December 1937, Blondie Hasler's talents were noticed and he was called back to England and appointed Fleet Landing Officer to the newly formed Mobile Naval Base Defence Organisation (MNBDO) based at Portsmouth. A secondary appointment as Assistant Editor of the *Royal Navy Sailing Association Journal* also enabled him to contribute to the growing archives of material on experiments with small boats – and, indirectly, to put on record some of his own achievements which modesty might otherwise have prevented him committing to paper and, of course, made the telling of his story far more difficult. Among the significant courses that Hasler attended and wrote about was one for the Davis Submarine Escape Apparatus held at HMS *Dolphin*. It did not take him long to appreciate that the use of this equipment could be extended far beyond its intended purpose.

When war was declared in September 1939, Hasler, now a Captain, was sent with the Royal Marines as a Landing Officer to Scapa Flow in the Orkney Islands. There he helped to install port defences and guns to protect the Home Fleet from German attacks. The following April, under orders from the First Lord of the Admiralty, Winston Churchill, the Fleet was directed to set up an economic blockade of Germany and prevent the export of vital iron ore from Norway after the country had been occupied by Hitler's army. A few weeks later, Hasler gained his first practical experience of a marine landing when he was responsible for putting men and equipment on the beaches of Skanland. Using two motor landing craft, MLCs 18 and 20, and a hand-picked team, he made his way through the narrow, twisting and fast-flowing Ramsundet Channel to the peninsula in a ground-breaking operation that has been described by J.L. Moulton in *The Norwegian Campaign, 1940* (1966):

> *Having embarked two crews, enough food, water and ammunition for at least a week and one anti-aircraft Lewis gun for each landing-craft, Captain Hasler's tiny force sailed on 23 May through this difficult passage under tow of two* Skoyter. *The ubiquitous* Skoyter *is best described as the Norwegian equivalent of the Scottish* Puffer *and, with one single-cylinder oil engine, they were about as*

manoeuvrable. Still they were to play an invaluable part in the whole campaign as Hasler and others would testify.

The amphibious mission was not helped by the fact that the two motor launches were almost obsolete vessels powered by water-jet propulsion that gave them a maximum speed of only 4 knots when fully laden. Landing two tanks and two field guns and tractors turned into a nightmare when the beach at Skanland proved to be too shallow with many rocks just below the surface. It took Blondie and his men over five hours to land their consignment: one of the tanks becoming stuck in the rising tide. As Hasler gazed on the helpless monster he realised how different things might have been if he had prior knowledge of the beach conditions. The thought would nag away at the back of his mind until, later, he was in a position to do something about it.

When Hasler was requested to return with a second load he took advantage of a car ferry landing point just along the coast and landed his precious cargo intact. While waiting at Saegnes for further orders, he decided to get the two launches adapted with additional, 14-foot long wooden bows that would enable troops to land on the shallow beaches without getting drenched in the surf. The little unit was consequently better prepared and aware of the potential dangers when ordered to take part in the attack on the Narvik peninsula on 27 May. Blondie paid special attention to local maps to find the least hazardous beach to disembark and under the cover of a heavy navy bombardment, his two launches made a total of eleven successful transfers of troops and armament in just over six hours. It was a remarkable turn in their fortunes after the first convoluted landing.

On several of the missions, the launches were subjected to sporadic enemy high explosive shells coming from the vicinity of the beaches. During one of the landings, a German post on the eastern side of the beach fired on MLC 20, killing one of the soldiers on board. MLC 18 had a narrow escape when the *Skoyter* that had been towing it was machine-gunned by a German Messerschmitt 110 flying over the invasion beaches, and set on fire. Blondie was able to divert the vessel just before the blaze reached the ammunition and exploded across the seashore. He was also called upon to embark troops from other areas and again came under machine gun and mortar fire. Another problem that Hasler had to contend with was the jet inlets becoming clogged with weed when navigating the shallow coastline. Such incidents necessitated the engine being idled while a member of the crew cleared the obstruction.

Within 24 hours of the initial landing, Narvik was in Allied hands and Hasler and his unit could return to base, their job well done. There was, though, little time for celebration. That same day on the coast of France, the evacuation of the British Expeditionary Force from the beaches of Dunkirk had changed the entire course of the war. Narvik was now no longer vital to Churchill in his new role as Prime Minister of beleaguered Britain. Blondie and his men were ordered to help evacuate the troops who would be so vital for the next stage of the war effort – at the same time destroying all the equipment, guns, vehicles and ammunition they had so arduously landed.

Hasler and his men were among the last marines to leave the Norwegian coast after the military force had been embarked on waiting destroyers. The team itself were taken on board HMS *Firedrake* for the return to Scapa Flow. Blondie was to recall later leaning over the rails meditating on the lessons he had learned during the past few days about small boat operations – positive and negative. His final memory, though, was of watching all the landing craft that had put in such sterling service under difficult conditions being sunk, one by one, by gunfire. It was, he wrote later and perhaps a little surprisingly for a man with such an affinity for small boats, 'an amusing ten minutes'.

When Hasler arrived back at Eastney, his natural modesty prevented him from filing a detailed report of his operations off the coast of Norway: beyond the bare facts required for the daily logs. Indeed, it was not until the Admiralty pressed the Royal Marines office in October 1941, that he was instructed to forward an account to the Adjutant General. Viewed in hindsight, this document can be seen to pinpoint the difficulties of staging an amphibious landing operation on a hostile shore and the urgent need for solutions, both conventional and unconventional, to the problem. Hasler makes it quite clear that he believed only combined operations utilising specially designed craft and specially trained men could hope to succeed. Whether he ever imagined he might become one of the main motivating forces behind the unconventional solutions that were now so clearly and urgently required, no one can be certain . . .

* * *

By the Spring of 1941, with Britain having withstood the threat of a German invasion thanks to the efforts of the RAF controlling the skies and the Royal Navy keeping the English Channel secure, Churchill turned his thoughts to occupied Europe. He instructed the resourceful Mountbatten as Adviser on Combined Operations to 'mount a programme of raids of ever-increasing intensity with the invasion of France the main object'. The Admiral was to make plans for combined operations and 'create the force, devise the appliances and select the site for the assault'. In March, Hasler, who in the interim had been made an acting Major, was put in charge of the Landing Company at the second Mobile Naval Base Defence Organisation formed on Hayling Island. His mind had evidently been working feverishly in the interim on how he could improve current amphibious techniques and equipment, as Ewen Southby-Tailyour explains:

> He was aware of the army's Special Boat Sections (attached to Lieutenant Colonel Bob Laycock's army commandos) and their use of Folbots to gather intelligence and conduct sabotage attacks in the Mediterranean. By coincidence, Lieutenant-Commander Nigel Clogstoun-Willmott, Royal Navy, had also been in Norway during that Spring of 1940 and had become equally as concerned as had Blondie (although they had not met in the fjords) over the lack of sensible beach intelligence and the absence of any plan, or method, to gain it.

Soon Hasler had an idea forming in his mind. In a paper written in May 1941, *Underwater Canoe Attack,* which he sent to Combined Operations Headquarters, he suggested using a combination of canoes and underwater swimmers against enemy shipping while it was in harbour. Such teams could be launched from an offshore vessel or submarine that would then wait to pick up the men after they had completed their mission. The idea would work, he felt, because of his knowledge that the army had suitable canoes and the Davis Submarine Escape Apparatus could be adapted for underwater tasks.

Although, curiously, Blondie's idea was turned down – in the mistaken belief that the necessary equipment for such attacks 'did not exist' – his lateral thinking caught the eyes of Mountbatten who shared Churchill's enthusiasm for encouraging what might at first glance seem like outlandish schemes. When Mountbatten asked to meet Hasler, the two men were soon busy discussing a whole range of covert methods that might be used in order to get raiding parties onto enemy territory in small boats. Their conversations also engendered a respect for each other that would last all their lives.

On 26 January 1942, Hasler was ordered to report to the Combined Operations Development Centre (CODC) at Southsea and begin the work that would lead to 'Operation Frankton' – the Cockleshell Heroes raid – and subsequently the less spectacular, but equally vital series of operations in Burma. First Blondie set to work on the collapsible canoe that was the key to all his plans. He initially code-named the 16 feet long, two-man, decked canoe 'the Mark II Tadpole' and based it on various boats he studied including Eskimo kayaks and the army's own Cockleboats. With a strong skin of three-ply, rubber-proofed canvas able to withstand bad weather and grounding, it was designed to weigh less than 100lbs, carry two 13-stone men and be paddled for long periods at between 3–5 knots.

Once several prototypes had been made the men of the Royal Marine Boom Patrol Detachment put them through a series of demanding tests on the Solent. These tests included 'boom dodging' – getting around solid obstructions – staged attacks on harbour installations and the surreptitious placing of limpet mines. It has been suggested that some of these operations were carried out without official permission to test their effectiveness because Hasler knew the ability to act stealthily would be an essential capability when the time came for *real* action. He received his own little taste of what such action might be like when he took out the Italian MTA from Eastney. The experience, though, did nothing to deter his passion for still more knowledge about the potential of small boats.

In his quest for the ideal canoe, Hasler did not allow himself to overlook the requirements of the men who would operate in the 'Cockle Mark II' – as the finished version became known – and it is evident that the guidelines he devised later formed the basic training programmes for the units that would fall under his jurisdiction: the Royal Marines' Special Boat Service (SBS), the Combined Operations Pilotage Parties (the COPPs), the Sea Reconnaissance Unit (SRU) and the secretive Royal Marine Detachment 385, all of whom would operate in the waterways and *chaungs* of the Arakan. Blondie's biographer, Ewen Southby-Tailyour, carefully lists these requirements in his book; their successful adoption by those who fought in amphibious operations off the coast of Burma is now a matter of record:

> Basic swimming lessons, basic seamanship, familiarisation with the local seas, Tommy-gun practice, pistol shooting, unarmed combat, navigation, the layout of naval dockyards and how ships are moored were all included. Nothing was left out: speed boat training; field sketching and note taking; limpet mine operations and the 5-pound depth charge; coding and decoding, until slowly, painfully slowly, the lessons would begin to include camouflage and operational approaches to an objective when training in the different methods of attack and attention would be meticulously taught, rehearsed and practised.

On 16 August 1942, in a document stamped, 'Most Secret', Acting Major Hasler was able to inform his superiors that the RMBPD was now 'capable of undertaking at short notice any form of specialised small boat operation'. His timing could not have been better because the War Cabinet Chiefs of Staff in London were becoming increasingly concerned about the Axis merchant ships operating from Bordeaux transporting naval and military materials to Japan. It was another defining moment in Blondie's life. Mountbatten informed the War Cabinet he had just the man to disrupt this service and put the fear of the unknown into the minds of their enemy. The Admiral had no doubt that Hasler and his men would be able to reach their destination – but nursed real doubts, which he kept to himself at the time, that they would be able to return after carrying out their mission.

'Operation Frankton' – Hasler's first amphibious mission – is now a part of Second World War naval history and requires no more than the briefest mention here. After a series of intensive training exercises around the mud flats of Hayling Island, five canoes of ten RMBPD men led by Blondie were launched from a submarine, HMS *Tuna* off the Girdone estuary in the Bay of Biscay on 7 December. Their orders were to paddle some 75 miles upriver to Bordeaux and attack German 'blockade runners' – the fast merchantmen being used to sail to and from Japan. Only two canoes made it to the harbour on the night of 11/12 December and placed limpet mines on four of the ships. Unhappily, Mountbatten's fears were confirmed when all the men, with the exception of Hasler and his canoe partner, a resilient Cockney Marine named Bill Sparks, were drowned or captured and shot. Blondie and Sparks were able to escape to Spain and from there made their way back to Britain, arriving in April 1943.

Although the 'Cockleshell Heroes' only managed to sink one of the ships, three others were badly damaged and the operation was deservedly rated a success both in terms of its impact and the effect on morale, although the cost in lives had been high. On Hasler's return – thanks to the efforts of members of the French Resistance movement helping the two men through the large number of German troops ordered to capture all the saboteurs – Mountbatten was delighted to be able to pass the news on to Churchill and write a citation about his protégé on 13 May:

> *Major Hasler's cool, determined and fearless leadership was in accordance with the highest traditions of the Royal Marines corps. He is strongly recommended for the highest recommendation possible for a feat of this nature.' [On 29 June 1943, the* London Gazette *announced the award of a Distinguished Service Order (DSO) to Hasler.]*

The repercussions of the raid were felt on both sides of the English Channel. The Germans reluctantly conceded that it had been 'the outstanding commando raid of the war'; while in Britain it quickly became a media sensation and source of inspiration for all those who shared Hasler's belief in the value of small boat operations. Blondie threw his energy back into the RMBPD, which had increased in size during his absence, though several planned operations had not materialised. Instead, Hasler's diary indicates that his time was frequently taken up with meetings sharing his expertise and experiences with Nigel Clogstoun-Wilmott of COPP, Lieutenant Bruce Wright of SRU and another forward-thinking Royal Marine like himself, Lieutenant Roger Courtney, the mastermind behind the SBS. As Southby-Tailyour has written:

> Towards the end of 1943, Blondie became aware that the COPP parties (except those earmarked for the invasion of Europe) and the SRU were being filtered to India, and while the Combined Operations Development Centre (CODC) continued to be the focus for innovative thinking in small boat operations, the European theatre itself was becoming less 'receptive' to such work. It did not come as a surprise, therefore, when Lord Mountbatten called for him from Dehli to co-ordinate small boat operations in the South East Asia Command (SEAC) under the catch-all title of the Small Operations Group.

Together these men of SOG, referred to in some quarters as 'Mountbatten's Little Navy', would be responsible for a wide range of covert operations on the Arakan blending their particular abilities to those of the other Banzai Hunters of the Coastal Forces. The pinprick that Blondie Hasler had delivered to the Japanese war effort by his attack was now about to become a full-bloodied thrust to the heart in the Far East.

7

RETALIATION AT HUNTER'S BAY

The Fairmile motor gunboat ML 854 edged its way cautiously into the tranquil waters of Hunter's Bay late on the evening of Sunday, 7 January 1945.* In the wheelhouse, the skipper, Lieutenant Reg Harris, peered into the darkness at the sweep of enemy-occupied bay he was entering for the second time in as many days. He hoped his mission would be less dangerous on this occasion, but was not over-optimistic as the tempo of events on the Arakan coast was now beginning to build up daily. Harris and the other men on board were investigating the possibility of an invasion of the horseshoe-shaped bay, in particular a landing on the Myebon Peninsula, a mile wide strip of hilly terrain between the estuaries of the Kyatsin and Myebon rivers. Their instructions were to identify where the Japanese troops were located and, if possible, their numbers and weaponry, to help make possible an amphibious operation that Mountbatten and his chiefs of staff had pencilled in for 'immediate action'. The 'top brass' wanted to exploit the seizure of Akyab and make a combined forces landing in order to cut off any Japanese retreat south.

Although it was difficult to see the whole bay in the almost starless night, Harris knew that it ran for about 30 miles from a point called Eastern Baronga to where it joined another bay, Combermere, with the dark shape of Ramree Island on the horizon. In between these two locations lay an intimidating complex of shallow bays, estuaries, rivers, creeks and *chaungs* and, behind them, treacherous mangrove swamps and a dangerously exposed floodplain. The Lieutenant had been especially briefed about the extensive area of intertidal mudflats at the northern edge of Hunter's Bay that were said to be dangerous to ships, even those with shallow drafts, at low tide.

A glance down at his map of the area updated only that morning told Harris that he was close to a part of the Arakan that contained some of the most

*On modern maps of Burma this area is designated as the Bay of Hanter.

notorious waterways occupied by the Japanese, including the Dainbon and Min *chaungs*. But the experienced and proficient veteran of the South African Naval Forces (SANF) now attached to the 36th Flotilla of the Coastal Forces was not a man to take chances. He did not need documents to tell him to be wary of the coral reefs fringing the coast or that the Japanese would probably be entrenched in all sorts of unlikely places waiting for unwary intruders. He had even heard that if his gunboat avoided the enemy, there were still crocodiles in these waters . . .

Apart from Harris' number two, Lieutenant T. G. Edmonds of the RNVR and a crew of eight, the gunboat was also carrying four hulking men who had been sat together in a huddle in the stern ever since the vessel had left its mooring off Akyab island earlier in the evening. They had resisted being drawn into conversation by the other ratings and seemed preoccupied with thoughts about their part in the night's operation. The quartet was, in fact, due to disembark when Harris got ML854 within striking distance of the shore – and then go looking for the Japanese.

As soon as the features of the land became clearer in the gloom, Harris eased back the boat's V12 engines from the 2,200 rpm he had used to make maximum speed to Hunter's Bay. Now came the tricky part of the mission, he told himself: to get the boat into the estuary without grounding it. The best way of doing this was to reverse, a method that had been proven with Fairmiles in many different kinds of coastal localities. Whatever happened, the skipper wanted his bow facing out to sea in case he was fired on and had to make a quick exit.

When Harris was satisfied he'd approached as close as he dare and was hidden in the lea of some big trees, he cut off the engine and ordered the bow anchor to be lowered on a rope to make as little noise as possible. He signalled to the four men. Without a word, they slipped a pair of canoes soundlessly into the water and paddled away into the night. There was nothing anyone on ML 854 could do now except remain at action stations and wait. Silence was essential and there was not even the chance of a cigarette for the smokers on board. A Jap sniper would have spotted any kind of light in an instant.

Among those left sitting on the boat as the minutes ticked by was a new recruit, Able Seaman Duncan Hill. He had joined Harris' crew only a short while before its first mission to Hunter's Bay on Friday 5 January. As he waited for the return of the landing party, Hill could not help running over again in his mind the dramatic incidents that had occurred two days earlier. He later committed the details to paper for a special anniversary edition of the *Coastal Forces Veterans' Association Newsletter* in January 1970.

Hill – known as 'Taffy' to his friends and shipmates – had been born in 1924 in Morriston near Swansea. Like Les Gunn and many of the other young men who served in the Arakan, he had been anxious to join up as soon as he was old enough. Indeed, he had a taste of the realities of war while he was still in his teens, when his school, Dynevor Secondary, was destroyed by a German air raid in February 1941. Fortunately, the bombing had occurred at night and none of the staff or pupils was injured. A year later, as soon as he was eighteen, Hill joined the Royal Navy and began training as an ASDIC operator, the transmitter-receiver device that sent out highly directional sound waves through the water. The equipment had not long been developed by the Anti-submarine Detection Investigation Committee – hence its initials – and was now the primary underwater detection device used by Allied escorts.

Taffy's first posting had been the cruiser, HMS *Suffolk,* on which he spent a year becoming proficient with the ASDIC. However, the life did not provide the young Welshman with the excitement he craved and while he was in port at the Naval base in Simonstown, South Africa, the chance for a change presented itself. Volunteers were being recruited to crew Fairmile motor gunboats under construction in Cape Town. His request for a transfer was granted and in 1944, Hill went to serve under SANF Lieutenant Jack Dunning in ML830 on the coast of India.

Unhappily, though, the boat was caught in a cyclone just off Madras and left stranded on the notorious Cocanada Shoal. All the crew escaped without injury, however, and Taffy requested a new commission – which was how he came to find himself on board ML854 in the Arakan. On the night of 5 January he was with Lieutenant Harris' crew when they were sent on a mission to spy on Hunter's Bay. On board were 'some high ranking Army and Air force officers, a Royal Marine Commando officer and several Indian Navy ratings' – to quote Hill – with the task of looking for anti-invasion obstacles in the Myebon estuary. The boat was about 600 yards from shore when, he says, all hell broke loose:

The whole operation had been observed by the defending Japs and as soon as the Fairmile changed from a stern-first approach to forward revolutions, it came under heavy fire from small arms and shells. Fortunately, the boat was constructed of wood, except for the bridge armour, and the shells ripped through the superstructure, one passed between the helmsman and the echo sounder in the wheelhouse – a distance of no more than one yard. Another passed through the top of the engine room underneath the feet of the midship Oerlikon gunners. Shells tore through tea chests in the coxswain's cabin and the Ward Room, whilst bullets lodged in the ship's sides.

Despite the ferocity of the attack, the crew of ML 854 did not forget their training and returned fire at the enemy positions on the shore while Lieutenant Harris powered away into the open waters of the Bay of Bengal. When safely out of range, the skipper was relieved to discover that only two members of the crew had been slightly injured. It was a small price to pay for having established that there were a number of dangerous obstacles in the water that would have to be removed before a landing could be attempted, and that the Japanese were clearly going to defend their hold on Hunter's Bay. For AB Hill's part, he had wanted some front line action and he had got it – and there was more to come.

The young Welshman was still mulling over the events of that night when a single flash signal broke the darkness. The two canoes were on their way back. He glanced at his watch and saw that over an hour had passed. As he helped the four men back onto the motor gunboat he thought their blackened faces looked as emotionless as when they had left. If they had known anything about the previous attack on the craft they were giving nothing away. It seemed the men had seen enough of the Japanese defences to report back to base.

For some time afterwards, 'Taffy' Hill remembered being impressed by the coolness and sense of purpose of the four men and wondering just *who* they might be. If he had heard the initials COPP he might not have been much wiser. In fact, the men belonged to a special small boat unit now operating on the Arakan with the curious title of Combined Operations Assault Pilotage Party. This nomenclature had been deliberately chosen to reflect the unit's secondary role: their primary one was beach reconnaissance, but any reference to this fact was feared to compromise their security. In operational orders they were generally referred to as the 'Coppists', while certain envious factions preferred 'Combined Operations Police Patrol' because of their furtive midnight missions. To John Fordham in *Secret Wartime Operations* (1969) this made them the providers of 'priority number one of the Burma war'. What *is* beyond doubt is that they were an extraordinary bunch of men.

* * *

According to Admiral Sir Philip Vian, the amphibious operations of the Arakan campaign 'would not have been possible without the Combined Operations Pilotage Parties who had been specially trained to reconnoitre the *chaungs* and possible landing spots before the operations'. He explains the reasons for his conviction in *Action This Day* (1960):

Looking for the Japanese – a typical mission for the Banzai Hunters on the Arakan.

In the depths of the Arakan – 'The Worst Place on Earth.'

A rare photograph of some of Major Firbank's 'navy' at anchor in Teknaf harbour.

Captain John Ryland, commander of the Arakan Coastal Forces.

A Fairmile B motor gunboat – one of the most effective craft used in the Arakan campaign.

Lowering a Landing Craft Support (LCS) from a transport ship on Davits was often a hazardous experience for everyone on board.

A group of Landing Craft Mechanised (LCM) carrying heavy artillery rehearse a landing.

Troops on board a Landing Craft Assault (LCA) prepare for a raiding mission against enemy-held territory.

Two of the wooden
Landing Craft Personnel
(LCP) beaching troops in
an assault operation.

A group of V Force men
on a dangerous
reconnaissance mission
along an Arakan river.

Allied forces on the Arakan were regularly subjected to Japanese propaganda urging them to surrender. The Japanese characters read, 'Any person carrying this leaflet will be accepted as a prisoner of war and will be given protection accordingly.'

To You The English Soldiers

You are like fishes caught in a net, without an outle The only faith left for you is Death alone. When we thi and give consideration about your loving wives, paren and brothers we could never carry on inhuman-like action Therefore stop your useless resistance. Throw down yo arms, and surrender. It is then that we will guarantee yo lives and will treat you according to the International Law.

How to Surrender to the Jpanese Forces

1. The surrenderers are required to come hoisting some white cloth or holding up both hands.

2. Carry the rifle on the shoulder upside down.

3. Show this bill to the Japanese soldier.

Nippon Army.

此ノ證携行者ハ投降者ニツキ保護チ加ヘラレタシ

大日本軍

Colonel Peter Young, a commanding and influential figure in the battle to retake the coast of Burma.

Royal Marine commandos undergoing training at Achnacarry in Scotland for the Arakan war.

One of the early successes for the Banzai Hunters was the recapture of Akyab Island, which had been devastated by the Japanese.

Above: Members of 44 RM Commando landing on St Martin's Island off the coast of the Arakan.

Below: A Landing Craft Support (Medium) similar to that skippered by Second Lieutenant Johnnie Lancaster.

Theirs was valuable and extremely dangerous work which involved stealing up the chaungs in canoes during the night or in the mist of early morning to sound for depth and mark the channel with buoys. It meant climbing ashore at low tide up the slimy banks to reconnoitre beyond them the prospect of assault across the firm or flooded paddy fields. At any bend or confluence the chaung might be mined or ambushed. Indeed the whole distance of this jungle water-maze was a sniper's paradise.

In fact, the necessity for beach reconnaissance to ensure the landing of Allied raiding forces as near their target as possible, with the odds on being detected as low as humanly possible, had been advocated by certain far-sighted individuals ever since the early skirmishes of the war. One of the prime movers of the concept of creating special units of men to carry out such 'spearhead' missions was a shrewd and clear-thinking Navigating Officer, Nigel Clogstoun-Willmott, whose beliefs – along with the unstinting support he would receive from Blondie Hasler – were to write another chapter in the history of amphibious warfare. The latest generation of a Dorset maritime family, he had joined the Royal Navy in the late thirties and was a Lieutenant Commander when war broke out.

Clogstoun-Willmott's campaign to give landing troops a better chance of success on hostile shores had been inspired after hearing about the experiences of an uncle during the Anzac landings at Gallipoli in the First World War, when the battleships HMS *Irresistible* and *Ocean* had been mined. His concern had turned to determination after serving on a Q-ship off Norway in 1940 and becoming aware that more than half the Allied ships lost had foundered on unsuspected shoals or rocks. A few months later when he was Fleet Navigating Officer in the Mediterranean Fleet he encountered the same problem rearing its ugly head. At what was a low point in the war, Clogstoun-Willmott realised three things: that the Navy was eventually going to have to land armies back on land; that some troops would have to be landed on beaches as all the harbours were enemy-held; and because the Navy's entire training was directed at keeping clear of the shore, it knew little about finding and disembarking on enemy-held beaches.

It was in 1941 when tentative plans were under discussion for an assault on the Italian-held island of Rhodes that Clogstoun-Willmott persuaded his superiors to allow him to swim ashore by night from a submarine and explore the gradients and composition of the beaches on which the attackers would have to land. The information he secured proved of great significance, as James Ladd has written in *Commando and Rangers of World War II* (1978):

As the submarine nosed around the island's waters for three days, often making one and a half knots or less, there were a number of unanswered questions in Nigel Clogstoun-Willmott's mind. Was that apparently empty fisherman's hut an abandoned home or a gun emplacement? Were there any hidden sandbars a dozen yards from the beach, for a man could drown easily in the eight feet of water beyond them as in eighty? Answers were essential and, in time, beach reconnaissance would become a scientific study of landing areas and their immediate hinterland – the littoral across which Clogstoun-Willmott's men would lead raiders and the van of invasions, guiding the landing crews with marker canoes and other devices that in part at least made up for these flotillas' limited experience of coastal navigation.

Despite his realisation of these dangers, the Lieutenant Commander had a hard job convincing the Admiralty to look further into the matter – a resistance based on the fear that any recce might leave traces of the visit that could give away an intended invasion landing-place. Undeterred, he persisted with his idea and in December 1942 was given the go-ahead to raise a small number of teams with the brief to 'find, reconnoitre and survey proposed landing beaches, mark them during landings and conduct assault force navigation'. He was allocated quarters for his recruits at Sandy Point on Hayling Island and met the like-minded spirit he had just missed in Norway – Blondie Hasler. All the support and encouragement he needed was given at once and unstintingly.

Clogstoun-Willmott decided to use the Yacht Club Buildings at Sandy Point and Chichester Harbour for developing his techniques of 'assault pilotage'. He set up a demanding routine of training for himself and his men including long distance swimming and a variety of exercises to promote physical endurance. These routines, according to a later report, were 'exhausting almost to the point of mutiny'. Another contemporary account describes the lengths to which the Lieutenant-Commander would go to preserve secrecy and his use of unlikely and often commonplace items to facilitate his work: 'He would swim onto beaches with his army compass strapped to his body and covered in periscope grease, while his torch was water-proofed in the rubber sheaths of issue contraceptives to conceal its purpose'.

All new recruits to the 'Coppists' were told by Clogstoun-Willmott that they would require 'the patience of an animal' and an absolute determination to get their reconnaissance reports back to base. They would need to build up great physical strength and endurance to survive and would have to go much further than the normal raider or saboteur. For some operations, they might be brought close enough to a coast to swim ashore, but for other longer and riskier missions a special canoe was devised. It had a canvas canopy buttoned around the paddler and an air bladder in the cockpit.

For this aspect of his work, Clogstoun-Willmott found Hasler's help and advice invaluable – as it was when he came to make decisions about the outfits to be worn by his team. Initially, each man wore a heavily greased jersey and long john underwear: an obviously bizarre combination that is said to have caused what proved unwise remarks by other navy ratings. These, though, soon made way for a full-length rubber suit designed by Siebe Gorman with a watertight helmet, wrist and ankle fittings and rope-soled 'fishermen's' boots. When the men of COPP were sent to the Arakan, however, with its much warmer temperatures, these outfits were discarded for thin overalls.

The suits, fitted with special pockets, enabled Clogstoun-Willmott's men to carry an impressive array of equipment including infra-red homing devices, underwater writing tablets, pocket lead-lines, beach-measuring lines, night-reading compasses, waterproof watches, stiletto knives, revolvers (usually a Colt 45 in a waterproof holder) and the inevitable torch in its 'intimate' receptacle. Some men were also equipped with a 'Bong' stick – a metal rod that conducted underwater sounds that could be picked up by ASDIC receivers as far as 12 miles away – as well as the occasional No 36 SUE (Signal Underwater Explosion) grenade. One former member of the unit has even insisted that bottles of pills were sometimes pressed on men before setting off on a particularly hazardous mission which bore the inscription: *Instantaneous Death Tablets: To be Taken with Discretion.*

According to Lieutenant Ruari McLean of the Royal Navy Volunteer Reserve who was a member of one the earliest COPP units, Clogstoun-Willmot realised very early on that his men would more often than not have to work at night, which presented its own particular problems. But solutions were soon found, thanks to the help of Hasler among others, as McLean has written in his entertaining autobiography, *Half Seas Under* (2001):

> The best way to land on an enemy-held beach at night without being observed, he decided (with the help and experience of some friends with whom he had already been practising it) was for two men to be carried to the area by submarine, motor boat or even aircraft, be launched in a two-man canoe which would paddle to the outward edge of the surf, and for one man then to leave the canoe and swim into the shore. The most difficult part would probably be for the swimmer to find the canoe again, and for the canoe to find its carrier. For this, most rigorous training was required.

The ideal number for a unit, Clogstoun-Willmott decided, was five officers and six or seven men. They should include a trained navigation or hydrographic specialist, a naval officer in charge of the equipment on which, of course, every member of the team's life would depend, and a Royal Engineer commando captain to reconnoitre the leeward aspects of beaches and their defences and exits. Collectively, these 'Coppists' would turn their leader's dream into a reality – but only after a lot more hard work as McLean has recalled:

> It needed the strictest training, the utmost adherence to rules and timetables, perpetual use of common sense and good luck. Failure meant death by drowning or capture by the enemy; and to be captured or leave the enemy any trace at all of our existence would prejudice the success of the subsequent operations involving thousands of lives. Experience taught us early that the dangers of detection by the enemy was negligible compared with the danger from the weather; the initiative always rested with us, the intruders, and we would be poor at our job if we ever allowed ourselves to be detected. But wind, sea and tide could be enemies with whom we had to reckon more seriously. The first COPP parties, anxious to justify themselves and at last do the job for which they had been training, launched their canoes in weather that made success impossible; and four valuable officers were drowned. We continued training for some months and it was eventually decided that we were ready for action.

A series of Combined Operation Pilotage Party missions in Europe – in particular precise surveys of the Normandy beaches during the winter of 1943 – finally convinced even the lingering doubters in the Admiralty of the value of Clogstoun-Willmott's concept. A further series of exploits in the Mediterranean on totally different coastlines proved equally invaluable as the tide of the war gradually turned in favour of the Allies.

Then, in late 1944, two COPP units, number 7 and 8, commanded by Lieutenant Peter Wild RN, were assigned to the Far East and sent to join the Coastal Forces operating off Burma. Despite the blanket of secrecy that covered their movements, Royal Marine files indicate that one of their first missions was a reconnaissance of Elizabeth Island in Hunter's Bay – a precursor to the raid in which Peter Young took part. James Ladd describes what turned out to be a rather inauspicious beginning to the Coppists' time on the Arakan:

> As the party neared the island they could see village fires ashore and sentries' huts – possibly the lavatories Japanese soldiers built at the end of the small

wooden jetties over the seashore. The night was bright enough for one of the men, Michael Peacock, to watch his colleague, Alex Colson, clamber over the sand at the back of the beach, where he was fired on without any warning challenge – the Japanese must have known anyone on these beaches was against them if he wandered around at night. Peacock swam clear of the beach but passed out, coming to while drifting across the bay with no one in sight. He struggled ashore, but three days later three islanders took no notice of the waterproof packet of letters offering rewards for his safe conduct – although there were several versions of text in different dialects – and he was handed over to the Japanese. He was taken to Rangoon, later surviving a three-day march as the Japanese tried to evacuate 600 POWs in the retreat.

However, the importance of the work of these latest recruits to the ranks of the Banzai Hunters was soon paying dividends for the Allied high command. The four men taken into Hunter's Bay brought back information of spiked and angled obstacles in the water around the Myebon Peninsula that seemed like clear evidence of the area's importance to the Japanese. The two senior officers charged with co-ordinating the assault decided to investigate in person. They were Brigadier Campbell Hardy, a veteran British Army officer who had led 46 (RM) Commando during the Normandy Beach landings – where he won a DSO – and Captain Martin Knott, an English-born signals specialist in the Royal Indian Navy, who commanded the RIN sloop, *Narbada*. Knott, a fluent Urdu speaker had been in the RIN for a decade during which time he had been responsible for 'leading a collection of sloops, frigates, ML's and other craft, manoeuvring his ships in narrow, muddy *chaungs*, and acting as mobile artillery in support of the Army in the Arakan operations', according to Bisheshwar Prasad in the *Official History of the Indian Armed Forces in World War Two: Arakan Operations 1942–1945* (1950). He was a man who knew the territory well and would later be awarded a DSO for his bravery.

Hardy and Knott had the necessary knowledge and experience to know exactly what they were looking for on the morning of 9 January when they left Akyab in the *Narbada* for Hunter's Bay. The ship's log indicates that they patrolled along the coast, seeing nothing very remarkable except a derelict steamer, which they decided to shell more in hope than expectation. However, when a concealed gun returned fire from the shore, the Brigadier recognised it as a British 2-pounder that had probably been captured by the Japanese at an earlier date. The *Narbada*'s guns continued to pound the shore, eventually silencing the big gun, but not before the ship had sustained slight damage from return fire and a couple of casualties with minor injuries.

The two men had been handed secret reports before sailing that the Myebon Peninsula was believed to be a 'concentration area' for Japanese reinforcements going north and for the wounded travelling south to Rangoon. From their observations, these stories seemed to be accurate. With binoculars and a high-resolution telescope they could see evidence of dumps of ammunition and stores; and the reports that 'two or three hundred soldiers of the Reconnaissance Regiment of the Japanese 54th Division' were believed to be in occupation seemed very probably true.

During their mission, Hardy and Knott also spotted a sand bar about 13 feet below the surface of the sea with the water shallowing just beyond it. There were, though, three sizeable muddy banks that seemed to offer the right facilities for a 'beaching', not far from a little village named Agnu lying on the southern tip of the peninsula. At low tide, the shoreline was covered by black sand and a combination of surface silt and thick mud. The fact that one of these banks was defended by 15-feet high stakes, 9 feet in diameter, positioned 8 to 10 feet apart in a straight line just above the low water mark some 300 yards from the 'beach', convinced the two men the sea bed here must be solid enough to take a landing.*

As the *Narbada* returned to Akyab, Brigadier Hardy began drawing up his report and making plans for a mission to be code-named 'Operation Pungent'. In order to take Myebon, he would need a flight of fighter aircraft to bomb the beach defences supported by shelling from the sea in order to obliterate the considerable Japanese force. Allied troops could then go ashore at high tide and mop up any resistance that remained. From what he had seen, Hardy knew that the landing *must* coincide with the high water mark if the invaders were going to be able to establish a workable beachhead.

D-Day for the assault was fixed for Friday 12 January with H-Hour at 8.30 a.m., the forecast high water mark. According to the records of 'Operation Pungent', No. 3 Commando Brigade embarked from Akyab with the *Narbada* and another sloop, the *Jumna,* carrying a commando force each. Four BYMs transported the third commando, while the fourth commando was carried by three LCIs. A further twelve LCMs and five LCTs moved the tanks, guns, bulldozers and other vehicles and stores necessary for the mission. The assault craft to take the men onto the beach – a total of 22 LCAs – were all towed by the fleet. Supporting naval gunfire was provided by the anti-aircraft cruiser HMS *Phoebe,* the sloop HMS *Shoreham* and five destroyers, *Napier, Nepal,*

---

*As a matter of record, Allied experiments later showed that these heavy stakes set to a depth of 6 feet into the seabed would have been able to resist the best efforts of an LCM driven at full speed with its ramped bow door down.

Pathfinder, Raider and *Rapid,* with air cover by Spitfires, Hurricanes, Lightnings and Thunderbolts of the RAF's 224 Group.

Before the assault took place, there was to be another trip to Hunter's Bay for the hard-working ML 854 and its captain Lieutenant Harris. A team of eight Coppists had to be taken to Myebon in the early hours of 12 January. Taffy Hill was again on board and remembered his third and perhaps most important trip to the ominous peninsula very vividly:

> *Our orders were similar to those of the previous mission – silence, obscurity and preparedness. Six members of the party, with blackened faces, were to land from their canoes and place delayed charges around the stakes to explode twenty minutes before the main landing force reached the beach, thereby creating a gap for the incoming commandos. The other two members of the party remained on board the ML in readiness to land with instantaneous charges should the original six members fail to return for one reason or another. However, the original six men returned in due course, their adrenalin rushing, claming success and informing the crew of the ML that the Japs were still there. They had even heard them talking.*

According to Hill's wristwatch, the time was just after 5 a.m. and dawn was beginning to break when their boat sped out of Hunter's Bay. All those on board were pleased that their mission had gone according to plan – so far. Suddenly they were aware of a flotilla of boats coming in their direction. It was the assault force and each man gave the thumbs up signal as the Fairmile rocked in the waves as the vessels passed. At precisely 6.30 a.m., all of them – ratings and Coppists alike – allowed themselves the first cheer of the night when the skies were rent with the sight and sound of the delayed-action charges going off on schedule. After the smoke, debris and foaming water had cleared, a 25-yard gap awaited the invasion force.

Commando Peter Young, once again in the attack force, experienced a mixture of emotions during the next few hours. The strafing by the aircraft and the shelling from the ships was a 'complete success' and the assault force was able to land with only sporadic opposition. The troops found many of the Japanese guns silent in their bunkers and the ground strewn with the corpses of enemy soldiers. Tragically, though, a number of the commandos lost their lives while wading ashore by stepping on hidden mines. A landing craft was also hit by a 75mm enemy gun that caused more casualties. Young's eyewitness report states:

It was just as well that the landing was a surprise. The tide began to recede rapidly and from the bridge of the Narbada, *I could see men toiling ashore in mud up to their armpits. When it came to the turn of 44 Commando they had nearly four hundred yards to wade. Under fire it would have been murder. There was a miniature peninsula to the left of the beach, joined to the land by a natural causeway of rocks. Seeing the misfortune of the rest of the brigade, I went round the outside of this peninsula and landed on the rocky neck. I was about the only person to get ashore dry shod!*

As the smoke cover gradually dispersed from the devastated shoreline, more than 100 tree trunks were revealed embedded further back in the mud. There were also a number of craters that had concealed anti-personnel mines: one of which had killed the Naval beach master. Laboriously, the fully armed commandos of 'Four Four' struggled ashore through the cloying mud that, as the tide receded, became a quagmire. Their anxiety to get ashore was heightened by the knowledge that the beach was a habitat for crocodiles and snakes, although as Tony Mackenzie has described, *nothing* could have made them move any quicker in the situation in which they found themselves:

By the time the marines disembarked, the water was almost at its lowest ebb. The landing craft, despite their shallow draft, grounded approximately 400 yards from the beach. The men of 44 stepped from their craft into waist high water and thick, glutinous mud. Marching across the Achnacarry heather during training, when a man's calf muscles screamed in agony was, by comparison, child's play. Hardly able to put one foot in front of the other through the knee high layer of mud which formed the sea bed, the marines toiled their way to the beach. The mud claimed boots and socks, literally sucking them off men's feet as they moved forward at snail's pace. Some men fought individual battles; others formed rugby scrums to overcome the clinging morass beneath the water. As the weary men neared the beach they were pulled ashore through the steeply shelving final few yards by ropes thrown by their comrades on dry land. By the time the unit had assembled on the beach, completely exhausted and covered in mud, it had taken over two hours to cover the strength sapping quarter mile from the landing craft to the shore.

Only the sheer physical strength and will power of the marines pulled them through the ordeal and it was an achievement of which they could all be proud. The tempers of some were not improved, however, when it was discovered they should have been landed on another, adjacent beach. It seemed that despite the on-the-spot report by the Coppists, a staff officer sitting comfortably many miles away at Divisional Headquarters had mistakenly identified the beach on which they found themselves and their equipment dumped in slimy sludge. The man's decision to land on one of the most treacherous surfaces on the Arakan had, it seemed, been based on a week-old aerial photograph . . .

* * *

Despite the messy landfall, it did not take the commandos long once they were on dry land to establish a beachhead and bring their equipment ashore. By nightfall, an ever-increasing area of the Myebon Peninsula was falling into Allied hands and the discovery of large quantities of food, clothing and blankets in bunkers and tunnels confirmed the strength of the opposition they had just routed. What, though, surprised the new occupiers was that the Japanese had made no attempt at a counter-attack. In fact, documents captured later would show that 150 Japanese soldiers out of a force of 250 on the peninsula had been killed that day. Only one wounded man was taken prisoner, but any hope of getting information from him was lost when he died in the dressing station at Agnu. By contrast, Allied casualties amounted to 45 killed and 90 wounded.

The following day, as the troops started to press along the peninsula to attack pockets of Japanese soldiers, the planners at Command Headquarters began preparing for their next objective on Hunter's Bay. It was to be a small naval base and supply point named Kangaw, just 8 miles from Myebon, believed to be heavily defended and important tactically to the Japanese. If taken, the enemy would no longer be able to evacuate the Arakan via its waterways. The base also stood at the junction of the enemy's lines of communication and a drivable track, the Myobaung to Tamandu road, which, if lost, would cut off their only other exit south through the An Pass. The Allied operation that took place at Kangaw would, in time, become known as 'the smallest beach-head of the war'.

The plan to capture Kangaw was actually a more ambitious and original one than that to capture Myebon – involving a strong element of surprise. Instead of the obvious route northwards up the Myebon River, it had been decided to go through the enemy's 'back door' by sending assault craft through 23 torturous miles of the Theegyan river into the Dainbon *chaung*. The entire stretch – 'longer than crossing the English Channel', as one participant would remark grimly later – was a waterway less than 100 yards across at its widest point. Near to Kangaw there was a vital wooded defence ridge designated as 'Hill 170', approximately 100 feet high by 700 yards long and 300 yards wide, which was surrounded by seemingly endless swamps. It was code-named with typical military wit as 'Brighton'. Once this position had been seized, it would obviously be easier for the attackers to secure the base and repel any counter-attack.

However, there could be problems for the flotilla packed with troops in reaching their objective if there were Japanese gun positions along the banks. Any passing vessel would be a sitting duck. Consequently the COPP unit that had helped to identify and reconnoitre this circuitous route was asked to carry out a further 'assault pilotage' before 'Operation Matador' was given the green light. This time, though, it was decided to send a bigger contingent – two Fairmiles, a pair of LCSs and a solitary BYMS – the party lead by Captain Knott, travelling on board Lieutenant Harris' ML 845.

The dangers of the route were brought home to the men on the five vessels very quickly. The BYM became stuck in mud and rocks less than half an hour after entering the river and an LCS had to be left behind to free it. As the remaining three continued, the other Fairmile, ML 855, also got bogged down in the treacherous mud and had to be left to free herself. Harris' motor gunboat and the last LCS continued for a further three hours. They finally came to a standstill within striking distance of their objective in the middle of banks less than twenty yards apart.

Captain Knott was keen to get a close-up look at the Japanese stronghold and slipped quietly away into the mangrove swamp, taking a COPP officer with him. The men on the two boats tried to settle their nerves with the thought that the Japanese would probably never have imagined their enemy approaching from this direction. They were all relieved, though, when Knott and the Coppist returned half an hour later, the Captain apparently satisfied with his foray. The return journey to the coast was equally tense, although the crew of ML 854 were able to help free their less fortunate colleagues on ML 855 and the three boats made for the estuary. When the trio reached open water just before daybreak, they were in for an unexpected shock, as Duncan Hill has written:

> The crew began to relax, but were suddenly brought back to reality. An ML in the estuary, unaware of the operation, opened fire on the returning raiders, disregarding the identification signal sent out by Aldis lamp. Not knowing that the fire came from a fellow ML, the mid-ship Oerlikon opened fire, only to be stopped by an order from the bridge. The shells landed in the superstructure and proved that the fire came from an ML – although our fellow craft later denied their involvement.

This unfortunate case of 'friendly fire' might have been viewed as an ill omen for 'Operation Matador', but the facts, thankfully, show the opposite. Indeed, the first bit of good luck occurred on 16 January when a patrol of 'Four Fours' on the Myebon peninsula found a box of Japanese military documents in the village of Gaungpy just after the Japanese had abandoned it. When examined by intelligence officers, the papers included maps of the enemy's defensive positions around Hunter's Bay between Myebon and Kangaw. They gave fresh heart to everyone preparing for action.

Launched at 1 p.m. on 22 January – a 'beautiful day of clear skies' to quote the official record – 'Matador' would subsequently go down as one of the fiercest and bloodiest battles in the entire Burma campaign. It would also prove a turning point in the conflict: the bravery of the Army Commandos and their colleagues of the Royal Marine Commandos securing another triumph in the Far East war. Among several honours awarded, pride of place must go to the epic courage of Lieutenant George Knowland, who earned the highest award of all, a posthumous Victoria Cross. John Winton has summarised the events, as the invasion fleet of fifty vessels burst onto Kangaw before firing a shot to avoid alerting the enemy until the moment they were ready to embark

The 'wrong way round' approach was a happy choice. The exertions on the Myebon peninsula and in the Myebon River suggested to the Japanese that an attack on Kangaw would be from the north. The convoys approaching in silence from the south achieved complete tactical surprise. Covered by fire from the Narbada, Jumna *and 'Z' craft, and by a smokescreen laid by B-25s of 224 Group RAF, the first commandos were ashore at 1.03. The landing craft played their parts with tremendous panache – it would have interested many experts to see an LCI with masts lowered, proceed into a* chaung *not more than fifty feet wide, cut its way through overhanging trees, disgorge her troops on a bank of not more than fifteen feet in width, and then be towed out stern first by two LCPs.*

A fascinating first-hand account of this landing has been provided by Lieutenant Stuart Guild who served as a naval liaison officer on one of the 'Z' craft. These curious boats were actually large, manoeuvrable, self-propelled barges that had previously been used for off-loading bigger ships. They had a draft of 3 feet, flat iron decks about 150 yards long and hand-winched loading ramps. Powered by two Gray marine diesel engines operating twin propellers, the vessels also had four gun platforms welded to the steel deck carrying 25 pounder guns. In an article written for the April 1980 *Gunner* magazine, Guild describes a critical moment in the assault that again demonstrates how narrow the margin was between success and failure in any operation in the Arakan *chaungs*:

> *The height of the mangrove must have obscured the ships from any higher ground observation. As we rounded one corner, we saw two wrecked 'country boats'. These were wooden motorised boats about 30–40 feet long used by the Japs. As we sailed up the* chaung, *a squadron of Mitchell bombers flew over and suddenly to the right front there was a tremendous 'crump' and a huge cloud of red dust arose as they dropped all their bombs (pattern bombing American style). Maps were hastily consulted as this was not where we expected them to land – and it was instantly concluded that they had dropped them in the wrong place!*

Despite the confusion, the 'Z' Craft continued up stream with the river growing ever narrower until it finally reached the 'beach' at Kangaw about three hours after the first commandos had landed. Lieutenant Guild dispatched four gunners to check for any enemy troops in the vicinity, while he carried out a recce as far as some rising ground. He returned to his vessel covered in mud but knowing a bit more about the area as he explained in his article:

> *The commandos were assaulting 'Hill 170' (code named 'Brighton'). Indian troops were disembarking from their LCIs and the beach came under fire from Jap artillery. Spasmodic shells splashed in the* chaung, *burst in the trees, or thudded into the mud without exploding. I remember thinking about a 'Dear John' letter when a shell splashed about 30 yards upstream from us! As the tide went out, the 'Z' craft tilted, so how effective we were I am not sure. However, we did give support at various times during that day and the next, with harassing fire at night.*

The indomitable Peter Young was also in the attack on Kangaw and committed his thoughts to paper:

> *The landing was through mangrove for about three quarters of a mile, leading up to 'Hill 170' which was swamped by the spring tides. Even the bunds [embankments] didn't make proper footpaths, being broken in many places. No tanks could be got ashore for the first few days. But we had air support, a lighter battery and a sloop. Motor launches and landing craft guarded the* chaung.

Peter Young remained in the heart of the battle for Kangaw and was one of the first to notice how easily the four commando brigades had become intermixed and were seen, uniquely, as a single fighting unit. The fact every man wore an identical green beret heightened this perception. Young himself also became the centre of a number of stories and though one may well be apocryphal – it does not appear in his biography – it is well worth the telling. A fellow officer is said to have seen him and a unit of commandos under attack from a seemingly endless number of Japanese and sent him an urgent message asking if he would like reinforcement. 'No thanks', Young is reported to have replied, 'We can see this lot off all right'.

As history records, Young and the other commandos and soldiers did indeed 'see off' the Japanese, withstanding several ferocious counter-attacks in which the enemy fought with 'fanatical, brutish courage which lacked subtlety and made little use of manoeuvre', to use his own words. After the action, 340 Japanese dead were counted in one area just a hundred yards square. For their part, the commandos lost 66 killed, fifteen missing and 259 wounded. The success of the assault on Kangaw prompted a message from Mountbatten that it was 'an outstanding example of inter-service co-operation'. The accolade was followed by a special 'Order of the Day' addressed to every Banzai Hunter who had taken part:

Through your exploits at Akyab, Myebon and Kangaw and the valuable reconnaissance which you made along the Arakan Coast, you have gained a reputation throughout the Corps for indifference to personal danger, for ruthless pursuit in success, for resourceful determination in adversity, which has been a source of inspiration to your comrades in arms. The Battle of Kangaw has been the decisive battle of the whole Arakan Campaign.

It was later learned that some 3,000 Japanese, of whom almost two thirds had been killed, had defended Kangaw. The importance of the victory could not be underestimated; nor the part played in it by Nigel Clogstoun-Willmott's COPP units whose work he described later with a sense of satisfaction as 'not unlike that of crews in Bomber Command'. The retaliation in Hunter's Bay had undoubtedly jeopardised the position of the retreating Japanese forces in Burma – in particular the 15th Army in the Irrawaddy Valley. The time had now arrived for another amphibious group to write their chapter in the story of the Arakan campaign. They would write it on the banks – or more particularly in the waters – of that famous stretch of river, the Irrawaddy.

8

THE IRRAWADDY WATER DEVILS

The Irrawaddy River is one of the most picturesque and legendary rivers in the world. Rising in the southern Himalayas, where its sources are the Mali and N'Mai rivers, it flows for 1,350 miles across Burma, dissecting the land from north to south, before emptying through a nine-pronged delta of mangroves and fresh-water swamp forests into the Indian Ocean. The river is Burma's most important commercial waterway, coveted by the local people, admired by visitors and fought over endlessly during its long history by the Burmese, the Kachins and even the neighbouring Chinese. Not without good reason has it been referred to as 'the cradle of Burma's civilisation' – nor that it should have played a significant role during the Allied Forces recapture of Burma in what became known as 'The Battle of the Irrawaddy Shore'.

The name Irrawaddy – today spelt as Ayeyarwaddy – is believed to derive from the Sanskrit word *airavati* meaning 'Elephant River' after those now largely extirpated animals once used in the teak trade. It is also notorious as one of the most heavily silted rivers in the world. Notwithstanding this fact, countless small wood and bamboo *bashas* cling to its banks or sprawl across the surrounding valley that has a drainage area of about 158,700 square miles and is covered by an enormous patchwork of rice fields. Ferries, barges, bamboo rafts and other vessels of all shapes and sizes ply the waterway carrying crops and passengers between villages and markets.

Along the riverbank, elegant monasteries rise now and then above canopied trees and there are also a number of ancient temples that contain a wealth of historic treasures. Foremost among these is the magnificent Shwegu Dagon Pagoda, a great cone-shaped Buddhist monument that rises 326 feet on the east bank of the Irrawaddy at Rangoon. The ancient building's magnificent spire is covered with gold leaf that can be seen from the river shimmering in the sunlight, while the interior is encrusted with precious stones. For centuries, the implacable monks in their saffron robes have had to watch carefully for covetous eyes among the millions who have come visiting.

The monument is, in fact, just one of the reasons why in colonial days before the arrival of the railways and the motor car, when tigers and leopards still roamed the area, the Irrawaddy became famous as 'The Road To Mandalay'. This great city in the north of the country with its fabulous palace has, of course, been celebrated in poetry by Rudyard Kipling, in song by Frank Sinatra, and in prose by George Orwell (*Burmese Days*), John Masters (*The Road Past Mandalay*) and several other major writers. Above all, it is a waterway filled with surprises – not least as serving as the natural habitat of a variety of marine and freshwater life including, surprisingly, dolphins and sharks – as both the Allied and Japanese forces who battled for control of it between 1942 to 1945 found out: frequently to their discomfort and often to their cost.

*   *   *

The Irrawaddy River became the focus of the war in Burma in January 1945 when Field Marshall Slim made plans to cross the great waterway, take the Arakan and capture Rangoon overland in what was named 'Operation Sob' – 'Sea or Bust'. The successes of the Coastal Forces, the commandos, marines and other covert units on the coast meant that the time was ripe for the 14th Army to mount an offensive against the Japanese using military, airborne and amphibious forces in a great push south. As Julian Thompson has written in *War in Burma, 1942–1945* (2002):

> Slim sought to bring the Japanese army to battle as early as possible, in a place of his own choosing where his superiority in armour and air power could be used to best advantage. He judged that the Japanese would fight hard to stop him reaching the Irrawaddy as this would give him the opportunity to destroy them on the Shwebo plain, north of Mandalay between the Irrawaddy and the Chindwin.

However optimistic the shrewd soldier was, he had reservations about the task that he kept to himself until years later when he wrote his own definitive account of the campaign, *Defeat into Victory* (1956). Hoping that the Japanese commanders 'had their eyes fixed on Mandalay while the 4th Corps approached the Irrawaddy', he admitted to himself:

> Success depended on what? Luck? A Japanese pilot streaking across the tree tops, an enemy agent with a wireless set crouched above the track counting tanks, or a prisoner tortured until he talked – and Kimura's divisions would move, the muzzles of his guns swinging towards our crossing places. Imagination is a

necessity for a general, but it must be controlled imagination. At times I regained control of mine only by an effort of will, of concentration on the immediate job in hand, whatever it was. And then I walked once more among my soldiers, and I, who should have inspired them, not for the first time or last, drew courage from them.

As Slim also knew, a vital factor in the success of such a mission was not just the ability to reach the Irrawaddy but also to *cross* it. He was in no doubt his adversaries would defend the crucial river ferociously and attempt to isolate his troops on the far bank where they could be picked off. The Field Marshall needed specialists at river crossings – and he needed them urgently. The answer to his problem came in the person of Lieutenant-Commander Bruce Wright, a resourceful and imaginative Canadian, and his Sea Reconnaissance Unit (SRU). As the New Year dawned, Wright suddenly found himself and his men 'needed in Burma as soon as we could get there', according to his own account of the next tense weeks in *The Frogmen of Burma* (1970).

Setting up this band of specially trained and equipped swimmers had been a long and often frustrating task, but now Wright believed they would have a chance to prove their worth in one of the most hostile environments in the world. The challenge for the SRU was to help facilitate what Mountbatten would later describe as 'the largest and most difficult river crossing I have ever heard of'. It was an achievement that actually had its beginnings four years earlier almost to the day on a snowy night in St. John's, Newfoundland. There, Wright, a former Canadian Forest Service employee and Sub-Lieutenant in the RCNVR, was on anti-submarine harbour patrol duties waiting for a posting to the convoy escorts in the embattled North Atlantic where German U-Boats were wrecking havoc on British shipping. After one stint of duty he was reading an article about the abalone divers in California and their adept use of paddleboards, 'single window' dive masks and swim fins, when a thought suddenly occurred to him. What if these swimmers were used in marine operations taking the battle to the enemy *underwater*. He later explained this new concept in his book:

A team of 'abalone divers' could be put overboard from a submarine lying outside the ASDIC loops. They would tow a cigar-shaped plastic mine that would not register on the loops and swim to the net. This they would pass by diving and cutting a hole to pass themselves and the mine through. Then they would proceed to their target and, after placing the mine, return the same way. It all seemed so simple . . .

Les Gunn, left, and the crew of LCS (M) 87.

The Chaung War – 1: An LCA in a tight position on the Arakan uses a mangrove bank to turn around.

The Chaung War – 2: A Fairmile and LCA on the hunt for Japanese troops, from a drawing by Lieutenant H. D. Rowe, an RNVR officer who served on the Arakan.

Major Blondie Hasler, inspirational leader of the Small Operations Group (SOG), and perhaps the most important of the unsung heroes of the Arakan campaign.

The captured Italian 'Explosive Motor Boat' that Hasler tested on The Solent with unexpected results.

Secrets of our Motorized Submersible Canoes

A ONE-MAN CRAFT for use in enemy waters at night was one of Britain's closely-guarded war secrets. Twelve feet eight inches in length, with a beam of 27 inches, it can be carried on the deck of a torpedo motor-boat or in a submarine. The flooding of the canoe is controlled by valves and, if necessary, it can loop-the-loop in 50 feet of water. Moving at full speed and ready to dive (1), it submerges until only the pilot's head is visible (2), and the run-up to the target is made under water (3). Alongside an enemy vessel (4) he is in position to fix an explosive charge to the hull; this canoe, with a cruising range of 30-40 miles at three-and-a-half knots, powered by electric motors, is camouflaged for service in the Mediterranean. The pilot (5) wears a water-tight rubbersuit and oxygen breathing apparatus.

Only after the war were the achievements of Blondie Hasler and his men made public in stories like this from *The War Illustrated*, 31 January 1947.

Men of SOG undergoing amphibious operations training at Hammenniel Camp in Ceylon (Sri Lanka) in 1944.

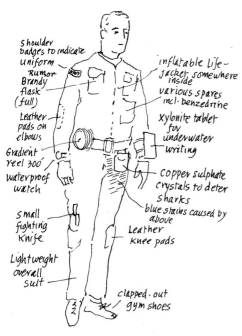

shoulder badges to indicate uniform
"Rumor Brandy flask (full)"
Leather pads on elbows
Gradient reel 300'
waterproof watch
small fighting knife
Lightweight overall suit
clapped-out gym shoes
inflatable life-jacket somewhere inside
various spares incl. benzedrine
xylonite tablet for underwater writing
copper sulphate crystals to deter sharks
blue stains caused by above
Leather knee pads

(Above) Lieutenant Ruari McLean of the Combined Operations Pilotage Parties (COPPs).

(Left) A sketch by McLean of the Coppists's operational gear.

One of the top enemy
hunting teams of the Special
Boat Service (SBS) patrolling
the Arakan.

Lieutenant Commander
Bruce Wright, the founder
of the Sea Reconnaissance
Unit (SRU) known as the
'Frogmen of Burma'.

Several units of the Small Operations Group played an important role in the vital crossing of the Irrawaddy River.

Marine commandos had to keep a close watch for crocodiles and water snakes while landing on the Myebon peninsula in January 1945.

Aerial photograph of the harbour at Kyaukpyu on Ramree Island as Allied troops prepared to retake the Japanese stronghold.

Another aerial shot of landing craft establishing a bridgehead at the Letpan chaung.

The armada of Coastal Force vessels approaching Rangoon i 'Operation Dracula' as the Arakan campaign draws to its dramatic finale.

The terrible aftermath of the Arakan war: thousands of Japanese bodies were found in the chaungs – shot, drowned o dead from disease and starvation.

Bruce Wright had been a swimming champion at university and appreciated the kind of extreme powers of endurance such a project would require. But he also sensed other uses to which such men might be put: underwater observation and beach reconnaissance, to name just two. As far as Wright knew, his concept was an original idea and he quickly prepared a report for his superiors, *The Use of Natatorial Assault and Reconnaissance Units in Combined Operations.* A year later – and after going through several naval hands – his manuscript finally reached the Admiralty in London. He was ordered to England and told to bring a surfboard, underwater mask, fins and a spring-loaded, arrow-firing gun to demonstrate to the boffins how his idea worked. The Sub-Lieutenant had only just arrived across the Atlantic when a story was published that he would later regard as one of the most curious twists of fate in his career:

An article had just appeared in a news magazine about a Japanese unit of trained swimmers, several hundred strong, that had been used with success in the attack on Hong Kong. I traced the story and found that a film of this unit in training was available through Intelligence sources in the United States. I used frames from this movie to illustrate my report. I suggested the use of several pieces of equipment that the Japanese apparently did not have.

Approval for Bruce Wright's idea came from the very top. Mountbatten had been one of those who had read his paper and suggested the Canadian should be allowed to recruit and train up a group of men to prove his ideas. He was to set up a base on Hayling Island and report to a certain Major R.M. Hasler. It was to prove a fortuitous decision for the Sub-Lieutenant who would find his superior wholly supportive of his ideas as Ewen Southby-Tailyour describes in *Blondie*:

On Sunday 10 April 1943, Bruce Wright's name first appears in Blondie's diary. He knew of Wright's existence, but on that day he first saw one of the new ideas that he had brought with him across the Atlantic. Blondie watched Wright demonstrate his paddleboard at their first meeting. He was sufficiently impressed to take him to London the next morning to develop further a few of the ideas and ask Dunlop's to produce special suits and fins to aid underwater approaches and attack. Bruce Wright was working on an idea that Blondie regarded as a minor incursion into his own field, but he saw the value and gave it free rein.

What Blondie saw was that Wright's proposal would use underwater swimmers for reconnaissance and sabotage duties in those places that canoes like his, and certainly heavier craft, could not operate. Mountbatten, too, recognised this logical progression, but insisted that Wright should work under Hasler's wing. A training syllabus was agreed – to be directed by Blondie who was also to be responsible for the selection of candidates. As both men agreed that endurance was going to be a primary key to successful underwater attacks, they made a series of lengthy swims together, covering 443 yards on one occasion on just one oxygen bottle. Within a matter of weeks, Hasler had given his unqualified blessing to the formation of Wright's 'Amphibious Reconnaissance Party' – a designation which would shortly afterwards be changed to the more familiar Sea Reconnaissance Unit.

The embryo unit was installed at Eastney Barracks, which had an indoor pool in addition to being located just across the road from the heaving, grey waters of the English Channel. Here the first 'operational swimmers' – a term Wright thought more appropriate than his own 'natatorial unit' and pre-dating the more familiar 'frogmen' – began training. Wright supervised the making of the masks and fins and was also able to get the well-known boat builders, Thornycrofts, to make a supply of sturdy paddleboards based on the Californian original.

Each day, the Sub-Lieutenant swam with his men, getting them used to the various pieces of the equipment they would have to use in operations. What he wanted most, he insisted to everyone, were 'sub-mariners' who would be able to undertake secret reconnaissance work, observe coastal terrain above and below water, and undertake missions as amphibious scouts or raiders in inland waterways. He expected that 30 feet would be the furthest down any diver would need to go, as anything deeper could almost certainly be regarded as of no importance to an amphibious assault.

As the days passed, however, Wright found that although all the recruits were tough, developed the necessary endurance and could navigate in all weather conditions, some were not natural swimmers. He took his problem to Hasler who advised him to spread his net further and seek volunteers from all three services. The response to his call for men for 'hazardous duty' in what was now classified as a 'Top Secret' unit was remarkably good. Within a matter of weeks Wright was again going through a rigorous selection process until he had a group of men he hoped would meet his demanding standards.

However, the Sub-Lieutenant soon began to realise he would never finalise his team if their training was confined to the cold and murky waters of England and suggested to Mountbatten that the clear seas and surf he needed were best found in southern California where he had first read about the 'abalone divers'. To Wright's delight – if some surprise – he was given the authority to decamp to the golden west coast of America. He was also promoted to Lieutenant Commander to put him on a similar footing to the other service personnel with whom he would have to liaise. There were – it was said – a number of officers with a reputation for being rather uncooperative and referring rather contemptuously to all small operations groups as 'private armies'.

The men of the Sea Reconnaissance Unit had no inclination to get involved in any inter-service rivalry, however, and were happy to be off across the Atlantic. There, at Camp Pendleton, a great stretch of arid scrubland fronting on the Pacific Ocean at San Onofre that belonged to the US Marine Raiders, they began the next phase of their training. Living in bell tents, the team of 'Brits' set to work to develop their skills in the clear waters and enormous breakers that rolled onto the beach. The conditions might have been idyllic, but Wright knew that mastery of the water would mean the difference between success and failure, life or death, when put into operation under battle conditions. The Canadian gradually whittled down his recruits to the core number who would comprise the SRU, as he explains in *The Frogmen of Burma:*

> We proceeded to teach our men the necessary skills and it was fascinating to watch their confidence grow. In a week they were going back and forth at will through ten-foot breakers. The added power of their fins and the ability to see what was happening through their masks, were all these adventurous spirits needed. Soon the officers were cautioning the over-confident. But there were also those who could not face it. They were R.T.U'd (Returned to Unit) and finally we settled on our target force of 40 men.

One of the most important tips Wright believed he could give his team concerned the effect of water 'stopping' bullets. In lectures and in the swimming pool he made a point that would be proved time and again to them later: they were safer in battle than any ordinary soldier because all they had to do was submerge to avoid small-arms fire. He also stressed how good the lightweight, manoeuvrable, hand-operated paddleboards were for unobtrusively carrying one or two men over distances that were too far for swimmers to operate efficiently, though too short and dangerous for canoes. Because the hollow boards only drew a few inches of water and were very fast, they were an excellent form of transport for a scout or raider in swamps and small waterways. With practice, he said, it would be possible to carry machine guns and limpet mines on the board. These were all pieces of advice the men who later served in the Arakan would remember with gratitude whenever they were making for a heavily defending objective or else escaping from a tight situation.

When operational training began, Wright organised the unit into four sections and appointed Captain E.H. 'Mick' Muldoon of the Irish Guards as his second in command. Muldoon, from Newcastle, had been recruited to the SRU after winning an MC in North Africa. A stickler for discipline who hated unnecessary delay, he was also capable of great outbursts of anger. Yet despite his temper, Muldoon was said to be the 'the sort who would lead a bayonet charge until the last man dropped'. The rapport between Wright and his 'Jimmy the One' – as Navy tradition referred to people of Muldoon's rank – soon became evident to the whole unit as their energy and leadership qualities proved to be one of the key elements in its success.*

The beautiful weather on the Californian coast made most operations a pleasure and mock paddleboard attacks planting limpet mines were followed by reconnaissance exercises and night raids on the Pendleton Camp in which the American marines took part with undisguised competitiveness – thankfully without any serious injuries to either side. Another valuable lesson was learned when trying to avoid the guards who patrolled the perimeter with ferocious 'war dogs' – a swimmer still wet from the sea gave off almost no scent and a soldier and his animal could pass within a few yards without detecting the intruder.

Dogs on land were not the only danger Wright's men came face to face with during their training. The Lieutenant Commander had been aware since coming to California that when operating in tropical seas they would encounter various species of marine life – and it was important to know what kind and how to deal with the dangerous sort. Colonies of sea lions that could become violent during the breeding season were familiar on the west coast, and octopuses up to 33 feet across were not unknown. The killer whale was another predator that hunted in the local waters. The only way of dealing with these terrifying creatures, Wright was told by his local contacts, was to get out of the water and into a strong boat as quickly as possible! The Canadian also knew he could not discount the possibility of meeting sharks. Off the coast of San Onofre, there were said to be a few small leopard sharks, but they were not ranked among the most dangerous members of the sea's notorious killing family.

*Captain Muldoon would later be credited with a major role in the successful crossing of the Irrawaddy in an extraordinary newspaper story by war correspondent Arthur Halliwell of the *Daily Herald.* In a front-page dispatch of 19 February, 'Swimming Daredevils Forge Road to Mandalay', the Irish Guardsman was said to have lead 'a death or glory squad of champion swimmers naked [sic] across the river on Monday night'. When Lieutenant Commander Wright was shown this report, he was incensed and lodged a protest with the Chief Censor that the publicity of his unit had 'blazoned all over the English papers the supposed secret use of swimmers' which would have been read by Axis contacts and relayed to their superiors, exposing the SRU to retaliation. He added that if Halliwell, a well-known reporter somewhat inclined to sensationalism, ever appeared in any of Wright's sections, 'he would be shot!'

Wright did, though, want his men to see the real thing up close and explained he would have to go to the Bahamas in order to complete their education. There, in a world of crystal clear seas and dazzling white sands, the men of SRU would be able to carry out the last phase of their training. The contrast of this new location and what lay ahead was not lost on Lieutenant Commander Bruce Wright, however. For in the Caribbean they could enjoy a slice of paradise while preparing – as he later wrote – 'for what then appeared to be one of the most dangerous jobs in the world in what would be the most advanced positions of the war . . .'

* * *

For security reasons, the 40 members of the Sea Reconnaissance Unit completed their training on Salt Key in the Bahamas. A remote offshore island, it was little more than a stretch of coral rock about a mile long with undercut cliffs 20 feet high on the south shore and a sea beach of white sand on the other. It was known locally as 'Treasure Island'.

While the men gained proficiency using the Davis Submerged Escape Apparatus, Bruce Wright gathered all the available information he could find on the dangerous creatures that be might encountered in coastal waters. He learned there were four: the killer whale, the larger sharks, the barracuda and the estuary crocodile. The SRU men had, of course, already seen the first type and were anxious to get a look at the next two. Stories about the fourth would come as a complete surprise to them all a little later.

Wright decided to test the received wisdom that blood in the water would attract sharks and barracudas. Several experiments were tried with different types of animal flesh, but singularly failed to attract a single marauder. The Lieutenant Commander needed to have second thoughts:

> *Something else beside blood was obviously required to make the sharks attack. I suspected that this might be movement. All my baits so far had been stationary lumps of flesh. This time I used live, but wounded fish. The wounds provided the blood and their struggles on the hook provided the movement. In two hours I had taken nine barracuda and one shark and on subsequent occasions I hooked and lost five other large sharks. Movement was clearly the catalyst that released the attack.*

Experiments in the water off Salt Key also produced two other important facts for the SRU swimmers to be aware of: armed, as they were, with just a small spear. It appeared that when more that one man faced a shark, it invariably swam away; while underwater explosions, far from driving off sharks, actually attracted them. Wright kept a careful record of all his unit's encounters with dangerous creatures – adding sting rays, moray eels, vicious jelly fish like the Portuguese man-of-war and sea urchins to the list – and after the war revealed his observations in an article, 'Releasers of the Attack Behaviour Pattern in Shark and Barracuda' published in the prestigious *Journal of Wildlife Management* (April 1948).

In the spring of 1944, however, such details were not the stuff of scientific journals but vital information for men about to risk their lives in dangerous waters in the Far East. All too soon, in fact, the balmy days came to a halt when a signal informed Lieutenant Commander Wright that a group of senior British officers were coming to the Bahamas to see how his unit was getting on. A full-scale night-time operation was hurriedly laid on, complete with a 5-mile journey on paddleboards carrying explosives, attaching limpet mines to a ship and an undercover beach infiltration to reconnoitre enemy positions. The exercise was a resounding success and the visitors left agreeing that a valuable new team was now ready to be added to the Allied war machine.

When Bruce Wright returned to London, however, he found everyone in authority bound up in the plans for D-Day. His mentor, Mountbatten, had left to become Supreme Allied Commander, and there appeared to be no one at the Admiralty interested in using the skills of the Sea Reconnaissance Unit. Excepting, that is, a rather unlikely scheme for dropping the men by parachute during the invasion of Europe as near as possible to the French coast for a 'do-or-die' operation. James Ladd has described this unsettled period of the SRU's existence:

> *Their sea training was completed by March 1944, but the previous winter the back breaking apparatus for the SCUBA (Self Contained Underwater Breathing Apparatus) had developed technical faults. The unit and other British frogmen had to use the Davis Submerged Escape Apparatus breathing oxygen. Operations proposed for the Aegean, Adriatic, Black Sea and the Danube were not carried through [and] a proposal to split the unit was resisted on grounds that at least 40 men were required for successful operations in any one theatre. But it was felt these powerful swimmers with a low silhouette on fast and manoeuvrable boards might just have a sea-borne role in the Far East.*

The summer and autumn of 1944 passed as Wright fretted about a posting for his men. Finally, in October, when he had almost given up hope, he was summoned by Mountbatten to Ceylon [Sri Lanka]. He was to be reunited with Blondie Hasler as part of the hush-hush Small Operations Group based at Camp Hammenheil, a depot near Jaffna, where groups of small units like his own were under training. Wright's spirits rose when he was told that plans were already advancing for the SRU to be used in operations in occupied Burma and Malaya. As soon as his men arrived by troopship, they were to begin training on the coast – where, it was said, conditions were similar to those they would encounter in action. It seemed to Wright that all the hard work he had put in was not to be in vain, after all.

The SRU settled into the tropical climate well after their experiences in California and the Bahamas and refined the use of their fins and paddleboards in the tropical estuaries and rivers. Among several mock exercises, they took part in a jungle reconnaissance mission that involved a pitched battle and the 'capture' of a headman from a native village. They were well prepared when Mountbatten paid a surprise inspection visit. The SEAC Commander was evidently delighted with everything he saw and Wright did not have to wait long for the next move. On 31 January 1945, he was summoned to a top-secret meeting. The 14th Army was approaching the Irrawaddy River and landings were being planed on Ramree Island off the Arakan coast. It was time for the Sea Reconnaissance Unit to fulfil its destiny.

*   *   *

Even before the men of the SRU reached Burma on 9 February, it had been decided they would be divided into four groups. Number 1 section, commanded by Captain Jock Elder, a Scot from the Black Watch, and Number 4 under another Canadian, Flight-Lieutenant Harry Avery, were to go to the Irrawaddy to a point about 20 miles downstream from Mandalay. Number 2 section, lead by Lieutenant Burton Strange of the RCNVR, would be sixty miles away near the ancient city of Pagan, with Number 3 under the command of the Lieutenant John Junor, RN, on the Arakan coast to prepare for an assault on Ramree Island. Wright himself planned to begin the mission with Number 2 section, though he would move around when and where he might be needed. Now, he told himself, his ideas were to be tested for *real*.

The General Staff had numerous blanks they wanted filled in for the coming Corps crossing of the Irrawaddy and we were to go to work the same night. Our forward position was three miles from the western bank of the river. Those three miles were a no man's land and the Japs, who held the eastern bank, sent patrols into it at night. Our job was to do a recce of the proposed embarkation point on the waterfront of the village of Kukyun. What was the grade of the bank? Was the soil firm enough to carry tanks? How close to shore could the four-foot draught boats and barges come? Finally, was there four feet of water around either end of an island that lay as a natural screen along the whole length of the beach?

The operation had to be carried out under the cover of darkness and, unsure of the movements of the enemy and the loyalty of the natives, Wright made his decision with careful deliberation. This was a mission for swimmers alone – and he knew he should lead by example and take one of the most skilful of his men, Marine Gilchrist. That night, the two men approached the river in battle dress, each wearing thin rubber-soled shoes, their fins under their arms, carrying an automatic pistol and commando knife each. Masks would obviously be of no use in the dark. As the Lieutenant Commander admitted later, he and Gilchrist were full of trepidation as they slipped into the jet-black river:

I had thought about crocodiles, but could get no information without giving away too much of our plans. We would have to risk them. There were regal pythons up to 30 feet long that lie at the water's edge at night, waiting to grasp and coil around anything that comes to drink. We would have to risk them, too. The Irrawaddy dolphin is a small whale that lives in this river. It would be harmless, but startling to meet when swimming at night. And last but not least, there might be Japs swimming like ourselves in the river.

It did not take the two swimmers long to determine that the water of the river at this point was shallow and no vessel drawing 4 feet of water would be able to cross. It took longer – several hours in fact – and a lot of swimming to find an embarkation point that was unobstructed and deep enough for the tank carriers to pass. Then, just as the pair were making their way as silently as possible through the watery gloom, a pin-point of light suddenly flashed across the water. Wright and Gilchrist froze in the water. When, finally, the light was extinguished, the two swimmers could only hope they had been mistaken for a pair of crocodiles! Finally, they felt confident they had all the necessary information and returned to the western shore just as dawn was about to break. Both were exhausted and shivering from the cold, but quietly elated.

The success of Wright's first SRU mission not only pleased him, but delighted the military authorities who promptly issued orders for another 'swim'. The following evening they were to take a detailed look at the channels between the sandbars of the main stream and the beaches on the Japanese side that might be used for a landing. The area was in a constant change of flux and it had been decided against asking the RAF to take aerial photographs for fear of alerting the enemy.

Wright knew the urgency of this mission and the distances involved called for greater speed than his swimmers could manage – he decided it had to be a team effort with ten men using paddleboards. As night fell, he lead the group across three miles of dank, muddy terrain shrouded in darkness, conscious every step of the way to the river of the contrast with the golden Californian coast where they had learned their skills. The ten men took silently to the waters and put all their training to good effect. Before sunrise, they were all safely back at base reporting having found three possible assault beaches, as Lieutenant Commander Wright's log of this particular mission indicates:

Points noted: 1. Locals swimming at No. 2 beach, i.e. no mines. 2. They dove directly off the bank indicating deep water close in shore. 3. Activity in hole in cliff over No. 3 beach – armed sentry noted at mouth of cave. Believed to be a gun emplacement.

These same SRU records indicate the thoroughness with which the men carried out their missions on the Irrawaddy during the next few hectic days. Their endurance and skills were tested to the full and resulted in a wealth of observation – the charts of beach approaches and gradients still exist today. The men also located sand bars and mud banks, river depths and underwater obstacles and, especially, the location of Japanese troops. Bruce Wright could claim later with every justification that no planner before ever had more detailed information for a river crossing.

Although all the patrols returned safely from their respective missions, there were a number of close shaves. Several times the men had skirmishes with the river dolphins, large water snakes and some other, indeterminate, river life. On a few occasions, the wakes of their paddleboards were apparently seen by Japanese sentries who flashed torches from the riverbank, but without apparently spotting anything. On one night, a guard persisted in playing his light near to a pair of stationary swimmers who were probably only saved by the sudden appearance of two other objects drifting by. The men's fear they were about to be attacked by crocodiles was only slightly mollified when they realised the shapes were actually a pair of rotting corpses that had probably floated down from one of the battles near Mandalay!

The evening before the crossing was due to begin on 14 February, Lieutenant Commander Wright remembered looking across the river at the ancient city of Pagan with the spires of its pagodas glinting in the setting sun. Try as he might to enjoy the beautiful sight, he could not help being concerned for his men who would be responsible for directing the troops of the South Lancashire Regiment to the landing beach. Indeed, just before the signal to go was given, the SRU's heretofore-perfect safety record was very nearly ruined:

> *Two Japs with shaven heads and wearing trunks were seen swimming back to the Jap bank immediately in front of the embarkation point. A man returning from a recce raised his Tommy gun and killed them with a single burst. The fire, however necessary, tightened many nervous fingers on both banks and my scout was still out. As he approached our bank, returning on a paddleboard from the final recce of the beaches, Rifleman Booth of the SRU was fired on by a machine gun. His board was hit but he escaped injury. This was the first time the SRU had drawn fire since its arrival in the area – and it came from our own side!*

The crossing of the Irrawaddy was not achieved without many problems and great loss of life as the various histories of the war in Burma have documented. In several instances, though, the problems were quite unseen. For example, because of the need for silence and secrecy, the pull chord motors on the South Lancashire Regiment's canvas assault craft had not been started in weeks and when the boats were fully loaded, a number refused to start. Some of the other older boats began to leak when weighed down with troops and struggled to cross the river. A number even had to be paddled with rifle butts, tin helmets and planks torn from the floor.

Almost inevitably because of these problems, a large section of the assault force was soon struggling in the river, a sitting target for the Japanese troops. Unbeknownst to the enemy, however, events were about to take a dramatic turn for the better thanks to the efforts of the Sea Reconnaissance Unit. They had managed to get another of the Regiment's companies over the river earlier under the cover of darkness. Bruce Wright takes up the story:

> *The whole assault was piling up on the great sandbank above Kukyun. The only exception was 'C' Company whose sneak crossing in darkness was our only success. At 0.35 Sergeant Cochrane and I had been on the two sandbars. When we heard the muted splashing of 'C' Company approaching in the darkness we turned on our lights. I had to wade over 100 yards downstream from the end of*

my bar to find sufficient water for the boats. I waited on tenterhooks for a long time for the burst of fire that would signal their discovery, but none came. They had landed undetected.

While 'C' Company held its position, reinforcements arrived in the shape of Thunderbolt fighters and Mitchell bombers, their strikes augmented by heavy guns and tanks. Relentlessly, the tide began to turn against the Japanese as their posts on the opposite bank were hit, their trenches flattened and an ever-increasing number of soldiers and snipers were killed. A vivid record of the crossing from the army's point of view is on file in the Sound Archives at Kew [No. 20474] recorded by Lieutenant Peter Noakes of the 1st Northamptons who crossed with the 32nd Brigade of the 20th Division:

We set forth like a crocodile of rubber dinghies with an outboard motor on the front one which kept conking out. We were met by machine-gun and mortar fire which was not very effective. A couple of nights before we crossed, a young officer was sent out to the far bank with two or three signallers in a rubber boat with an Aldis lamp as a guide to us. He was told to put a red filter in the lamp. The Irrawaddy current is quite fast, so navigation across at night is difficult. The red lamp was a brilliant idea. The RAF was asked to send their noisiest plane to patrol up and down the river to cover the sound of the crossing. This seemed to work and we landed on the far bank after a while. When we got out we found ourselves in four feet of water. We waded ashore and dug in on the beachhead. We came up against the Japs' infantry guns, we called them 'whizz-bangs', but we managed to turf them out and dig in.

The men of the SRU, having completed their part of the assault, could only watch from the opposite bank as history was made. The bridgehead opened by 'C' Company was expanded and reinforced and two days later it had been extended down to Pagan, allowing the Allied troops at last to cross the Irrawaddy in force and storm on to take Mandalay, as Slim had long planned. Bruce Wright provides the *finis* to his part in the events:

It was the longest opposed river crossing attempted in any theatre of World War Two and is reported to have moved Winston Churchill to a remark that was often quoted in South East Asia Command: 'Today we crossed the Irrawaddy with a bamboo pole and a piece of string'. It was a very proud moment for the men of the Sea Reconnaissance Unit.

The men of the SRU – who would later become a part of local legend as the 'Irrawaddy Water Devils' for their part in the crossing – might have been tempted to add to this reference to the two cheapest materials in Asia, a short postscript: 'and a mask, some fins and a lot of breath'.

* * *

Over the river, two days later, Second Lieutenant Kazuo Imai of the 12th Company 215 Infantry Regiment of the 15th Imperial Japanese Army was shell-shocked and demoralised. After arriving in Burma from Japan in November 1944, he had suffered mixed fortunes in the battles with Allied troops at Gangaw and Yesagyo, before being posted to Kyuigon opposite Myinmu in late January. Here his orders were to stand firm in preventing the Allied troops from crossing the Irrawaddy. Now the worst had happened: the enemy was over the river and he had new instructions to lead an attack team of 40 men against a group of Allied soldiers entrenched on a sandy stretch of the river bank beside one of the crossing points.

The time was late evening and despite an outward appearance of confidence, the Second Lieutenant was gripped by a sense of foreboding as he waited for the arrival of his commander, Lieutenant Midorikawa, to order the attack to begin. Before this could happen, however, the sudden cry in Japanese of 'Enemy in the river' broke the silence, to be followed by a flurry of tracer bullets and flare bombs that lit up the night sky. Kazuo Imai has recalled what happened next in his contribution to *Tales by Japanese Soldiers of the Burma Campaign, 1942–1945* (2000) one of the very few books to tell the story of the Irrawaddy crossing from the opposing point of view:

> *By the light of a flare bomb I saw several silhouettes of boats moving towards the beach from upstream. I could not judge whether they were boats that had drifted from the crossing or those of the enemy trying to attack us and I called, 'Light machine gun!' The black figure lying on the ground on my left answered, 'Machine gun out of order'. So I cried back, 'Disassemble and clean the gun'. Then I contemplated what I should do. Mortar bombs began to fall around us and I smelled burning powder.*

As the Second Lieutenant lay on the ground he saw the silhouette of a man fall from a boat that was nearing the beach. The sound of a machine gun rattling nearby made him realise that the enemy had several firing points on the plateau in front of him. A mortar bomb exploded almost on top of Imai and for a moment he thought his world had ended. When he looked up again, shots from somewhere else nearby were whizzing past him:

I noticed that bullets from our medium machine gun were hitting the sand in front of me. The machine gunner was dead with his head down, still pressing the trigger knob. A shadowy figure pushed aside the gunner and started to fire. A very bright flare shone on him and the enemy machine guns targeted the gun; our second gunner was shot in the face and lay prone. Undeterred, a third gunner took the position and fired and soon the ammunition ran out. I heard a voice. 'No bullets!' said the voice of the commander, Lieutenant Midorikawa, 'Machine gun retreat'

The attempt to stem the tide of Allied soldiers crossing the Irrawaddy was clearly failing, Lieutenant Kazuo Imai realised in that moment. But it was not so much the failure that bit into his soul that day, but hearing the word 'retreat'. He had never heard it before and it seemed to be sounding the death knell to Japanese ambitions in Burma. He could not know that the fortunes of war had, indeed, turned and that within weeks one of the Imperial Army's strongholds on the Arakan, Ramree Island, would also be echoing to the same call as it, too, was taken thanks to a third unique group of Banzai Hunters.

INVASION OF CROCODILE ISLAND

Ramree is the largest island along the Arakan coast, covering 520 square miles. Shaped rather like an inverted pistol with its barrel pointing north towards Combermere Bay, it is 50 miles long and 20 miles across at its widest point, with a southern hilt consisting of almost 10 miles of continuous swamp and wilderness. Like much of the Arakan when seen from the air, Ramree looks deceptively peaceful and empty of people with dense swathes of trees sweeping down to the west coast on the Bay of Bengal. A single dirt road runs along the coast – in places, even along the beach – swinging eastwards past occasional small hills and rock clusters towards the town in the centre that provides its name. Mile upon mile of surf are also visible breaking onto the sands, interrupted by the occasional *chaung* and a handful of small coastal villages and hamlets like Minbyin, Kangwe and Mayin. In January 1945, however, as Mountbatten and the Allied commanders made plans to wrest it back from the Japanese only the airfield at Kyaukpyu (pronounced Chalkpu) at the northern most point and the town of Ramree some 12 miles from the mainland, gave any hint that it was an enemy stronghold – or that it possessed a fearsome reputation above and beyond that given by its latest occupiers.

Here, though, on the island some 60 miles south of Akyab where the Coastal Forces had launched their series of remorseless operations to gain control of the Arakan, history was about to be made. Stationed on Ramree were almost 1,000 Japanese soldiers of the 2nd Battalion of the 121st Regiment commanded by the dour and humourless veteran Major Matsu. Since the Japanese occupation in 1942, it had been used as a training base that had given their men knowledge of the terrain and conditions that would be invaluable if the need to defend it occurred. The beaches had been heavily mined, too, and gun emplacements dug into large rocks overlooking any beaches considered potential targets. Major Matsu also had at his disposal field artillery, well-fortified bunkers and troops reputed to be tough fighters. All were invisible to the naked eye. Furthermore, Ramree was said to be 'a noisome place' inhabited by vicious mosquitoes, scorpions, snakes, and, in the swamps, as many as 1,000 enormous salt-water crocodiles that were said to be the most dangerous in the world.

It would, in fact, take two operations by the Allies to capture Ramree: 'Operation Matador' to seize the harbour and airfield at Kyaukpyu and 'Operation Block' to drive the enemy into the swamps in the south. Both would prove to be groundbreaking missions. 'Matador' was the 'largest amphibious operation yet attempted in the Arakan', in the judgement of Vice Admiral Sir Arthur John Power writing in 'Naval Operations in Ramree Island Area, 19 January to 22 February, 1945' (published in the *London Gazette,* 26 April 1948). 'Operation Block', on the other hand, would be a combined services manhunt in which the Army would attempt to force the Japanese into the swamps where the Navy and RAF would destroy them and their boats as well as preventing any vessels being brought to their rescue. It would prove to be 'one of the most ruthlessly executed minor operations of the war', to quote John Winton, who adds that 'all Allied forces were briefed to shoot on sight'.

In total, several thousand soldiers, commandos, marines and navy personnel would be involved in taking the island which was regarded as vital to the Allied cause to provide a base for air support of the 14th Army as it pushed south from the Irrawaddy and out of range of the airfields in India. There would also be more work for the COPP teams, the men of the SRU, and several of the Coastal Forces, including the 152nd Minesweeping Flotilla attached to the British Pacific and East Indies Fleet whose swashbuckling exploits had already earned them the nickname of 'Churchill's Pirates'.

To begin with, though, the success of the two operations owed a great deal to the reconnaissance work carried out by another of the small amphibious units belonging to Blondie Hasler's Special Operations Group. They were the Special Boat Service (SBS), whose secretive and highly dangerous work has been recorded by one of the men who took part. His name was Major Richard Livingstone and his own career and that of the men he led to Ramree are an essential precursor to the story of the invasion . . .

* * *

The man responsible for the creation of the SBS was Lieutenant Roger Courtney, another of the larger-than-life characters from among the ranks of men who put their unique talents and extraordinary personalities to good use for their country during a time of war. Referred to by friends and colleagues alike as 'Jumbo', he gave little away about his childhood beyond the fact that he had developed his passion for adventure along with the attitudes of a maverick while he was growing up in East Anglia. Roger had gone abroad while still in his teens and for a while was a gold prospector and big game hunter in Kenya. It was while he was serving in the Palestine Police Force – where he rose to the rank of Sergeant – that Courtney became fascinated with river travel.

In the mid-thirties, the young Englishman bought himself a Folbot – a kayak-style, two-man canoe named after the company that had invented them in 1933 – and soon became a very competent sailor. So much so, in fact, that he decided to sail the boat, which he had named *Buttercup,* on his own the entire length of the White Nile from Lake Victoria to Egypt. He armed himself only with a single spear – much to the amusement of the many natives he encountered on his odyssey. Not content with this expedition, when he got married in 1938, Courtney took his new bride canoeing down the River Danube for their honeymoon. His familiarity with the Folbot – and his growing sense of its potential – was firmly in his mind when the war broke out and he joined the King's Royal Rifles Corps and was seconded to No. 8 Commando. It was after one particular day of training in a Scottish loch that he got the idea for a 'raiding and reconnaissance force' using Folbots.

Roger Courtney's idea was initially greeted with scepticism – but he set out to prove the doubters wrong with a series of daring exploits. He used several handy Scottish harbours to demonstrate how it was possible to approach ships unseen in his Folbot and either steal a souvenir or leave a chalk mark on the stern. He was also able to show how when one of these narrow boats was seen on end in poor weather with its two-man crew lying flat, they looked exactly like a floating log. Similarly, when approaching an enemy boat in complete silence, it was possible to fire at the target at almost point-blank range before anyone on board was aware of their presence. Courtney's persuasiveness paid off and just as he turned forty, he was promoted to Captain and given instructions to recruit a dozen men for the first Folbot Troop. They were to operate initially under the auspices of No. 8 Commando.

In early 1941, as part of the troop's training programme, Courtney took his men to his old stamping ground, the Eastern Mediterranean, and established a base at Kabrit on the Great Bitter Lake. Although the group soon became quite skilled operators, they had to make do with very rudimentary equipment. There were no wetsuits – normal uniforms had to be worn – while torches with socks over them provided a crude signalling system. The men's only weapons were .45 automatics or Tommy guns.

For identification, the members of the unit all wore a green beret and a shoulder flash, 'Commando SBS', as they had been labelled. According to one story, the name had been chosen to fool *Wehrmacht* radio operators who might be listening in on British military communications. It was believed the Germans would have little interest in such a prosaically named outfit when there was so much else going on! Courtney, his reputation as a maverick well established, tried to adopt a motto of his own, *Excreta Tauri Astutos Frustantor,* but had to settle for 'Not By Strength, By Guile'. However, no setbacks of any kind were going to dampen his spirits or the sense of optimism that so endeared him to his unit. One member, Lance Corporal James Sherwood, is on record at the Sound Archives at Kew reminiscing:

> He [Courtney] was a very tough sort of man, very self-reliant, full of a love of adventure. Not a blustering, swaggering sort of pistol stuck in the belt type of bloke, but a straightforward man with an adventurous spirit. We liked him and would have been prepared to go with him anywhere.

Among Captain Courtney's early exploits was a reconnoitre of the Italian-held island of Rhodes where he became the only man to set foot on the island. The plan for a landing was, of course, stillborn when the invasion was cancelled. One good feature of the exercise was his meeting with Lieutenant Commander Nigel Clogstoun-Willmott who was also surveying the beaches with his Coppists. The men spent two invaluable months together going on missions, swapping experiences and forging a life-long friendship. Courtney was sorry to they had to part company when he and his men were moved to Alexandra to join the Royal Navy's 1st Submarine Flotilla – but was anxious to see action.

In late June 1941, after a series of dummy exercises, the SBS, now with the strength of all 47 ranks, carried out its first solo mission. This involved a journey on the submarine, HMS *Urge,* to Sicily where a two-man Folbot team landed on the coast and blew up a railway tunnel. This success was followed up by similar attacks on enemy bridges and aqueducts, several reconnaissance missions and even landing a number of secret agents and bringing out escapees from behind enemy lines. Their most dramatic feat was rescuing 200 Australian soldiers from Crete who were laboriously pulled through the water by ropes out to three waiting submarines without a single man being lost.

By the end of the year, the number of Special Boat Service members had risen to 60 and so successful were their missions that Courtney was dispatched, albeit reluctantly, back to England to recruit and train No 2 SBS which was officially established on 1 March 1942. The Captain devised a punishing seventeen-week training programme with the little boats that also included weapons practise and even parachute jumping. Among the new team he sent out to help in the North African landings in November 1942 was his own younger brother, Godfrey, who played a major role in reconnoitring the North African coast before the projected invasion. The unit later guided the assault force onto the Algerian beaches. Further operations off Italy, Norway and France saw the SBS – now a force of some 160 expert swimmer-canoeists – carrying out spying missions and night raids. There was even a daring attempt to sink some enemy vessels in Oran harbour using miniature torpedoes launched by hand from the Folbots.

In June 1944, three SBS units of twenty all ranks were posted to Burma to form another key part of the Small Operations Group. One of Courtney's first recruits to the second SBS unit, Major Richard Livingstone, was put in command. In the next year, Livingstone and his men would become the busiest of all the Folbot teams, taking part in over 80 operations on the Arakan coast. Both paddle canoes and motorised craft were used along with vastly improved personal equipment and armament. They also worked in tandem with the COPP and SRU growing familiar together with life on the coast of the 'white man's grave'.

To those Special Boat Service men who relished their operations with the same enthusiasm as their founder, the only regret was that Courtney himself was not there to see his ambitions fulfilled. Instead, this remarkable man of many parts had to settle for a desk job with the British Military Administration in Somaliland. He was still in his beloved Africa when he died in 1949.

* * *

Richard Livingstone shared the enthusiasm of his mentor for small boat operations, but none of Courtney's eccentricities. Both, though, were thoroughly dedicated soldiers who were not afraid of danger and carried out their missions to the letter. Livingstone was born in September 1915 and educated at Marlborough and Corpus Christi College, Oxford. In 1941, he volunteered for the SOE (Special Operations Executive) and transferred to the Commandos a year later. Hearing accounts of the SBS and their need for new recruits, Livingstone took up Roger Courtney's invitation to join. After completing his training, he was sent with the new unit to Gibraltar where it was attached to the 8th Submarine Flotilla.

After two years in the Mediterranean, Livingstone returned to England in 1943 to become second in command at the headquarters of the SBS at Hillhead on the Solent where, like Courtney before him, he came under the influence and patronage of Blondie Hasler. From this base, Courtney took part in two raids on the French coast that, he said later, helped prepare him for work under fire in

Burma. Late in 1944, and now commander of 'C' Group of No. 2 SBS, he was posted to the Arakan. In December, the Captain and his men began the reconnaissance missions to the coast that would lead to the invasion of Ramree – 'a god-forsaken place remembered by most of the men as "Crocodile Island,"' to quote Lance Corporal Sherwood.

The focus of several of the amphibious missions that first month was Laws Island, a small hilly outcrop just a mile across in the bay from Kyaukpyu harbour. Travelling by Folbot, they scouted for information about the Japanese evidently ensconced beneath the covering of jungle on Ramree. It was essential to try and avoid being spotted by the enemy and although there were a few skirmishes, the 'watchers' suffered no fatalities – a measure of the skill imparted to the swimmer-canoeists by their founder, Roger Courtney, as James Ladd has written:

In December 1944, the SBS made a number of forays to Laws Island, going into the tunnel of mangroves where the river outlets were hard to find even on a moonlit night and Japanese motor sampans patrolled with searchlights. They could see the Japanese sentries on Ramree and noted their routines and kept up a constant flow of information about the enemy's positions and movements.

The diaries that Major Livingstone meticulously kept of these operations offer a more intimate account of what it was actually like going on to the two islands under the very noses of the Japanese. These missions, consisting of up to nine teams of two SBS men per Folbot, were transported by MLs from their base at Teknaf across Combermere Bay to a suitable point off the small chain of islands that shelter Kyaukpyu. There they would be 'slipped down' into the sea at dusk. Livingstone's account of an operation that set out on 14 January 1945 is one of the most vivid of the whole Arakan campaign and was described by him in an essay, 'Burma: The War of Stealth' (1966). It begins with the journey of the unit to the coast of Ramree in two Fairmiles of the 55th Flotilla: ML 440 commanded by Lieutenant Jack Zappert, and ML 474 skippered by Lieutenant Ken Baber. Livingstone's orders were to investigate a report that the Japanese were about to withdraw from the island; that there were only about fifty troops at the airfield; and little resistance to an attack was likely. The Major was about to discover that the *facts* were actually very different indeed:

This time, we had chosen the cove under Catherine Bluff as our slipping point and the MLs lay rocking on the smooth swell with their engines humming as the boats were slung over the side, meeting the water in a surge of phosphorescence, and we climbed down into them as they bobbed alongside. Torch, binoculars, R/T set, weapons, rations, water-bottles, were passed down and stowed away, and last of all the long paddles. One by one the boats pushed off and took up their stations, the crews raising their paddles as soon as they were ready to go. We got away at midnight, following the narrow channel between Tankharo Island and Sinbaik chaung, slipping along between the steep, wooded heights with a strong tide under us. After a couple of miles, we saw a fire blazing among the trees on the Tankharo side, casting a red glare across the channel. Remembering an earlier report about Jap watch fires and Burmese lookouts, we stopped paddling and let ourselves drift slowly past on the tide. There were several men round the fire, but they did not see us.

The party arrived at Laws Island just before dawn. The Folbots were beached in a sandy cove fringed by bushes and the men waited in silence until the sun began to rise. The morning was spent carefully reconnoitring the island – establishing that the story the Japanese rarely visited any of the islands around Kyaukpyu seemed to be correct – and several hours observing the harbour across the bay with binoculars and a high-resolution telescope.

The SBS men got their first surprise when it became clear that the town, which had been reported as ruined and overgrown, seemed undisturbed with clusters of red-roofed houses rising intact above the trees. There were also bunkers at strategic positions and wire defences along the beach. Soon, a constant stream of people could be seen moving towards the town. At first glance, this suggested to Livingstone they might be going to market – then, more likely, that they were the members of a forced labour gang. Convinced that he should try and get to Kyaukpyu for some first hand investigation, Livingstone consulted his map and made plans for four teams to pay a visit during the ensuing night.

The party made the mile-long crossing at 9 p.m., landing near Careening Point, hiding their boats in the undergrowth before moving off. Livingstone had told the interpreter brought along for the mission, Corporal Ba Than of the Burma Intelligence Corps, that he wanted to go to the Zaing *chaung* about 2 miles inland. There he hoped to find someone with a good knowledge of the Japanese occupiers. Encountering a group of fishermen around a fire at the other side of the point, Ba Than negotiated a fee with one of the younger men. The boy agreed to lead the party and took them along a narrow jungle path and across some dry paddy fields until they reached the village. At the home of the headman, Livingstone was introduced to a venerable old man with a white moustache:

I began by telling Corporal Ba Than to make a soothing speech to the effect that we were friends who had come to drive the Japani away, and that when this had been done, there would be peace and prosperity for the people of the island and the whole of Burma once more. We needed his help in telling us all about the enemy, and that when we came back, we would remember those who had helped us – and also those who had not.

According to the Major, the Burmese relayed this information word for word while the old man nodded sagely. There was a lengthy silence after the interpreter had finished speaking, before the headman replied that everyone on the island was tired of the *Japani* and would be glad to see the *Ingaleik* back again on Ramree. Livingstone's account continues:

We then got down to the actual situation at Kyaukpyu and the old man gave us a lot of information. He said there were about 300 Japanese at Gonschwein on the sea side of Kyaukpyu. They evidently had guns and had conscripted everyone to dig defences – not at all what the Allies were expecting. The Japs seemed to have behaved fairly well, but had ruthlessly rounded up everyone, young and old, fit and unfit, for forced labour. They had 'encouraged' the recalcitrant by pouring boiling water in their ears. There was a lot more useful stuff about enemy movements, motorboat supply routes, etc., but not much about their actual positions. After an hour and a half it was time to go. I said that the General wanted to talk to someone who knew what was going on in Kyaukpyu. The headman objected strongly and said that the Japs would have his head: naturally, if a disgruntled villager reported the transaction, and he had said nothing about it, he would get short shrift. I replied that the General's orders must be obeyed and that, incidentally, there would be 50 rupees for anyone willing to come as well as 20 rupees for the headman. Eventually our fisherman-guide, whose name was Aung Chan U, agreed to come, if he could hand the money over to his wife before leaving. So I produced my money-belt and the interview ended with polite obeisances all round.

Swiftly paddling back to Laws Island, Livingstone was pleased to find that in his absence his men had found another eager informant. His name was San Hla Baw and he had been a clerk in the District Commissioner's Office before the arrival of the Japanese. Then he had fled to the island with his family – his wife, aged mother and five small children – for fear that they would all be massacred. The Burmese spoke very precise English and was able to add to the information

Livingstone had received from the headman and Aung Chan U. It seemed that the whole 121st Regiment was on Ramree and armed with artillery. The Second Battalion was in the Kyaukpyu area; there were two companies on the beach at Gonschwein; and the remaining troops were heavily entrenched on Mount Peter and Black Hill. San Hla Baw added that the Jap headquarters were hidden in a cave temple and pointed out the exact locations of two of their biggest guns.

Roger Livingstone could hardly believe his luck at getting such priceless information. He was now in possession of a virtual blueprint of the Japanese whereabouts on Ramree. He could only imagine the delight with which his superiors would receive this news. To be absolutely sure, though, he told the former District Commissioner's Office clerk that he wanted to take him back to Corps HQ:

San Hla Baw objected strongly to coming with us. For an hour we argued with him, flattered him, offered him rewards. I did not want to carry him off by force if it could be avoided. Then his old mother told him to pull himself together and 'be a man' (Braganza's translation). Finally, he agreed, on the promise of a chit from me, a chit from the General, 50 rupees and a new suit of clothes!*

That night – 18 January – after four days on Laws Island, the party climbed back into their Folbots and paddled for four hours to the rendezvous at Catherine Bluff where Lieutenant Jack Zappert in ML 440 was awaiting them. As soon as the SBS men were spotted, Zappert dispatched a radio message to ML 474, waiting at the alternative rendezvous point, Pagoda Rocks, to come and take on board the remaining men. Dawn was coming up as the two vessels with Major Roger Livingstone and his tired but extremely satisfied teams began their journey back to Teknaf. One man who would have been particularly pleased at the outcome of the operation was, of course, a world away – but there was no denying it represented another realisation of Roger Courtney's idea dreamed up on that chilly Scottish loch.

* * *

The Allied attack on Ramree Island to seize Kyaukpyu was code-named 'Operation Matador' and took place on the morning of 21 January. The force was

*San Hla Baw was later rewarded for his vital information with a trip to Calcutta where he was officially thanked on behalf of the Allied Forces. A few days after this, he returned in triumph to Ramree on the bridge of the battleship, HMS Queen Elizabeth.

well armed with intelligence: for apart from the SBS, the SRU and Coppists had also been busy. No. 3 Section of the Sea Reconnaissance Unit, led by Lieutenant John Junor, had surveyed the mangrove *chaungs* behind the island, overcoming their disappointment at not being involved in the bigger mission of their other teams on the Irrawaddy; while the COPP units had explored the proposed landing beaches and confirmed they were heavily mined and covered by artillery.

The Assault Force Commander, Major General C.E.N. Lomax of the 26th Indian Division who was supported by the Naval and Attack Forces Commander, Captain E. Tyndale Cooper, gave the green light for the assault. A force of considerable size had been assembled and would be preceded by a heavy and hopefully accurate bombardment campaign by sea and air that would batter the enemy before a single Allied soldier set foot on land. Although the attack had actually been planned, mounted and carried out in fourteen days, it was, as Vice Admiral Sir John Power said later, 'the largest amphibious operation yet attempted in the Arakan'. After all the clandestine amphibious operations of the Banzai Hunters, it was now the turn of larger vessels to make their appearance. The constitution of the assault force certainly makes impressive reading.

Accompanying General Lomax's 26 Indian Division were the 4th Indian Brigade under Brigadier J.E.R. Forman with battalions of The Green Howards, 13th Frontier Force and 17th Rajput Regiment; plus Brigadier L.C. Thomas's 36th Indian Brigade with three battalions, the 16th Punjab Force, 8th Gurkha Rifles and a second battalion of the 13th Frontier Force; lastly, the 71st Indian Brigade, commanded by Brigadier G.G.E. Bull with men of the 1st Battalion of the Lincolnshire Regiment, 5th Battalion 1st Punjab and the 1st Battalion of the Royal Garwhal Rifles. In all, this was a total of nearly 7,000 troops. The men were embarked from Chittagong between 17–19 January on the personnel carriers, *Egra, Ellenga, Nevassa* and *Salwee,* and the infantry landing ships *Ikauana, Itola* and *Winsang.* Standing by to give the force air support were four squadrons of B24 Liberators and 24 P47 Thunderbolts of the American 12th Bombardment Group under the command of Air Vice Marshal The Earl of Bandon, commander of 224 RAF Group.

The sheer size of the naval assault force was designed to intimidate the occupying forces as much as possible. Heading the bombardment force were three destroyers, *Pathfinder, Rapid* and the Australian HMAS *Napier* skippered by Captain Eric Bush, with all his experience of the Normandy landings, supported by the RIN sloops, *Flamingo* and *Kistna.* In their lee were 24 LCAs, 18 LCMs, 8 LCPs, 4 LCSs, 3 LCTs, 2 LCIs and Landing Craft Headquarters 261. The attached force was made up of twelve Fairmile MLs, 7 BYMs, an LCM depot ship, and one

LCT maintenance ship. Two escort carriers *Ameer* and *Raider* also sailed to join the attack from Trincomalee on the afternoon of 18 January, followed by the cruiser HMS *Phoebe,* and the veteran battleship HMS *Queen Elizabeth,* commanded by Captain G. Norman.

The appearance of the huge battleship was intended to boost morale as the members of the force prepared to land on Ramree. What very few people knew at the time was that the *Queen Elizabeth's* presence was entirely due to the sharp eyes of the SBS. A letter written by Mountbatten years later in February 1969 reveals all: 'As soon as Livingstone reported the guns in the Rocky Temple Caves, I signalled immediately to Ceylon ordering the C-in-C to send up heavy bombardment units. *Queen Elizabeth* got the order to raise steam within less than an hour . . . the army could hardly believe it!'

The beach selected for the assault force to land lay between Georgina Point and Dalhousie Point near Kyaukpyu. H-Hour was set for 9.30 a.m. at low water – and the sudden appearance of the massed ranks of ships of all sizes proved a total surprise to the Japanese troops, as Admiral Sir Arthur John Power has written in 'Naval Operations in the Ramree Area, 19 January – 22 February, 1945' published in the *London Gazette* on 5 April 1951:

> *The pre-assault bombardment began when* Queen Elizabeth *opened fire at 8.30 – using her main 15-inch armament in action for the first time since the bombardment of the Daranelles' forts thirty years earlier. She had a most reassuring effect on the assaulting troops of the 71st Indian Infantry Brigade; the sight of the battleships and the explosions of her 15-inch shells on a commanding ridge to the west was the most heartening to all concerned. At 9.15,* Phoebe *and the other bombarding ships opened fire and again all troops were delighted by the effect on the hillside. Meanwhile, four squadrons of* Liberators *bombed enemy positions covering the beaches and Thunderbolt fighters bombed and strafed the beaches themselves.*

It was soon evident that the Japanese had completely misjudged where any Allied attempt to retake the island might occur. They had the greatest concentration of their forces at Thames Point on the west coast and in Ramree town. After the first wave had reached the beach near Kyaukpyu at 9.42 a.m., the second wave joined them at 10.15 and within the hour, the occupiers were being driven south in considerable numbers. A number stubbornly defended their positions and were deliberately bypassed – in particular those in entrenched posts such as the Yanbauk *chaung* – and left to the ensuing troops who would surround the Japanese and wipe them out or force them to surrender in their own time and at the cost of least casualties.

The beach landing was not without its problems and tragedies, however. Just after 11 a.m., LCA 2086 hit a mine and sank with the loss of 23 of her contingent of 32 troops and two crewmembers. Another vessel, Fairmile ML 891, which came to the aid of the survivors, also struck a mine and three ratings were killed. The main cause of the trouble was the fact that only four of the BYMs had been available for minesweeping duties: one had been used to tow a barge and two others to transport parties of sappers. Those who did ultimately reach the beach had their work cut out to remove the explosives left behind by the fleeing Japanese.

One of the men who took part in 'Operation Matador' was Chief Petty Officer Engineer, Alf Forshaw, of BYM 2008 of the 152nd Minesweeping Flotilla. He and the other crews of the minesweepers based on the Arakan were often at the centre of hazardous duties during the recapture of the coast. Forshaw remembers that the captain of 2008, Lieutenant George Draper, often had problems getting provisions – and fresh water was so scarce it could only be used for cooking purpose. Any man found with a clean shave would be put on a charge. Alf has explained all this in a fascinating account of life on a BYM during the battle for Ramree in the *Merseyside RNPSA Magazine:*

We had sailed in an arc across the widest part of the Bay of Bengal escorted by a couple of destroyers to put off any Japanese observers. We were by then completely out of food, water and fuel. Beside the presence of the battleship, HMS Queen Elizabeth, in the anchorage, there was Royal Naval Auxiliary supply ships. The 2008 being the then flotilla leader, we led the approach to the Auxiliaries to replenish with food, water and fuel. But the Auxiliaries refused to take our lines, saying that the supplies were for Royal Naval ships only – even though we drew their attention to the fact that we were flying the white ensign. Our skipper consulted the crew, as he wanted the OK for him to use a little fresh water so that he could wash and shave as he was going on board the Queen Elizabeth, which was carrying Admiral Walker. This he got and then put forward our difficulties to the 'Top Brass'. In double short time, signals were being flashed to tankers and supply ships so that we got our supplies! Coming alongside the Queen Elizabeth, we must have lived up to our name as 'Churchill's Pirates'. When the tidy matelots on the 'Big One' looked down on our ship full of unshaven, fierce-looking crewmen, with a wealth of coloured bandanas on their heads, I wonder if they thought they were going to be boarded!

By the time darkness fell over Ramree on 21 January, Allied Forces were well established on the northern half of the island. The 71st Brigade was moving quickly south down the west coast, supported from the sea by destroyers and sloops, while the 4th Brigade made the airfield secure and took on shore over 100 vehicles and 70 tons of stores to support the troops. Three days later, as the Japanese were being driven inexorably south and faced either trying to escape to the mainland or make a last stand on the edge of the mangrove swamp, General Lomax and Captain Bush inaugurated their second plan, 'Operation Block'. This would put the once all-powerful occupiers into a position of no return, as Bruce Wright of the SRU has written in *The Frogmen of Burma:*

> *The Japs retreated to the southern tip and there a decision was made. Who made it we do not know: was it Major Matsu on the mainland, or the senior officer present? At any rate there would be no surrender. Survivors would cross the ten miles of mangrove swamps to the mainland and rejoin their unit. This was a true samurai decision, as these swamps had never been crossed by men on foot before – and the Japs knew all about the crocodiles. Our intelligence considered the swamps impassable and the Japanese trapped. Some enthusiastic type, with experience of the Italians in the Western Desert behind him, happily constructed POW enclosures several acres in extent to hold prisoners. He obviously knew little of the Japanese soldier . . .*

The methodical survey of the area beyond Ramree town that had been carried out by the men of the Special Boat Section was invaluable in the sardonically entitled 'Operation Block'. Its intention was, quite simply, to trap and slaughter hundreds of Japanese soldiers between the advancing Allied troops and the dangerous swamp behind them. The plan called for further reconnaissance by the SRU and COPP units to find the best location where the 'block' might be set up. After several rapid missions to the wasteland, a passageway was found where the tide ran out at night and mortars, machine guns and rifles could be set up. Captain Tyndale Cooper, put in charge of the operation, decided to establish two 'blocks': the longer 'North Block' extending from the Thanzit River through a confluence of *chaungs* nick-named with typical British humour 'Piccadilly Circus', to the Kaleindaung River; and the 'South Block' which ran from the Taraung *chaung* to the town of Ramree itself.

To support the gunners on the banks of the river, two destroyers were brought into range, HMS *Paladin* and HMS *Pathfinder* – the latter skippered by Lieutenant Commander T.F. Halifax who was in command of operations in 'North Block' –

and a fleet of small boats operating in close proximity to one another including eight Fairmiles, five BYMs, four LCSs and LCI 279 from which Lieutenant H. Friend was in charge of 'South Block'. According to Alf Forshaw, their mission was ever afterwards referred to by the men in the flotilla as '*Chaung* Hopping', although such a euphemistic expression could not hide the terrible fate that awaited every Japanese soldier as they began falling into the trap from 9 February. Admiral Sir Arthur Power, writing in the *London Gazette,* could scarcely disguise his own horror at what happened to the fleeing enemy:

> *During the day as well as the night; acres of thick impenetrable forest; miles of deep mud; mosquitoes, scorpions, flies and weird insects by the billion and – worst of all – crocodiles. No food, no drinking water to be obtained anywhere. It can hardly be possible that in their decision to quit the island the Japanese could have been fully aware of the appalling conditions which prevailed.*

The records of the 71st Brigade indicate that on the first night two sampans packed with Japanese soldiers were sunk in 'South Block' and every man lost. The following day, several more sampans and a motorboat were destroyed in 'Piccadilly Circus' and the Fairmiles lurking on the Thanzit River destroyed 23 boats while an RAF attack accounted for 40 more. During the night of 11–12 February, two more sampans full of despairing Japanese were sunk and the same fate awaited four more boats the following evening. A brief attempt at retaliation by Japanese Hamp-Zeke 32 aircraft from the mainland on *Pathfinder* and Lieutenant Friend's LCI 279 did nothing to halt the slaughter.

When the Allied patrols began to suspect that some of the Japanese were trying to slip through the 'block' by swimming or on hastily constructed rafts, Captain Tyndale Cooper gave orders for the *chaungs* to be illuminated at night. From 15 February an array of searchlights, flares, signal projectors and Aldis lamps – anything that could be found in the stores of the vessels, in fact – was pressed into service. Five boats were caught in the glare that very night and not a single enemy soldier lived to tell the tale. Even more desperate men made attempts to cross by daylight the next day and all were killed or driven back into the swamps. On the night of 18–19 February, two formations of enemy craft tried to make a dash across the Mingaung *chaung* – but again virtually all were sunk and at least 100 soldiers were killed.

Nothing, though, seemed to stop the stream of crazed men from coming on to their deaths. According to observers on the Allied vessels, many of them were in the most piteous condition and hardly able to walk on their grossly swollen feet.

Some were even barefoot and lacking toes from stepping on mangrove shoots. Each morning revealed the rivers littered with corpses being fed on by predators, including the voracious crocodiles. Yet, despite the heavy toll, there were undoubtedly still hundreds of Japanese on the island who remained unaccounted for long after the conflict on Ramree was over. And, if we are to believe an enduring legend, most of them fell victim to the crocodiles in what has been claimed to be the 'World's Worst Crocodile Disaster'.

* * *

The story that hundreds of Japanese soldiers may have been killed and eaten on Ramree by enormous saltwater crocodiles appears to have begun in the *London Gazette* in its account of the war in Burma, published in April 1948. The periodical refers to the reptile, known as the *Crocodylus porosus,* as the largest in the world, able to grow to a length of about 25 feet and possessing a reputation as 'the most savage of all human-eating crocodiles'. Although the creature is believed to live mainly in rivers and estuaries, it has been known to venture out to sea and some have even been seen over a hundred miles from land. The *Gazette* added that this particular type has the patience to become almost invisible to an unsuspecting victim – lying with only its eyes above water – and looking just like a floating log until its huge teeth suddenly snap with deadly effect.

In the decade after this reference, several writers claimed to have been told by men who served in 'Operation Block' that the night of 19 February had been 'one of the most horrible they had ever experienced'. The sound of gunshots picking off fleeing Japanese soldiers had been interspersed with the screams of wounded men being crushed in the jaws of huge crocodiles. The noise of the threshing reptiles as they pulled the bodies apart or fought over the limbs made for what one man described as 'a cacophony of hell'. At dawn, the vultures arrived to clean up what the crocodiles had left. According to these reports, of the 1,000 Japanese soldiers known to have been on Ramree at the time, only 20 were subsequently found alive.

The crocodile story next found its way into *The Guinness Book of Records* under the heading of the 'World's Worst Crocodile Disaster' giving the number of dead Japanese as 'c.900' and seemingly confirming it to have been fact. These facts, though, did not convince one man who was serving in Burma at the time and had already begun to suspect the story was a myth – albeit one based on an element of truth.

The man's name was W.O.G. Lofts, one of the foremost researchers of the twentieth century, who devoted much of his life after the Second World War to investigating a number of its more unusual and obscure stories. Bill had served in the Royal Artillery as a squaddie and had mixed emotions about his experiences in the Burmese jungle. He hated the oppressive climate and long, damp periods of inactivity during the monsoon. One such period had, though, ignited his passion for research when he came across a discarded copy of a *Sexton Blake* novel. Bill read the action-packed crime story at a sitting, but was surprised to find there was no indication as to who had written it. He decided he would like to find out when he returned to London – and in 1947 started his quest for the anonymous, the esoteric and the mysterious that made him so highly regarded among researchers and writers.

I was one of these authors and spent many enlightening hours with Bill Lofts while he expounded his knowledge on a wide range of topics. Of particular interest to him was the conflict in the Far East and, for obvious reasons, the campaign on the Arakan. When, on his death in 1977, he bequeathed his archives to me, I found a considerable amount of the information and a number of the photographs that now appear in this book. He had also reached a conclusion about the story of the crocodile massacre.

As Lofts did on every occasion when carrying out research into the war, he first checked Army, Navy and RAF records dealing with Burma in February 1945. Nowhere was there any confirmation of a large number of Japanese troops being eaten by crocodiles on Ramree Island. Certainly there was every indication that the fleeing enemy had suffered terribly in the swamps from mosquitoes, scorpions, all kinds of blood-sucking insects and some of the most venomous snakes, including Russell's Viper, King Cobra and the Banded Sea Snake. It appeared that a few of these men, unable to get food or fresh water, suffering from malaria, beriberi and dysentery and on the point of collapse as they crossed the *chaungs*, may indeed have fallen victim to crocodiles – but certainly nothing like the 900 suggested by *The Guinness Book of Records*. Re-examining the *London Gazette,* he also found a note that the Allied forces had been 'unable to completely seal off all exists from the swamp'.

Bill discovered, too, that although the *Crocodylus porosus* is not above eating carrion and human flesh, it would have taken a very large number of these reptiles to dispose of so many bodies in such a short space of time. In pursuit of the truth, he even made contact with some of his former compatriots in the jungle, now members of the Burma Star Association. Several had returned to the scenes of their service and, by coincidence, another group was on the point of going there. Primed with Lofts' questions, these men spoke to a number of Ramree residents who 'discounted any suggestion that large numbers of soldiers fell prey to crocodiles', according to his notes. One veteran said that a tour guide told him that even among the Japanese veterans who had returned to Ramree, not one had ever mentioned a crocodile massacre.

Lofts' file reveals that at least one other writer came to share his conviction that the story was untrue, an American, David Finkelstein. In an article, 'Tigers in the Stream' published in the *Audubon Magazine,* May 1984, which Bill attached to his own notes, he underlined one telling line by the author, 'I believe that the majority of Japanese troops escaped to rejoin the rest of their army'.

Whether the legend of the crocodile slaughter is true or not – and this is certainly a story that will go on being discussed for many years to come – the war was nearing its end for a great many of the Japanese on the Arakan. And by sheer coincidence, on the day of the alleged massacre, the first enemy prisoner was taken allowing some of the Banzai Hunters to finally have a chance to see one of their elusive adversaries up close and personal.

10
FUGITIVES ON THE ARAKAN

The evening patrol on Sunday 18 February began like many others recently for Lieutenant William Matthews and the crew of the Fairmile gunboat ML 437. It was now over three weeks since 'Operation Block' had successfully penned the Japanese into the mangrove swamps on Ramree Island and although the number of stragglers still trying to escape to the mainland had decreased considerably, the men on board all the boats navigating the rivers and *chaungs* of the Arakan had been ordered to keep their eyes open. A number of enemy troops who had not been killed were believed to be at large in the swamps and dense undergrowth and near the end of their tether. They were still armed, though, certainly desperate for food and fresh water and as far as anyone knew, as fanatical as ever.

The moon was low in the sky and there was a slight mist across the Mingaung *chaung* as ML 437 moved quietly along its predetermined route. The boat was running smoothly despite having put in three busy years of service for the Burma RNVR. Built originally in Rangoon and towed to India, it had been commissioned in May 1943 and joined the 59th Flotilla of the Coastal Forces in time for the latest attempt to retake the Arakan. Lieutenant Matthews of the Burma RNVR – 'Willo' to his friends – was proud that he had created a hardworking and efficient crew who had been on constant duty since 'Operation Block' had begun.

ML 437 had, in fact, already seen its fair share of action and although the level of tension as the boat crossed the *chaung* was not as high as it had been a couple of weeks earlier, Mathews had his searchlight on, constantly sweeping the darkness. He knew that not far away another boat, an LCA, was also on a patrol, and he did not want to stray into its arc of fire. In the darkness, just one itchy trigger fire could easily cause a nasty case of friendly fire and he had already had cause to write a report about a potentially dangerous situation he saw arise during the assault on Ramree – a situation he worried could happen again with much larger numbers of vessels involved in operations. His salutary words are now on file in the National Archive and are a clear indication of the hectic pace of missions on the Arakan:

An alarming feature of the operation was that the various craft operated by different authorities were working on the same night in the same enemy waters without any knowledge of who the others were or what they were doing. This ML had instructions to rendezvous with two unknown MLs for an unknown purpose off Sagu Island before proceeding through the 'gates' into Ramree Harbour. Those MLs were not there at the appointed place and time, having, it is understood, no knowledge of this arrangement. It was then decided to anchor and not approach the narrows until after 22.00 when there would be less chance of being spotted, secrecy being of paramount importance to the COPP party. Duly set course for the 'Gates' at 22.15 and there right in the narrows sighted four craft, three appearing to withdraw inside and one coming out. After being challenged and identified (flashing obviously and unavoidably visible from ashore) the latter proved to be a BYMS who had swept three MLs, not two, through the 'Gates', but did not know their numbers or what they were doing. He was also as surprised to see us as we him. Fortunately also the visibility was good, otherwise there might have been a sorry shooting affray since operational orders for Arakan Coastal Forces in enemy coastal waters have usually been to assume all craft sighted as hostile except where other own craft have been known to be operating, in which case full information has been given.

On that Sunday evening in February it was not just other boats or a still dangerous enemy that Matthews and the other crews of the 59th Flotilla had to be on the lookout for. An increasing number of dead bodies, blown up like balloons in the steaming heat, had been found drifting on the tide. They were a nauseating sight and not easy to sink, even with accurate gunfire.

It was now nearly 8.45 a.m. and the skipper could see that a strong flood tide was rising in the Mingaung *chaung*. His binoculars were trained towards the east when something caught his experienced eye. At first glance, it appeared to be a log drifting upstream in the direction of a mangrove island. Then a flash of white reflected in the searchlight. It looked as if something was clinging to the wood. Matthews adjusted the focus and narrowed his eyes. A man, almost naked, his arms wrapped around the log, was being rocked from side to side by the flowing tide.

'Man in the water', the skipper shouted to his number two, Leading Seaman John Bond, and pointed to where the beam of light had just swept. The searchlight was instantly swung back and now the figure on the log was unmistakable. It was about 75 yards from the boat and the man seemed to be trying to get across to an island that others had attempted to reach on previous days. Immediately the man realised he had been spotted, 'he cried out and kept up a constant wailing', to quote the Lieutenant's log.

Matthews swung the wheel of the Fairmile around to pursue the fugitive. He knew how anxious Coastal Forces were to capture a prisoner before anyone else did – and could see the man would probably reach the island in a matter of minutes. As the ML got closer, John Bond shouted at the figure to grab the lifebelt that was being thrown over the side. 'He was either unable or unwilling to approach', the log continues.

But 'Willo' Matthews was not going to lose his prize. He ordered Bond and three other men to drop the boat's dinghy over the side and go and grab the swimmer. For a moment he thought he had made the wrong decision when a round of gunfire split the silence across the *chaung*. Just as quickly, though, he realised it was the same kind of outburst he had heard lots of times before and must be the other patrolling LCA that had probably spotted something in the water. He shouted at the men in the dinghy to hurry. The figure on the log was now about 200 yards away and the others on ML 437 watched excitedly as the little boat hunted down the fugitive and caught hold of him just yards before he reached the island.

The bedraggled man who was helped on board the Fairmile a few minutes later was a sorry sight. He was covered from head to foot with insect bites and his feet were swollen into raw masses of flesh. His clothes had almost literally rotted off his back and legs. It was all the crew could do to prevent themselves from being sick at his stench, though curiosity quickly got the better of their revulsion. They were, after all, the first men on the Arakan to have taken alive one of the 'ferocious little yellow bellies' that had been their invisible enemy for so long. Lieutenant Matthews's log takes up the story again:

Convinced he would be shot, the prisoner, who was already weak, was in a state of extreme trepidation. He was thought to be a sergeant and taken to the Mess Deck where he disclosed that he had been the first to attempt the crossing. He had five companions who he also expected to attempt it, but there had been some firing which had frightened his companions back into the mangroves.

With the help of one of his Indian crew members who understood a little Japanese, Matthews promised the man good treatment for himself and his companions if they gave themselves up. The Lieutenant told the wretched figure that no boats would come to their rescue – even if they did reach the other side – and there they would surely die in the swamps from hunger and thirst. He offered the man a deal. He would be given food and drink if he would go on deck and call his name and tell the other soldiers they would be safe if they gave themselves up. Still shivering despite the blanket now draped around his shoulders, the man nodded his agreement.

For the next half an hour the Japanese shouted out his name, Asahima, and the words, '*Atsumare! Atsumare!*' ('Surrender! Surrender!') as ML 437 cruised up and down the Mingaung *chaung*. As his voice grew weaker, Matthews realised it was probably a futile exercise. The Japanese soldier obviously had no idea whether the other men were still in the area or had already made the crossing. He had admitted making his bid for freedom some considerable distance from where he was seen and by then had been in the water for a couple of hours battling the tide. Matthews decided there was no point in going on, especially as dawn was about to break. He reversed ML 437 from the *chaung* and took his hostage back to Kyaukpyu.

It was not until the following morning when Lieutenant Matthews had handed over the Japanese to a British Intelligence Officer, Captain J.S. Barden that anyone found out just how valuable the man was. He was a 42-year-old Captain, Tokuishi Asahina, of the 54th Medical Unit, attached to the II/121 Japanese Infantry Regiment. He had been on Ramree for a year in command of the army's medical services. According to his story, on 12 February after the RAF strafing and Army assault on the island, his commanding officer had given the order to his 600 troops: 'Every man for himself!' However, as a result of the attack, there were very few boats left undamaged and Asahina and five companions had decided to 'go eastwards through the mangrove swamps in the hope of getting somewhere'.

After three days of blundering through hostile terrain with little idea of where they were going, all of the men had run out of their supplies of rice and fresh water. On the sixth day of the trek, Asahina lost touch with the others and soon began to fear that the chances of any of them surviving were very limited indeed. He was angry, he said, at his Divisional Commander's failure to evacuate him from Ramree and spare him all the suffering he had to endure while on the run. He had no idea whether his superior was alive or dead and believed the man to be a liar as he had often insisted to his men that the British always tortured and killed their prisoners. The Captain said that all these factors – and because he was a non-combatant – 'release me from my vows to the Emperor'.

At the end of their conversation, Captain Barden asked Asahina if he would go out again on the Mingaung *chaung* a further time to try and find the other five fugitives. In the words of the Intelligence Officer's account, the prisoner 'took the most unusual attitude for a Japanese soldier of agreeing'. Barden's report concludes:

The prisoner's conduct was extremely good. His main reaction seemed one of bewilderment at having got away with his life and gratitude for good treatment. He never showed the slightest intention of attempting to escape or to commit suicide, although until his capture he had quite believed that the British shot all their prisoners.

On 20 January, Captain Asahina was returned to the scene of his rescue on another Fairmile skippered by Captain Eric Bush. Barden went along to interpret and ensure the recovering Japanese did not have second thoughts about his 'dishonourable' decision to co-operate with the enemy. Bush later recalled the trip in his book, *Bless Our Ship* (1958):

I can hear Asahina's raucous voice as I write. I can see him, in borrowed clothes much too big for him, peering over the bridge screen. 'Atsumare!' he shouted all the time as he called on his men to surrender. The sun rose high and sank. But not a single Japanese appeared. At sunset, I returned to base, telling the blockers to get on with the killing.

* * *

As the build up of men and armaments continued on Ramree for the next stage of the Allied advance, there was the little matter of the string of small islands along the Arakan coast that might be occupied by Japanese troops to take into consideration. Slim and his officers did not want remnants of the Imperial Army causing problems behind their lines – and especially not from islands where they would be able to make surprise strikes by day or night. It was obviously a job for the Small Operations Group to reconnoitre the islands that varied in size from tiny outcrops to some that were larger and covered by dense foliage. A number were certainly big enough to harbour small garrisons of men, perhaps even an entire battalion.

The COPP forces were the most active of the three amphibious groups on these missions, their surveys and intelligence reports more often than not drawing blanks. The motor gunboats of the 59th Flotilla also visited a number of the offshore islands to gather information from the native population. A few provided unexpected surprises.

One of the first islands to be investigated was Cheduba, a heart-shaped stretch of open terrain and dense jungle, lying 12 miles to the south of Ramree. Initial reports estimated there were 200 Japanese soldiers and five field guns in place.

The force obviously had to be destroyed or they would pose a constant threat to the western flank of its recently captured neighbour. It was therefore decided to launch what John Winton has described as 'the only purely naval assault landing in the war', code-named 'Operation Sankey'.

The Royal Marines of the East Indies Fleet supported by the 707th LCP Flotilla would carry out the assault on Cheduba. The marines sailed from Trincomalee on 23 January in three cruisers, the *Newcastle, Kenya* and *Nigeria,* and two days later rendezvoused off Ramree with another group of vessels, some of which were still at anchor after having taken part in the assault on the island. These included the destroyer, *Rapid,* the cruiser, *Phoebe,* six LCAs, two Fairmiles, two LCMs and the four BYMSs just released from minesweeping duties. The force split into two: the *Phoebe* and three other cruisers designated to provide cover from the Bay of Bengal, while the remainder sailed to Searle Point, the most northerly point of the island.

Accounts of the operation state that the first wave of troops went ashore at 8.48 a.m. – to 'a crushing disappointment'. It seemed the Japanese had anticipated the coming of the assault force and there was no opposition waiting them after all the careful planning – although there was plenty of evidence that the island had been occupied. The enemy headquarters in the town of Cheduba showed every sign of a hasty withdrawal: there was a fire still smouldering under a pan of cooked eggs. Items of uniform hung in many of the *bashas* and a number of documents were discovered only partially hidden in a trench. The sense of anti-climax of 'Operation Sankey' was not, in fact, lifted until several days later when the mystery of the deserted island was solved.

It appeared that news of the fall of Kyaukpyu had reached the island just hours after the Allied landing and the local commander had decided to evacuate his men to the mainland. Six rather reluctant Japanese out of the total contingent of 200 had been left behind, apparently without any substantial weapons to defend themselves. These men had 'gone native' and were later found dispirited and hungry, dressed in Burmese clothes, hiding on the east coast of the island. Their lack of knowledge of Japanese movements once their colleagues had left Cheduba, made them virtually useless as informants.

Two other inhabited islands to the north of Ramree, Round Island and Sagu Island also required investigation. A cautious approach to the first by a pair of 59th Flotilla launches found the natives coming eagerly to the beach to offer information. They said groups of Japanese soldiers had visited the island to recruit labour for digging trenches on Cheduba and had rounded up men from Thetleyun village, beating up anyone who refused to go. The island had not been garrisoned, however, unlike Sagu where the previous August a unit of 50 Japs had dug themselves in at Oogabyin village. There they had built an observation post and were in possession of a large field gun and several mortars.

This Japanese activity had been spotted by an RAF reconnaissance flight on 3 December, but no action was taken until the first week of February when ML 391 commanded by Lieutenant Maung Yaw and Lieutenant Matthews' ML437 fired on the observation post and put it out of operation. Although the Japanese infantrymen escaped injury, shells hit two villagers. The enemy had then evacuated the island, again leaving behind a party of six men. When the two motor gunboat officers met the natives of Sagu, they were told no one knew where these *Japani* had gone or even if they were on the island. The natives had been forbidden to enter certain proscribed areas on pain of death or having their villages burned to the ground. Despite a thorough combing of Sagu Island, though, no trace of the occupiers was found and their fate has remained a mystery to this day.

On 16 February 44 Commando were the first to land on a little cluster of islands just to the west of Ryuwa. This group 45 miles down the coast from Myebon had been thoroughly surveyed by COPP units before the decision was taken to land the 53rd Brigade as the first step of a 12 mile advance northward up the An River to encircle more Japanese. Reports of this operation indicate that it was the unobtrusive work of the Coppists and the accurate hydrographic charts of the previously unsurveyed river ways produced by the *Nguva* and MLs 1248 and 1368 – completed in just a matter of days – that allowed the operation to go ahead within a week of its inception.

The speed of this action and the successful seizure of the islands was undoubtedly helped by the Coppists placing 'Control Positions' in the *chaungs* to indicate the way for the landing craft – all named with typical British humour after English public schools including Charterhouse, Winchester and Eton – followed by a pin-point RAF air strike and a bombardment from the sloops *Flamingo, Jumna* and *Narbada*. Within 24 hours, Ryuwa itself had been taken, again with a minimum of casualties. Although the Japanese countered with shell and mortar fire during the next three days, the sustained firepower from the three sloops – firing over 9,750 rounds – ultimately bombarded the enemy out of existence.

According to John Winton, although the operations to clear the islands along the Arakan coast of Japanese troops were almost completely successful, 'not more than a score of them were ever taken prisoner and they were all found to be semi-dehydrated and in a very low physical condition'. Where the operations were more successful was in gathering Japanese Army documents which revealed escape routes and gave a clear indication that the enemy was now more focused on retreat than attack. It certainly raised the spirits of men in the Coastal Forces who had endured months of conflict on the Arakan, as Tony Goulden who served with them has written in *From Trombay to Changi* (1987):

> *As February ended and March [1945] began, the strain on all the ships, officers and men began to show in the gaunt, drawn faces of the officers, and the white ratings had huge patches of gentian violet covering septic prickly heat around their armpits. Almost everybody had scabs covering sores on their elbows and very many other places. Half a bucket of water a day was not enough and the lack of fresh food was a factor. On one occasion, Mountbatten visited the 56th Flotilla. His aides brought a supply of fresh food on the previous day, but Commander Howard ordered it to be set aside and arranged for the usual food to be served. At that time most of the cooks knew 56 ways to served corned beef. After the meal, Mountbatten enquired whether this was their normal diet. Afterwards the food improved.*

* * *

Another of the jobs that fell to the amphibious groups operating on the Arakan coast through the winter of 1944 to the following spring was rescuing British and American airmen shot down by ground fire or Japanese fighters into the estuaries and river ways. A number of the stories of manhunts for Allied pilots on the Burma coast have been told in other books about the Far East conflict, including the exploits of Pilot Officer 'Tommy' Thompson who was shot down near the Akyab Peninsula and hidden from the Japanese by the local Chittagonians, and the adventures of the crew of a crippled American *Liberator* that landed on the aptly named Foul Island and were rescued looking more like Robinson Crusoes than airmen by the observant crew of a motor launch patrolling the area. Perhaps, though, the most dramatic rescue of all was a combined operation in April 1945, which for no apparent reason has been largely overlooked.

The pilot in question was Warrant Officer John Campbell, a 21-year-old New Zealander who was attached to No 258 Squadron. He had been flying an American Thunderbolt when the kind of disaster occurred that every airman over the Burmese jungles dreaded. On the morning of 2 April, he had been reconnoitring almost at ground level over the Mayu River looking for Japanese fugitives when he accidentally struck the mast of a moving rice boat and crashed into the river.

Campbell was a fresh-faced young man from Auckland who had signed up in the Royal New Zealand Air Force the moment he was old enough in 1943. After qualifying for his 'wings', he had travelled to Britain to join the RAF and soon after was posted to India. He had barely got used to flying missions over the Arakan when the Allied forces took Ramree and 258 Squadron was transferred to Kyaukpyu. The landing strip was still in the process of being mended – like much of the rest of the town – when a new wave of operations against the Japanese began. Because of the state of the runway, only fighters could use it and Campbell was not sure whether he should be pleased or anxious. (In fact, it would not be until 15 May that transport and bomber aircraft would again use Ramree.)

The Warrant Officer had, though, come to admire the qualities in the P-47 Republic Thunderbolt that the squadron was flying – the very qualities that were going to save his life. Despite its somewhat bulky appearance, the aircraft was a fast machine and its massive Pratt and Whitney 2800 'Double Wasp' radial engine could develop around 2,300hp and reach 422 mph in level flight. After it had entered service with the US Air Force in 1942, the Thunderbolt's semi-elliptical wing, razorback canopy and great manoeuvrability had made it popular with pilots who nicknamed it 'Juggernaut'. By 1945, the P-47 had proved its capabilities in several of the theatres of war as a bomber escort and solo fighter: it could carry 2,500 lbs of rocket bombs on eight launchers under its wings and belly and had the same number of 50 calibre machine guns protruding from the leading edges of its wings.

Campbell had 'never seen such a monster before' when he was checked out on his P-47. He knew it was reputed to be the heaviest aircraft in the world – weighing over five tons even before it was loaded and outweighing many twin-engined aircraft – and at the controls soon discovered that the weight was most noticeable when a loss of power or lift occurred and its nature 'changed to one of a descending rock'. This, though, proved to be good for landings if the approach was made with a fair amount of power and then cut back, allowing the aircraft to settle immediately and 'stick' to the runway. For such a big aircraft it also had a very impressive range of 2,350 miles.

Perhaps what was even more important to young pilots like Campbell was the fact the Thunderbolt had a well-armoured fuselage and a reputation for being able to withstand a tremendous amount of damage and stay aloft to get the pilot back to base. In Europe, particularly, 'The Mighty Jug' had proved its remarkable survivability rate with over two thirds of all planes sent on risky ground attack missions returning home safely. When Warrant Officer Campbell began flying over the densely forested, swampy terrain of the Arakan he hoped his P-47 would live up to its reputation. When he crashed on his 21st mission, he had every reason to believe it did.

According to the subsequent RAF account of the crash, Campbell had been following the winding passage of the Mayu River when a native boat had suddenly loomed into sight as he was flying round a corner. Although he banked at once, he had been unable to avoid hitting the vessel's mast and, momentarily losing control, belly-flopped into the water. The report compiled by Captain Bob Houston of the RAF Public Relations Unit continues:

> He [Campbell] succeeded in extricating himself with only minor injuries and swam to the west bank. There he was set upon by hostile Mughs who stripped him of his effects, including his escape gear. They then let him go and he made his way through the jungle and across the spine of the Mayu hills to the western side where, at Donbaik, which was an enemy headquarters, he ran into a Japanese patrol. He eluded them in the dark and went into hiding in a bamboo thicket near Thawin chaung. There he was found, befriended and concealed by the Muslims.

News of this extraordinary sequence of events reached RAF sources on 10 April. As the air force had no capability to undertake rescue missions in the jungle, the details were passed on to SOG where the information found its way to the resourceful Denis Holmes in Teknaf. He immediately sent a message through one of his scouts that Campbell must stay where he was and not attempt another escape. A preliminary mission in a motor launch to find a suitable landing place on the Mayu coast near where the young Canadian was hiding had to turn back when bad weather caused the boat to hit a rock and develop a list that made it impossible to continue. To make matters worse, the damaged boat was spotted in the bright moonlight by a Japanese bunker post that opened fire – but was fortunately out of range.

The boat struggled back to Teknaf where Holmes found a note waiting for him. It was scribbled on an empty cigarette packet and read, 'Am OK and waiting for you'. Campbell was obviously safe and Holmes decided that as the monsoon season was imminent another rescue attempt must be made as quickly as possible. This time, though, they would take a more direct route from the small island of St. Martin's, lying about 6 miles south of Teknaf. Known locally as Narikel Jinjira, it was generally referred to as 'Coconut Island' because of its abundance of coconut trees. It had sandy beaches, picturesque reefs and a number of tiny islets ranging from 300 to 1000 feet that were known locally as 'Siradia' or 'separate islands'. Near the main town of Uttarpara was a shallow lagoon connected to the sea at high tide by a narrow channel. Large flocks of birds, mammals, reptiles and amphibians also thrived there because – unique among all the islands along the

Arakan coast – it had been 'completely untouched by the war'. Certainly, St. Martin's looked like paradise to Holmes and his men when they landed on the western coast on 21 April.

The men would all have liked to take advantage of the island's beauties, but those who knew the Arakan realised the *chota* monsoon could arrive at any moment and when it whipped up the water around the estuaries on the coast, navigating small craft was fraught with danger. A voyage at night would have the additional problem of finding locations in the inky darkness after crossing the 13 miles of sea that separated St. Martin's from the Mayu River.

Their anxiety for Campbell was increased when another message was delivered by one of Denis Holmes' spies. It, too, was written on a cigarette packet and bore just three words, 'Please come quickly'. The messenger said that the Japanese seemed to have got wind of the fugitive pilot and were going from village to village intimidating and physically abusing people to get information about his whereabouts. The Chittagonians would obviously only be able to keep him out of the Japanese forces' clutches for so long. The party knew they had to go *now*.

Because of the hazards of heavy surf around the beaches, Holmes' decided to make the crossing in a sailing boat, the *Stella,* with a sail-rigged *kisti* in tow to negotiate any rough water in the Thawin *chaung.* If the surf proved too rough, a couple of good swimmers would be sent in attached to rope lines. Thankfully, though, the sea moderated during the crossing and a mile from the coast the shore party were able to transfer to the *kisti.* Observing complete silence, the men slid like shadows into the *chaung.* Captain Houston describes how weeks of frustration turned into a triumph for Denis Holmes and his unit:

Led by a local guide, he and another scout moved warily along the dark beach. Within an hour they were back, triumphantly carrying the distressed pilot. The kisti *was turned about and launched, but now had to fight a harder battle against the stiffening wind and more threatening breakers. She became waterlogged and hands were soon wet through and hard put to keep her baled out and hold a course with the paddles. At last they were safely through by resolute effort, but made slow progress against the now adverse wind until at last, after half an hour's arduous paddling, they discerned the dark shape of the* Stella.

There was no doubt Warrant Officer Campbell had endured a harrowing experience – he was pale and emaciated and wearing only a ragged shirt and *lungyi.* His nightmare had only been relieved by the kindness of the Chittagonians, he told his rescuers. They had hidden him meticulously – not to mention at great risk to themselves – and kept him alive on a diet of rice and dried salt fish. This, unfortunately, had made him sick during the early period of his 24 days on the run, hiding and surviving close run-ins with the pursuing Japanese.

When the *Stella* docked safely at Maungdaw after a crossing that got increasingly rough, an RAF doctor was waiting to check the young New Zealander before offering him a bath, a shave and a change of clothing. His rescue was certainly one of the most tortuous undertaken during the Burma campaign and deserves credit as another important achievement by the Banzai Hunters of the Arakan.

*   *   *

What was destined to be the final amphibious operation on the Arakan was set for 13 March. Code-named 'Operation Turret', it was to be a landing at Letpan near the Mai *chaung* in order for Allied troops to move inland and capture the Taungup Pass. This would effectively encircle the Japanese 55th Division and the remnants of the 54th Division retreating from Ryuwa. Viewed with the benefit of hindsight, 'Turret' can be considered as probably the best organised and executed operation of all the coastal campaigns. To be fair to the planners of the earlier missions, though, this achievement owed a great deal to the success of D-Day in Europe the previous year. The tactics and lessons learned from 'Operation Overlord', the battle for Normandy on 6 June 1944 when almost three million Allied troops had crossed the English Channel to occupied France in the largest seaborne invasion in history, had taken time to filter around the world to Burma.

The details of the brilliant combination of reconnaissance work, massive air and naval bombardments followed by an early morning amphibious assault that overwhelmed the well-entrenched German forces had been a masterstroke by its main planner, the American Commander, Dwight Eisenhower. And, certainly, Commodore A.I. Poland, who had taken over on 24 February from Rear Admiral Martin as the new Naval Force Commander in Burma, had 'Operation Overlord' very much in mind when he began to plan 'Turret'.

The evidence of the American influence on this operation is, in fact, to be found in the typewritten copy of the plans drawn up by the Commodore and his officers – 48 pages embossed 'TOP SECRET – Not to be allowed to fall into the hands of the enemy' – now on file in the National Archives. Whoever placed this document in Kew has earned the gratitude of historians for ignoring the remark at the end, 'On completion of the Operation these Orders are to destroyed'. Although the explanation for the survival of the pages is probably attributable to the final proviso, 'Certificates of Destruction are not required'.

The objective of 'Operation Turret' is simply stated: to land 4th Brigade Group and the 26th Indian Infantry Division on both banks of the Mai *chaung* and establish a bridgehead at Letpan. The joint commanders were to be Captain Tyndale-Cooper – designated Senior Officer Assault Group – Major General Lomax and Squadron Leader J. Rashleigh. The Navy would be at the forefront of the task, their amphibious force consisting of the destroyer, *Haitian,* the 'B' class infantry ship, *Barpeta,* 40 LCAs, 35 LCMs, twelve Fairmiles, ten BYMSs, eight LCSs, five LCIs, three LCTs, three LCPs, and the store ship, *Bandra.* The bombardment group would be made up of the *Cauvery, Eskimo, Jumna* and *Roebuck* with RAF support by six squadrons of Thunderbolts and two of Hurricanes that would 'carry out cab rank patrol' until midday. Both Lomax and Tyndale-Cooper would sail on the *Haitian* and, says the document, 'in the event of either becoming a casualty', Major H.G. Powell would assume their duties.

The operation was to be launched from Kyaukpyu with the troops embarking in five convoys – 'Nan', 'Oboe,' Peter,' 'Queen' and 'Roger' – between 9–13 March, proceeding to a navigational position off Fitzwilliam Island. On 12 March fixed white lights would be placed at the entrance to the Mai *chaung.* Folding boats with hurricane lamps were also to be left at prearranged positions by Fairmiles. The document lists a series of call signs for all vessels ranging from 'Batsman', 'Curate', 'Dusky' and 'Sugar'; as well as providing detailed instructions of the order in which the assault waves were to be formed up. It comments, 'Should morning mist or any cause make the approach impossible, all assault convoys will be anchored by order of the S.O.A.G. (Tyndale-Cooper)'. Doubtless to inspire its readers, a footnote has been added with typical naval élan, 'If opposition is met, LCSs and close support Fairmiles are to engage opportunity targets'.

This concern about opposition was based on an 'Intelligence Summary' appended to the document prepared by COPP, SRU and SBS teams under the heading, 'Jap dispositions affecting the Assault Landings'. As always, there were detailed surveys of the various proposed landing spots with information on their length, depth, gradient, mud quality, numbers of trees, scrubland and mangrove swamps, not forgetting their suitability for the draughts and landing ramps of the LCAs. Even tidal and astronomical information was included, not to mention such *minutiae* as the amount of inches a man might sink at any particular locality. Finally, the nitty gritty evidence about of the enemy:

> It is believed that the initial assaults will be opposed. It is estimated that the Japs
> may have in the Letpan area between 400–500 troops, some guns and perhaps

some small tanks. One 75mm gun near the beach has engaged a Fairmile and mortars have been fired from the vicinity of the chaung. *It is thought that there are more guns in the assault areas, but so far they have not yet fired.*

The focus of all this attention, the town of Letpan, was a curious mixture of the picturesque and the embattled. The cluster of houses and buildings bore the scars of bomb damage, although there were still many of the tall letpan trees, *Bombax ceiba,* (Silk or Red Cotton Tree) that had given the community its name clustered along the banks of the *chaung.* Standing over 40 feet tall with blood red flowers, these trees had come to symbolise the conflicts that had occurred in this part of Burma for centuries, and at the same time they provided the people with a rich harvest. Almost since time could remember, they had been used for canoes, the bark in rope making and the hairy seed capsules for stuffing. Even the young flowers could be eaten as vegetables or used in traditional medicine.

A number of the buildings in Letpan were known to have been occupied by the Japanese and showed signs of their careless occupation. Many of the streets were criss-crossed with trenches and gun posts. One large building was still open to the elements more than a year after an RAF Hurricane had attacked it. The plane had been flown by Squadron Leader John Foan, who had won an OBE for his bravery in supporting 14th Army troops operating in the nearby jungle. His attack on Letpan on 2 April 1944 during an offensive recce and the disruption it caused to the Japanese concealed positions, gun emplacements and river craft had undoubtedly saved the lives of many Allied soldiers operating in the area.

It was eight squadrons of Squadron Leader Foan's colleagues flying Hurricanes and Thunderbolts who roared out of the early morning sky above Letpan at 9 a.m. as 'Operation Turret' was sprung on the Japanese occupiers. Barely had the formations passed overhead, when the guns of *Jumna* began to blast shells onto the area rapidly followed by fire from the three other ships. At 'H-Hour', 9.30 a.m., the first wave of the 4th Indian Infantry Brigade entered the Mai *chaung* to find the enemy troops still frantically gathering themselves after the unexpected barrage from so close at hand.

Corporal Frank Orton was among this first wave of troops in the 2nd Green Howards to set foot on the north bank of the Mai *chaung*. He and his company had sailed the previous day from Kyaukpyu on the *Barpeta*. Frank, who was from Sheffield, had been transferred the previous year from the Yorkshire and Lancashire Regiment to C Company of the 2nd Battalion of the Green Howards. After a period of jungle training at Ranchi in India, he and the others had moved south to Burma and just after midnight on 13 March found themselves sailing from Ramree on the veteran 'B' Class ship that had been a troop carrier in the First World War and converted to an Infantry Training Assault Ship in 1939. Orton remembers the moments the *Barbeta* came under fire with great clarity:

> *She was a tough old ship. She'd been everywhere from Bombay to Karachi, even on the Tobruk ferry service and in the Persian Gulf. She made the landings at Kyaukpyu and Letpan, which meant going up narrow rivers. You always had to keep an eye out for Japs on all sides trying to pick you off if you stuck your head up too high on the decks. There must have been a couple of hundred of us on the deck for the landing at Letpan. I'll never forget the sound of shrapnel pinging off the hull.*

Orton also never forgot the curious sight of two Lee Grant tanks belonging to the Duke of Wellington's Regiment going ashore – only one of which had an engine. The mobile tank was landed from an LCT and then reversed up to the second LCT that was carrying the other motorless vehicle. It was towed off and put into position to use its gun against any possible attack. At that moment, 'Operation Turret' seemed to Frank like a curiously apt label for the assault.

Among the other landing craft putting down troops on the beach that day was Second Lieutenant Johnny Lancaster's LCS No.87 with Les Gunn in the crew. The little ship had been part of convoy 'Peter' and had sailed at a steady 8 knots from Kyaukpau in company with two of the minesweeping BYMSs and a string of LCAs. Les also has a clear memory of the moment:

> *By the time we got there, the first troops had gone ashore and we could hear the sound of guns going off all over Letpan. The Japs were given a real pasting and it was not long before we heard they had pulled out. Some people said they didn't seem to put up much of a fight. During the night, two of the hill positions on the Mai chaung were captured by our troops. The next morning the rest of the men came on shore and the whole brigade advanced south down the coast road. The Japs were obviously on the run.*

The records of the war in Burma show that the Japanese had indeed retreated after the fall of Letpan – although this was not to be quite the end of their resistance. Certainly, the fighting qualities of the Japanese 55th Division had been pushed to breaking point and the pursuing Allied soldiers soon discovered the remnants of their enemy had escaped through the Taungup Pass. There was, however, some crucial work still to be done on the most southerly point of the

Arakan coast. This would be the task of another amphibious group whose exploits have, curiously, been overlooked or dismissed in most accounts of the retaking of Burma. It is the story of the semi-secret Detachment 385 – the fourth and final of Blondie Hasler's SOG units – that brings the war of the Banzai Hunters towards its remarkable finale.

11

THE 'BOOTNECKS' HAVE LANDED

Captain Bill Bowie of Royal Marine Detachment 385 had experienced nothing like it before. He and his six-man team of 'Bootnecks' as they were known had only just landed on the moonlit beach when one surprise after another began piling in on them. First, it had been the ominous shape of an ancient building with a tower like a spear perched on a rocky headland, and then the sight of a row of heads peering with grim intent from a cluster of weapon pits. The marines had immediately dropped onto the white sands, their guns at the ready. It had taken the captain some moments to realise that the building was actually an old pagoda with a golden spire and the figures were amazingly realistic dummies with straw heads and bamboo shoulders impersonating Japanese soldiers waiting threateningly for any invaders. These initial surprises as the unit landed on the southern coast of Burma near Chaungtha on the evening of 22 February would not be the last of the night for them either.

The men were the first of the Detachment to take part in an amphibious mission on the Arakan. Their target area lay on the Irrawaddy Delta of fields and waterways and was the nearest spot on this shore to the city of Rangoon, just 115 miles due east. According to their orders, the objective of 'Operation Attempt' was 'to snatch one or two locals, preferably the village headman, with a sample of the enemy force from the village of Chaungtha'. For Captain Bowie, his second in command, Lieutenant Peter Colville, and the five marines, they might well be arriving late into the Small Operations Group operating on the Arakan, but they had the training, the expertise and especially the determination to play their part in the push for Rangoon.

The section had left Akyab harbour on the early evening of 21 February in Lieutenant Maung Bo's Fairmile ML 414 of the 59th Flotilla. They had made good progress at 12 knots until they approached a 'scraggy group of islands', the South Calventuras Group, close to their destination. As the crescent shaped beach with the outline of the Yoma Mountains forming a backdrop came into sight, Captain Bo gave orders for the engine to be cut to 'dead slow' to reduce exhaust noise as much as possible and avoid alerting any enemy troops. Captain Bowie, standing beside him in the wheelhouse, describes in his operation report that is now on file in the Royal Marines Museum at Southsea in Hampshire how the first mission of Detachment 385 men got under way:

Although we were at least four miles off shore the exhaust noise seemed so thunderous as to wake the dead, so we escaped below to put on our make-up and dress for the ball! When we came on deck again we must have looked very funny, but nobody laughed; it was our first operation. There was an awkward swell running and the unpleasant movement of the ML plus the excitement had made most of our party sick. By some miraculous or instinctive navigation (for there was nothing to fix on) the Burmese CO, Lieutenant Bo, anchored in the pre-arranged position three miles northwest of the pagoda. We lowered our surf boat into a roughish sea and it was a real pleasure to get away from the interminable rolling.

The 'real pleasure' of the six men was, however, rapidly dispelled when they landed on the sands of Chaungtha Creek – meaning 'Pleasant Stream' in the local dialect – firstly by the ominous pagoda with its golden spire towering above them and then by the 'fright' of the dummy guards. Fortunately, as Captain Bowie noted, 'no one loosed off' and the men were able to bury their escape packs on the beach – which turned out not to be sand but made of crushed oysters and shells – and left one of the Fairmile crewmembers to look after the surf boat for their return journey.

The section had been briefed before leaving Akyab that Japanese troops were believed to be stationed in and around the pagoda, so Captain Bowie ordered the men to form a V-formation and make a wide berth of the rocky promontory. They then made their way through a stretch of jungle for some minutes until they broke into open countryside. Just ahead they could see an isolated building and stealthily surrounded it.

Inside the hut the marines found three men who, after their initial shock at seeing the intruders, began nervously answering the Captain's questions. The villagers said there were about twenty enemy soldiers in the pagoda and the Japanese headquarters were about half a mile inland on the slopes of a hill. The beach was regularly patrolled, the trio added. Satisfied with this information, Bowie and his team set out for the headman's house and – they hoped – the prize they had come all this way to secure. However, the third surprise of the night awaited them as they left the house, as Captain Bowie has vividly described:

We were only about 300 yards away from the cover of the village when we heard voices on our left and saw it was a party of people walking across a paddy field. We froze, hoping they would pass to our rear. Any movement on our part at this stage must have aroused suspicion. As they came nearer, I saw there were about eight Japs in uniform and another three in lungyis. *Their original course would have led them about 50 yards to our rear, but for some unaccountable reason they changed course and bore steadily down on us, unsuspecting and busily chatting away. I gave them every chance to sheer away but inexorably they came on. I remember saying quietly to myself, 'This is it!' and then to the section, 'Fire!' Bullets flew and confusion reigned for several minutes. The section opened out shooting, bayoneting, knifing and stripping this party. One marine was putting in some good work with his bayonet and as he passed me during the mêlée, he remarked in a tone of not unjustifiable pride, 'Right in the gullets, sir!'*

After several minutes of close combat, the Captain sensed he would have to call a halt. Six of the enemy lay dead, but several more were escaping and would surely run off to report the attack. Bowie knew that the headman's house was still at least a mile away and to reach it, grab the occupant and return to the beach would take more time than he had available before the arrival of Japanese reinforcements. He shouted to his men, still fired up with their success, that they had to retreat to the beach *now*.

Finding Chaungtha Creek proved harder than expected and the Captain was forced to split the section into three groups. He was just beginning to worry about the appearance of the enemy at any moment when one of the men indicated he had found the beach. As the party gathered on the sands, the first signs of dawn were beginning to show on the horizon over the Bay of Bengal. Bowie concludes his report:

We signalled with a green torch for the surf boat to come in and take us off. We found out later that the boat had actually beached some 30 seconds before we made it down the beach towards it, this in spite of the good visibility. We shoved off and negotiated the surf successfully and soon sighted the ML without having to resort to any homing signals. Once in the ML we were soon under way and – fortified by a stiff tot of rum – we slept.

So ended 'Operation Attempt'. It may not have been a complete success, but it *did* result in a number of enemy dead without loss and some very useful intelligence on enemy strengths and locations. The only sad aspect is that this and the subsequent missions of Royal Marine Detachment 385 – like those of a number of the other military groups so aptly named the 'Forgotten Army' – have been largely overlooked and their achievements omitted in the story of the war in Burma. The record deserves to be set right.

* * *

The story of 385 Detachment is once again inextricably linked with Blondie Hasler and the unit was the fourth SOG unit whose collective work strengthens the claim of his importance in the ultimate Allied triumph in Burma. However, the group's role is barely recorded outside the archives of the Royal Marines Museum and those few comments about it in war histories are less than fulsome and even less appreciative. The otherwise excellent historian, Julian Thompson, in his *War in Burma 1942–1945,* is typical of these when he writes:

Detachment 385 was a Royal Marine unit trained in Ceylon by Lieutenant-Colonel Hasler and became operational in March 1945. The 122-strong Detachment consisted of canoeists and parachutists. This unit seems to have been dogged by misfortune. Of the eighteen operations it carried out, eight were failures and three of the remaining ten were only partly successful.

Thompson's judgement of 385 is actually incorrect in the date it became operational – as we have already seen with 'Operation Attempt' – the type of men in its ranks and his assessment of the outcome of their operations. He is, though, quite right in crediting Blondie Hasler as its guiding light and stating that it was formed to strengthen the three other SOG forces with a projected total of three troops. In fact, the origins of the largely forgotten group go back almost two years to 18 December 1943 when Hasler was appointed by Mountbatten as Officer Commanding Special Boats Units, South East Asia Command, as Ewen Southby-Tailyour has noted:

This title only lasted a few days, for on 25 January 1944, he was reappointed Officer Commanding Small Operations Group. For internal Royal Marines administrative reasons, though, he was to be re-appointed on 24 April to RM Detachment 385, but remained, de facto, OC SOG until its official formation under a Royal Marines Commandant on 12 June 1944.

The first anyone knew of 385 was just before Christmas 1943 when a rash of intriguing notices began appearing on Royal Marine notice boards in Britain calling for volunteers for: 'Hazardous Duties – Must Be Swimmers'. Records indicate that about 160 officers and other ranks took up this challenge and were sent to the Royal Marines' Hemsley Camp, near Havant in April 1944. There a rigorous training programme of assault courses, night and day marches, weapon training – including the use of revolvers, automatics, Tommy guns and Sten guns – knife fighting, unarmed combat, map reading and various other skills quickly whittled away the unsuitable applicants.

Two months later, the first officers of Detachment 385 were sent out to Ceylon for training with Hasler at the Hammenheil Camp on the northern tip of the island near the town of Jaffna. The arduous conditions tested the men to the utmost – two being forced to quit from exhaustion – and in June, Major John Maxwell was appointed Commanding Officer. Maxwell, an Irishman, who became a close friend of Hasler, shared his convictions about the importance of small boat units and the role they could play working behind enemy lines. Hasler, for his part, thought the piano-playing, Irish folk-song singing, larger-then-life Maxwell, 'one of the trickiest things ever sent out of Ireland who can make it out of any tight spot if anybody can'.*

In July, just over one hundred officers and other ranks that had passed the training programme in Havant arrived at Columbo. Transferred to Hammenheil Camp where they lived in tents, the numbers were reduced again with initiative and survival tests, along with courses in jungle training, small boat handling and seamanship in the waters of the nearby bay. When Maxwell and his officers were finally satisfied, 385 Detachment was divided into three troops each consisting of approximately six officers and 25 other ranks, mostly NCOs. Their training was completed with intensive instruction in underwater work with snorkels and oxygen cylinders, simulated attacks on ships and harbours, and demolitions using gun-cotton plastics and plastic explosives. Specially staged battles were followed by trips to Trincomalee harbour and airfield and even a climb up the 7,360ft Adam's Peak!

A member of the unit, Corporal Ron Walker, another young man who joined the marines just four weeks after his 18th birthday, survived the tough courses at Havant but found life at Hammenheil even tougher, as he has recalled:

*Despite Hasler's optimism, Major John Maxwell was subsequently captured on an intelligence gathering mission, 'Operation Copywright', to Phuket Island off the west coast of Siam on 9 March 1945. He was held as a Prisoner of War in Singapore until 20 July when, in an act of terrible barbarism, he and two other British POW's were beheaded on a hill to the north of Pasir Panjang by two Japanese officers. The pair, named as Captain Ikoda and Lieutenant Kajiki, later committed suicide at Rengam on 26 December 1945.

Training was basically split into two parts: canoe and weapons work and jungle training. Dealing with jungle training, this started very soon after our arrival. Various 'hikes' took place by day and night through jungle areas to which we were invariably trucked with a number of river crossings. I recall a night exercise taking place soon after our arrival during which we 'lost' one corporal. His body was found next day, but we were never told how he died. Drowning and/or crocodiles were believed to be the reason.

Walker was in Major Maxwell's troop on several training exercises including a rendezvous with a Catalina seaplane, an RAF air-sea rescue mission, and several sea journeys in small collapsible canoes. Later, the men of 385 were supplied with two-man Mark III Folbots equipped with outriggers and became proficient in using these in a number of night runs off the north coast of Ceylon towards Port Pedro travelling distances of between 10–15 miles at a time. Corporal Walker says the men trained hard in the nifty little boats, always taking the greatest care to avoid shallow coral reefs as these could rip the bottom out of the craft. During this period, they had an unexpected visitor, he recalls:

Several months after we had started, we had a visit from Sir Malcolm Campbell of 'Bluebird' fame. He had apparently invented a petrol motor with a flexible shaft at the end of which there was a small propeller. The idea was that one could approach the shore with it fixed to the stern and if a quick getaway was required, it could be unhooked and clipped to the bow. Without letting the old boy down, we demonstrated that our 'paddle' approach was faster and quieter than his motor and one deep pull on the blade enabled us to depart before his motor could be unclipped!

Like everyone who came to the Far East, the men of 365 had to get used to the climate and risks of disease. The comparatively small number who did succumb are said to have been anxious to get back to duty and usually left the sick bay in a matter of days having been signed off with a UTD – 'Unknown Tropical Disease'. The entire unit dressed in shorts, bush shirt and bush felt hat, with a blue beret usually worn on operations. A popular pastime during training were regattas and at one Christmas Day event Blondie Hasler joined in and apart from demonstrating his skills on the water also instituted a model sailing boat competition that he won by some distance.

The records of 385 Detachment indicate that tight security was maintained around their training and the missions they undertook when transferred to Burma in February 1945. Men like Ron Walker admitted that they knew nothing of the operations in which they were not directly involved. Often they were not even aware of one taking place until after it was over – when the only indication anything had taken place was an empty bunk or rumours of a missing officer or other rank. Certainly no one in the detachment was encouraged to discuss their work: a fact that has undoubtedly contributed to the lack of information about the men and their time in Burma. It is, though, undoubtedly worth looking through the Royal Marine files to make it more widely known . . .

*   *   *

Once the decision had been taken in February 1945 to make Detachment 385 operational, all three troops were assigned missions under the code-name 'Operation Attempt'. At the same time as Captain Bowie was arriving at Chaungtha, Troops 2 and 3 had also made the 200 mile journey from Akyab and were landing on the same stretch of coast. Number 2 Troop, commanded by Major Duncan Johnston, were assigned 60 miles further south at the village of Ngayokkaung; while Captain A.H. Harris' section beached at Sinma, almost exactly equidistant between the other two locations. All three had the same objectives of trying to snatch one or two locals – ideally the headman – and discover the location and strength of enemy troops. The outcome for both would, though, be very different.

Major Johnston of Troop 2 had been a marine since 1933 and served in Egypt and the Middle East during the early years of the war. Before joining 385, he saw action with the V Force behind Japanese lines and brought with him valuable knowledge about Burma and small boat clandestine operations. A big man who commanded the respect of his troops, Johnston led from the front when his ten-strong party were dropped from Lieutenant Tommy Cole's Fairmile 415 and paddled 3 miles to the shore. The men were eager for action as they pressed through mangrove swamps towards Ngayokkaung.

According to a subsequent report of the operation by Lieutenant P.E. Waugh, the section were walking in single file and were about half a mile from their destination when a shot rang out from the direction of the beach. Major Johnston was naturally concerned about being cornered and decided to turn back to investigate. On reaching the position where they had left the boat, the marines were suddenly peppered by shots and had to dive for cover. Lieutenant Waugh continues:

> *It was obvious that we could not signal the boat to collect us as originally*
> *intended because it would then be exposed to enemy fire. So we moved about*
> *100 yards down a subsidiary chaung from which Major Johnston decided that*
> *we could swim back to the boat. At this stage, Corporal B.G. Smith was lost,*
> *believed drowned. A search was made for him without success only attracting*
> *more Japanese fire. The chaung was only 50 yards wide, but in the general*
> *excitement several chaps forgot to inflate their Mae Wests [life jackets] and*
> *although they had orders to ditch any heavy gear which might impede them, the*
> *inclination of a well-trained marine is to hang on to his equipment, and this*
> *resulted in some of them getting into difficulties whilst swimming across.*

Worse was to come for the troops on the other side of the *chaung*. As the men began to approach the boat, another burst of fire caught the line unawares. Major Johnston, as always at the front, took several shots and fell to the sand, dying. According to Waugh, a decision was made for the men to make individual dashes for the boat, but the sound of Lieutenant Cole's Fairmile firing its Bofors at the Japanese gun positions stopped everyone in their tracks. When these enemy guns fell silent, the men of 385 piled into their surf boat taking the body of their dead leader with them. They reached the Fairmile fifteen minutes later, a sad and deflated party, collapsing onto the gunboat's deck as it headed out to sea. The following day, at 3 p.m., off the coast of Cheduba, Major Johnston was buried at sea.

Although the achievement of this section has been written off as a failure in most accounts – and it certainly cost the Detachment its first casualties – the official record does state, 'The party were rumbled ashore and were ordered to retire before the village was searched. Intelligence was obtained on the disposition of the enemy forces in the area, which *could not otherwise have been obtained*'. [My italics]

Better fortune awaited Captain Harris' eight-man party who were also landed from a Fairmile, ML 418, in the centre point of the 'Operation Attempt' target area. A Burmese liaison officer, Captain Dallah, who was very familiar with the area and knew that the Japanese coast patrols here were watchful and efficient, accompanied Troop 3. Once on shore, the men trekked for approximately 2 miles to Sinma. The report of Captain Harris states:

> *While I was getting my bearings and deciding on the best way to take to the*
> *village, Captain Dallah suddenly leapt to his feet and with his Sten at his*
> *shoulder, shot into some bushes, hissing threats in his native tongue. I signalled*

to the others to stay put and went to investigate. Well concealed in a bush and armed with a fish spear and a chopper were two very unhappy looking Burmese, utterly terrified. Dallah questioned them quickly.

It seemed that the landing craft had been spotted offshore by the Japanese who had ordered a number of the natives to keep watch for them along the coast. The two boys did not know whether to be more afraid of the *Japani* or the British invaders with their blackened faces and deadly weapons. Captain Harris made a quick decision. It would be better to return with the two Burmese than risk falling into the hands of a Japanese patrol. He ordered the boat lying offshore to be signalled. It was a decision he was glad he had made when the section were all safely back on ML 418:

One of the first things the prisoners disclosed when they were on board and been furnished with cigarettes, blankets and food, was that half a mile north of our landing point was a battery of guns which, from their description, must have been every bit of 755mm, three of them. This news tended to speed our withdrawal.

Whatever their individual value, the combined achievement of the three sections of Detachment 385 in 'Operation Attempt' were measurable in terms of the intelligence that had been gathered and also the experience gained by every marine that took part. The months of tough training had clearly produced a fourth, fully functional SOG unit more than capable of working alongside Hasler's three other groups – and ready for more missions. Indeed, the remaining months of the war in the Far East would see them expanding the scope and range of their operations to include landing clandestine forces, rescue missions, setting up coastal dumps, shore reconnaissance, further intelligence gathering, picking-up and dropping agents and 'snatches'.

The troops continued to use motor launches on most missions, occasionally augmenting these with a Catalina aircraft of the RAF's 240(D) Squadron stationed at Redhills, Madras for Operations 'Slumber', 'Subtract' and 'Bruteforce I & II'. Four HM submarines *Thresher, Rorqual, Torbay* and *Thule* were called on for operations 'Copywright', 'Noah', 'Meridian', 'Cattle', 'Clearance', 'Baker', 'Carpenter', 'Graph' and 'Defraud'. A pair of destroyers, HMS *Roebuck* and *Paladin,* were also recruited as carriers on the rather inappropriately named reconnaissance mission, 'Operation Fairy'. These tasks took the men of the three troops from the Gulf of Siam to the Malacca Straits, to Malaya, Sumatra, the

Nicobar Islands and finally to Penang as part of Force 'Roma' (short for Royal Marines) when it was occupied in August.

During the remainder of March and April 1945, however, they were kept busy making their own special contribution around the southern tip of the Arakan as the 14th Army moved relentlessly on to Rangoon.

* * *

'Operation Chaungtha II' directed at the town of Bassein on 17 March had been inspired by the events that occurred almost three weeks earlier on the same coast. It involved several of the same personnel, with Captain Bowie again in charge of the shore party. This time, though, the troops were undertaking a far bolder operation – the simulating of a beach reconnaissance to make the Japanese believe that a 'landing in force was imminent'. Their supplementary orders are still extant in the documents relating to the mission in the Royal Marines Museum under the heading, 'Deception Recce':

> *To plant ashore delayed action Very lights at Chaungtha. To drop offshore a signalling device in order to lead the enemy to think that a part of the force was in difficulties.*

Bassein [today renamed Pathein] was the main town of the delta region and just 25 miles inland. Dominated by a fort built by the British in 1852, it could be reached by a winding tributary of the Irrawaddy that flowed from Chaungtha Creek and capable of taking quite large vessels. Alternately, there was the Pathein River meandering by southwards on its 75-mile journey to the Andaman Sea. A harbour served both waterways, having been developed over the years to service the teak, bamboo and rice trade – the growth of which had earned the region the reputation of being the country's 'rice bowl'. Bassein was also at the end of a railway line from the north and after the Japanese occupation had become an important supply and support centre for their troops in the area. It was also strategically placed less than 90 miles from Rangoon.

Captain Bowie had once again familiarised himself with the locality before he and his second-in-command, Colour Sergeant S.G. Wilkins, and four men landed in two canoes a couple of miles to the north of the pagoda at Chaungtha. They had been put down from Fairmile ML 415 on which Captain Harris had sailed with them as officer commanding the operation. With them was the 'device' that was intended to fool the Japanese, as Bowie explains in his report:

*Sergeant D. Crozier, who was attached from D Force, busied himself with his
tricks. The device to be left on shore was a simple holding bracket on a stake,
accommodating three ordinary Very cartridges with a delay of 30 minutes. The
'Herbert' floating device was a wooden box with electric bulbs and reflectors
facing outwards from each corner. Inside was a cunning arrangement of balls in
cylinders and a number of batteries, the whole being fitted with a self-destroying
charge. When placed in the sea, the movement of the water rocked the box and
contact inside was made and broken, so the lights flashed on and off
accordingly. The device, when seen at a distance at night, gave a very good
imitation of badly sent or imperfect Morse signals.*

Once on the familiar beach, Captain Bowie led Sergeant Crozier to a suitable point
in the shallows, after which he and the others ran about making footprints in the
sand to indicate that numbers of men had passed by. As soon as the device was
primed, the party returned to their canoes and prepared to head back to the motor
launch. At that moment, however, a sudden surge in the tide caught the men
unaware and one of the boats was capsized. Not wanting to delay, Harris ordered
everyone to swim out to sea taking the upended boat that could be righted when
out of firing range. As they struggled to make progress against the surf, the captain
switched on a red light on his lifejacket to summon help. Precisely what happened
next has remained a mystery to everyone who landed on Chaungtha beach that
March night, as Bowie later wrote in his report:

*I noticed to my consternation a red light flashing out to sea about 100 yards up
the beach. This was not part of our plan at all and I began to wonder vaguely
whether some other 'private army' was muscling in on our party. This classic
example of wishful thinking soon faded and I concluded that the person or
persons flashing the light were not on our side.*

Fortunately the crew of the Fairmile had spotted their plight and they were soon
being hauled from the surf. As ML 415 began to pull away from the coast, the
'Herbert' device was dropped into the sea about a mile offshore. As soon as it had
'rocked' the first Very light into action, Captain Harris congratulated the party and
gave orders for an immediate return to Akyab at 'top speed'.

The official record of 'Operation Chaungtha II' states that the 'activity on the
beach' and the evidence found there by the Japanese would have convinced them
some kind of beach reconnaissance had taken place. It adds, 'It is reasonable to
suppose that the cumulative effect of activities on 23 February ('Operation

Chaungtha') and 18 March was to lead the enemy to believe that a landing was imminent and while it is difficult to confirm precisely the success of any deception activity, this operation is considered successful'.

Captain Bowie, though, was left to puzzle over the mystery lights. Later he made a note of his conclusion:

The only explanation I can offer for the intruding red light flashing to seaward in competition with mine, is this. About a month before some rucksacks of escape gear had been left behind by one of our parties at Ngayokkaung. Among the contents were red jacket life lights. I think it is reasonable to credit the Japs with a good guess as to their use and to notify all coastal defences to use red lights to lure future cloak and dagger parties to their doom. Precisely why no fire was opened on us while we were ashore or in the water near the shore is a problem which, probably, we shall never solve.

* * *

The success of this first 'Deception Raid' by the men of Detachment 385 prompted the decision to use them again on a similar raid in a completely different location to further confuse the occupying forces and cement the fear in their minds that an invasion of the whole delta was imminent. 'Operation Pagoda Point' on 24 March would prove to be their last operation on the Arakan before the fall of Rangoon.

The place chosen for this strike was one of the most beautiful spots on the Irrawaddy Delta, Thamihla Kyun, a small island about 6 miles off the southern-most point of the Arakan coast lying in the mouth of the Bassein River. Just 3600 feet long and 2395 feet at the widest point, the Burmese name translates as Diamond Island – a well-deserved title with its rocky reef and low cliffs, patches of open grassland and undisturbed beaches that have been home for generations to a wide variety of animal and marine life, in particular as the nesting habitat of Green and Loggerhead Turtles. Today, the island is a wildlife sanctuary; but in March 1945 it was believed to be the location of a secret Japanese radar station and was pockmarked with craters from RAF bombing raids.

The intention of 'Operation Pagoda Point' was two-fold. To leave on the island a canoe containing marked maps and air photographs to fool the Japanese; and, secondly, to try and establish whether a radar station *did* exist there. The evidence about the CD station was contradictory and reconnaissance raids by the RAF and scouting missions by the Army and Navy had failed to substantiate the claim. The only facts, such as they were, had been provided by an Army Intelligence Officer, Major Tom Ferguson who had landed briefly on Diamond Island the previous autumn and had to leave hurriedly when he was 'pursued by Jap planes that had presumably been called up by the radar', to quote Captain Derek Oakley in his book, *Behind Japanese Lines* (1996).

The Detachment 385 party of five men lead by Captain D.R. Fayle were taken to a position just over a mile to the west of the landmark known as Pagoda Point. There, at 8.10 a.m., they were embarked in a motor surf board carrying two canoes – one of which was to be left at anchor about 40 yards from the beach. As the unit prepared to leave, there appeared to be no signs of life on the island. But then the situation changed dramatically, as Captain Fayle says in his report:

> *The surf boat and canoes were lowered and were in the process of being lashed together for towing when aircraft were heard approaching from the south east. They appeared to circle over us and to make off in a northerly direction. At 20.30 hrs flares were dropped to the northwest at a distance estimated to be two miles. It was considered that we had not been seen from the shore, for if we had, there seemed to be no reason why the aircraft should not have seen us and dropped the flares much closer. It appeared probable that we had been picked up by the suspected radar ashore which had passed an inaccurate bearing to the plane dropping the flares. In view of this, and the comparatively short distance in flying time from the nearest enemy airfield, it was decided that it would be unwise for the ML to linger in the area.*

Before returning to Akyab, however, the canoe with its false documents and a suitably broken paddle was set loose to drift in the direction of Diamond Island. The report of the operation concluded: '['Operation Pagoda Point'] did not entirely fulfil its object . . . but that the enemy were aware that a stealthy operation was in progress and very likely found the canoe is almost certain. In this respect the operation could be considered successful'.

Just *how* successful the men of 385 Detachment would not know for some time. But pinpointing the location of a probable radar station so close to the estuary outside Rangoon was of vital importance as the SEAC High Command prepared for the land and sea assault on the major city now only miles away. For this last phase of the capture of the Arakan an operational code-name was selected straight from the pages of English literature. It was an iconic name belonging to one of the most bloodthirsty characters in fiction – Count Dracula.

12
FINALE: 'OPERATION DRACULA'

There were several reports in the media towards the end of the Second World War that German troops had fought alongside the Japanese in the Far East. After the spectacular victories of the Imperial Army in 1941–2, it was argued – largely by sensation-mongering journalists, mostly Australian, for the benefit of their readers – that the despised and ridiculed 'little yellow men' could not have won without the help of Hitler's crack forces. It was claimed that Luftwaffe bombers based in Saigon had sunk the British destroyers, the *Repulse* and *Prince of Wales*, and the Japanese tanks used in Malaya and Burma had been commanded by German officers. In fact, although long-range U-Boats journeyed between Germany and Singapore on a number of occasions carrying weapons technology and strategic materials – and a German submarine *did* sink the SS *Lucy Muller* in the Bay of Bengal in April 1944 – the Nazis and the Sons of Heaven never fought side by side on land, in the air or at sea.

Among these accounts is a tale that a trio of German Naval officers who had been serving in Burma as advisers on coastal offensive and defensive operations, were spirited away on board a submarine that arrived at the mouth of the Rangoon River only hours before the Allied army, air and naval forces were preparing to close the trap on the Japanese troops still in the city in late April 1945. Yet again the story is untrue and is thought to have been concocted from a mis-understanding of the term for the Allied sea attack, code-named 'Dracula', and a mistaken belief that the infamous vampire count of literature was a German and had escaped his pursuers by boat. Count Dracula was, of course, from Transylvania, although he did travel by ship from Europe to find a new life in England. There is no suggestion, though, that the planners behind the mission to take Rangoon thought about the likelihood of any such gossip when naming their plan. If they had anything 'supernatural' to fear, it was the onset of the terrifying monsoon season expected on or about 5 May.

It had always, of course, been Admiral Mountbatten's plan when recapturing Burma to carry out seaborne hooks from India over the Bay of Bengal, attack down the coast of the Arakan, before finally striking from the sea to take the biggest prize of all, Rangoon, the capital, largest city and chief port of the country. It was a plan very much in the old British military tradition of the indirect approach and just the kind of bold *coup* that would receive the blessing of Winston Churchill back in London who was busy finishing off Hitler's 'Thousand Year Reich'. The Prime Minister, Mountbatten knew, was determined that Britain should be seen to recover her lost territories by her own military power and once Rangoon had been taken it would be possible to mount an operation to recapture Malaya and sweep up the South China Sea to Borneo and Hong Kong.

From an immediate point of view, Mountbatten was aware that if the mission to take Rangoon was successful, it would cut the lines of communications of the Japanese armies in Burma and undermine their whole position. In the words of John Winton, 'By the spring of 1945, the capture of Rangoon had come to resemble the search for the Holy Grail – long sought after, always disappointed, always just over the horizon'. Now everything was about to change, as Louis Allen has explained in *Burma: The Longest War:*

> The Royal Navy decided the timetable for 'Dracula'. For an amphibious force to be safely landed at the mouth of the Rangoon River, it was thought essential to keep at a distance any possible incursions by the Japanese Fleet (highly unlikely, in fact) and, to ensure this, a carrier force of four destroyers (Saumarez, Venus, Vigilant and Virago), four escort carriers (Emperor, Hunter, Khedive and Stalker) and two cruisers (Phoebe and Royalist) was assembled. The 21st Aircraft Carrier Squadron provided fighter cover for the convoys. Close tactical air support was the RAF's province and 224 Group now had a wing in Kyaukpyu and one in Akyab from which long-range fighters could operate. Eight Liberator squadrons and four Mitchell squadrons, all from the USAAF, were to provide heavy bombing support.

Despite the presence of all this heavy armour, Lieutenant General Sir Philip Christison who had been put in charge of the actual landing in Rangoon knew that because the 14th Army was fast approaching down through the centre of Burma, everything had to be put in place quickly and he had very little time to refine his plans or obtain more information about Japanese positions on the Irrawaddy peninsula. His thoughts are contained in the National Archive file 80/15/1:

> But having done so many ad hoc operations, I had no fears and told Mountbatten I could do it. Observers sent over from the European landings were

horrified! Captured documents showed that the Japanese believed 12 April to be the latest date for us to attempt a sea-borne operation against Rangoon. There were three snags. Both the Japs and the RAF had heavily mined the Rangoon River, which would have to be swept. The sandy shoals meant that landing craft would have a 31 mile run-in; possibly in choppy water; and Elephant Point, at the mouth of the river, was defended by coastal artillery and dual-purpose machine guns which would make minesweeping impossible.

Planning for the assault began on 8 April on Ramree Island and was as *ad hoc* as Christison had anticipated: under canvas, using boards for tables, boxes for chairs and oil lamps for lighting. There was, though, always the compensation for the planners of the beach nearby for a relaxing swim. The fleet began to gather off Kyaukpyu with the assault troops of the 26th Indian Infantry Division and the 2nd Gurkha Parachute Battalion being readied for action at their bases. The Assault Force Commanders included familiar names from the Arakan: Rear Admiral Martin, Flag Officer Force 'W'; Major General H.M. Chambers, commanding the 26th Indian Division; and Group Captain H. Pleasance of the RAF. The Assault Group Commanders were Captain Tyndale-Cooper, with Brigadier L. V. Hutcheson, Captain T.S. Bell and Brigadier I. Lauder.

The men of Coastal Forces who had been attached to 'Dracula' – in particular the 13th and 14th Fairmile Flotillas who would be at the very forefront of the operation – had their own particular difficulties to worry about. The tides around Rangoon were known to be so strong at certain times of the year that the movements of the LCMs, LCTs and LCAs would have to be carefully controlled. In addition, because of the river depth and the mines laid by the Japanese, the assault craft would need to be lowered well to seaward of the river entrance and supporting gunfire during the actual attack would have to be provided by LCSs and some Landing Craft Guns (LCG) which had recently arrived in Burma. These purpose built craft designed to direct fire against beach positions and surface attack for first-echelon landing troops were 192 feet long, heavily armoured with 25lb plating and armed with two 4-inch QF Naval guns, two 20mm guns and two 2 pounder pompoms. The boats were powered by a pair of 500 hp Paxman diesels giving a maximum speed of 11 knots, crewed by two officers and thirteen men and a gun crew of three officers and twenty marines. They had been created especially to be beached and become an effective stationary gun platform.

The predicted state of the tide on the planned D-Day, 2 May, also meant that the whole convoy would arrive off the Rangoon River in darkness. To meet the deadline and travel the 480 miles to their rendezvous in the Gulf of Martaban off Rangoon, the assault force was dispatched from Akyab in six convoys on 27–28 April, with the 7th and 37th Minesweeping Flotillas following on the next two days. John Winton paints a rather inauspicious picture of the beginning of the operation:

Despite some breakdowns and leaking craft, the convoys arrived off the Rangoon River in good order, but bad weather, on the night of 1–2 May. It was a time of full moon, but the sky was almost completely overcast and there were heavy and frequent thunderstorms. The whole operation was conducted under the gloom of a meteorological phenomenon known as the 'Dracula Depression.'

In the gloom, even with the aid of binoculars and telescopes, it was impossible for most of the men at sea to make out anything of the famous ancient city lying 30km away. Rangoon was known to be a place that bore the signs of a troubled past: destroyed by fire in 1841 and extensively ruined in the Second Anglo-Burmese War of 1852, it had been rebuilt by the British on the lines of London only to be heavily damaged again by an earthquake and tsunami in 1930. Yet despite the bomb damage inflicted by the RAF, still rising above the wreckage was the golden dome of the enormous Shwe Dagon pagoda. Built in 585BC, it had turned what had originally been a small fishing village, Dagon, into a special place of pilgrimage for Buddhists. The community had been renamed 'Yangon' in 1753 by King Alaugnpaya following his conquest of lower Burma – the name derived from the words *yan* for 'enemies' and *goun* meaning 'end'. The British, in turn, anglicised it to 'Rangoon' and made the city into a trading centre for rice, teak and oil. Now as the invaders screwed up their eyes for any sight of the harbour and complex of buildings – which many imagined to be packed with ferocious Japanese ready to die rather than give an inch – some of the men in the assault vessels hoped it soon *would* be the end.

A few of the older hands, shivering in the darkness, rubbed their hands together to keep warm and wondered *why* the enemy had not yet shown himself.

* * *

Unbeknown to those who were preparing to go on shore from the assault fleet off Rangoon, an RAF pilot flying over the capital the previous day had returned to base with a curious piece of information. As the man had swooped over the battered streets and buildings he had seen some English words scrawled in white paint on the roof of the city's jail. Even before his eyes had fully focused and taken in the message, he was aware of a second phrase.

The first, in huge capitals, read 'JAPS GONE'. The second, which he immediately recognised as RAF slang, said 'EXTRACT DIGIT!'*

The pilot circled just once and headed back towards the Bay of Bengal convinced his eyes had not deceived him, but not sure of the implications. Had the Japanese *really* gone? They were nasty, devious little bastards, he knew, and this might be a trick. Whatever the truth, he would report what he had seen at his debriefing and then the decision about what to do next would be up to others.

In actual fact, the initial stage of 'Dracula' had already begun that same morning. A force of Gurkhas had been dropped by a flight of Dakotas some 5 miles west of Rangoon at a well-known landmark called Elephant Point. Their task had been to knock out any Japanese coastal guns – but the mission did not go without mishap, as Major General S. Woodburn Kirby has described in *The War Against Japan* (1961):

> The drop went well, but the parachuted Gurkhas were unlucky later. They marched to within two and a half miles of their objective, the guns at Elephant Point, which was being bombed by Liberators. Some of the bombs fell short and caused over thirty casualties among the paratroops, at which the Visual Control Post cancelled the bombing. Late afternoon saw the Gurkhas, after a trudge through torrential rain, on top of the Japanese gunners. There were 37 of them, and only one survived. The landing craft were now free to come in, once a channel had been swept through the mines.

Despite this unhappy beginning – and the puzzling report of the RAF pilot – Mountbatten and Slim were both certain there was no going back on the invasion of Rangoon – and no time to be lost. Slim had always been convinced that Rangoon would be hotly defended, admitting later in his memoirs, 'It was difficult to get information of Japanese intentions'. The General could not believe that the city would be abandoned without a fight and even worried that suicide garrisons might be left waiting for his men. If he had been privy to the thinking of Lieutenant General Tanaka Shinichi who was then unavailingly trying to find a way of stemming the Allied military advance on land, he would have known that he was correct and the Imperial Army veteran wanted Rangoon to be fought for 'street by street, house by house and even temple by temple if necessary'. Shinichi is said to have boasted in a message to his High Command, 'We have over a million troops in South-East Asia and we will throw every soldier into the battle'.

---

*In some versions of this sighting the words are said to have been a single phrase – 'Japs gone – Exdigitate'.

The officers in Rangoon, however, saw only annihilation from land, sea and air.

At 2.15 a.m. on the morning of 2 May, the go-ahead for 'Dracula' was given and after the BYMS minesweepers had swept the approaches and laid marker buoys, a stream of bombers droned towards the old city and saturated the beachheads. Out at sea, sheeting rain and heavy swells got up, making life unpleasant for naval man and soldier alike. Lieutenant Stuart Guild, who had taken part in the action in Hunter's Bay, was again among the invasion force – though not on a Z-Boat this time – and has provided another invaluable account of the day published by *The Gunner* magazine (May 1985). In his preamble, Guild says that the build up of information on the enemy batteries at Elephant Point was 'quite frightening', and all the men he spoke to were surprised that 'we seemed to be going straight in the front door'. Nonetheless, they sailed in convoy to Rangoon on HMS *Glenroy,* a ship converted to carry assault landing craft, and were duly embarked:

> *In pitch darkness we paraded on the deck, my party of four plus a platoon of the 9th Jat Regiment, boarded the LCA, and were lowered into the sea. The invasion fleet was some 21 miles off the river mouth. We were told it was the longest assault in an LCA (6 hours sailing). The sea was not that calm and had a swell that was barely noticeable on the assault ship, but was really rough in the LCA. I had never been sea-sick in my life, despite a number of sea voyages, but it was not long before my breakfast and that of many others was in the bag provided and lost.*

The rest of the journey was no less unpleasant for Guild and the others. The engine of their boat broke down and after wallowing helplessly for several minutes, the LCA was taken in tow by a faster and more powerful LCI. However, the wash of their rescuer quickly flooded the lame LCA and with dawn just beginning to lighten the sky, the whole party were forced to abandon the assault craft and join the infantry on the LCI for the remainder of the journey. In making the difficult crossing from one buffeting vessel to another, Guild slipped and was left hanging upside down on a rope until he was dragged onto the LCI by one of its crew members. The Lieutenant continues:

> *We sped up the mouth of the river, past Elephant Point, which the Gurkha paratroopers had captured at first light. The LCI beached and being 'extras' we disembarked, after the correct passengers, down the front ramps on each side of the bows, straight into the lens of an Indian cameraman! How should one look at the camera on coming off an assault boat? It was then that we realised we*

were on the wrong beach – one further north to where we should have been – so we had to set off down the right bank of the river to join our friends from the other LCAs.

If Lieutenant Guild thought he had experienced enough surprises for one day, when he and his men finally reached the beachhead where they *should* have landed, he could not have been more wrong. The evidence was obvious everywhere they searched. There was no sign of the Japanese.

* * *

There has been a considerable amount of debate since the Allied forces took Rangoon on that rainy Wednesday, as to just *who* was first into the abandoned city. The evidence would suggest it was neither a military or naval man, but an RAF pilot on a reconnaissance mission over the city sometime early in the afternoon. He was Wing Commander A.E. Saunders, the commanding officer of 110 Squadron, flying a Mosquito. From the air, it seemed to him as he passed overhead, that the place seemed empty of Japanese. On the spur of the moment, he decided to go down and have a look. However, Saunders' decision was not quite so easy to carry out, as Louis Allen has written:

He [Saunders] took his Mosquito over Mingaladon airfield and tried to put her down, but found to his dismay that Allied bombing had been so effective that the runway was full of craters. Nonetheless, he landed, damaging the Mosquito enough to prevent him taking off again. He and his navigator then made their way to the goal where the earlier pilot had seen the fateful message about the departure of the Japanese.

The appearance of the two RAF men in full flying kit striding into the open gates of the prison was a sight that none of the thousand prisoners of war still there ever forgot. Immediately, the men who were in various stages of poor health began clamouring for news of the invasion. Saunders was able to assure them that help was near at hand. In reply to some questions of his own, the Wing Commander was told that the Japanese guards had left on the night of 29 April. A notice, signed by the garrison commander, was shown to him. It read:

From tomorrow, 30 April, you are free to move as you wish. Enough food and medical supplies have been left behind for you. The British-Indian forces will soon be in Rangoon and you can wait for them or not as you choose.

It must have been the most humiliating notice for any Japanese officer to write, Louis Allen has observed, though curiously sympathetic and even kind for a man whose life until that moment had been one of unyielding devotion to his emperor. Allen completes the story of the audacious RAF officer:

With superb panache, Saunders walked out of the jail, made his way to the docks, and commandeered a sampan. In this he blithely sailed down the Rangoon River to meet the incoming launches of 26th Indian Division which picked him up on the morning of 3 May.

The story of the 'first man into Rangoon' delighted the media and quickly made its way to Slim's headquarters. It brought a smile of satisfaction to the General's face, which he remembered when he came to write his memoirs:

We were rather pleased about this in the Fourteenth Army. If we could not get to Rangoon first ourselves, the next best thing was for someone from 221 Group, which we regarded in all comradeship as part of the Fourteenth Army, to do it.

A rival claimant – at least in the eyes of some of the British newspaper war correspondents and photographers – was a member of the crew of a Fairmile who jumped ashore that same squally, wet Wednesday. His name was Second Lieutenant Jack Harley, a member of the crew of ML 269 of the 14th Flotilla skippered by Lieutenant Peter Royal. The story added a human-interest touch to the wordy accounts of the recapture of Rangoon – although, in fact, it was actually incorrect in several respects.

The photograph of a Fairmile motor gunboat with her gun crew gesturing triumphantly at the camera – published on 18 May in the *Times of India* and *Daily Telegraph* among other papers – was certainly part of the same Flotilla, but actually ML 269 commanded by Lieutenant J.H. Brock. The reporters made a great deal of the fact that the Fairmiles of the 13th and 14th Flotillas had taken part in another great landing on the beaches of Normandy at D-Day – after which they had undergone a major refit and been transferred to the Arakan. In fact, both Lieutenant Brock's boat and ML 269 had been added to the strength in Burma, as Tony Goulden has pointed out in his privately published book, *The 13th and 14th Fairmile Flotillas in Burma* (1989) which sets the record straight about Jack Harley's little piece of history-making during the taking of Rangoon:

ML 247 picked up a pilot from a sampan at Elephant Point. They led the way up the river with an LCI on their port side, on the forepeak of which a sailor played the bagpipes. Second Lieutenant Harley on Peter Royal's ML 269 arrived off the Irrawaddy for 'Operation Dracula' with the rain coming down in solid sheets. Visibility was almost zero, but improved as the MLs led the convoy up the river. They were expecting opposition that never came. As they got nearer the town, they could see sunken ships and damaged cranes. As they got nearer the quay, just astern of ML 247, Peter Royal shouted to Jack Harley to get ready to leap ashore. Jack duly jumped ashore and made fast to the bollards, becoming the first naval man ashore, fulfilling an ambition of Peter Royal, who was none too popular with his senior officer for some while.

The First Lieutenant of another Fairmile that tied up at the same jetty just a few minutes later also achieved another 'first' when he clambered up a lamppost and flew a Union Jack in the city for the first time in three years. By a curious twist of fate, Rangoon had been recaptured – just as it had been lost – without a shot being fired. To those who went ashore in the first few hours after the landing, a kaleidoscope of images awaited them – along with news that the assault had not been made entirely without casualties. Captain W.S. Knight, a Forward Observer Bombardment officer, whose job was to spot for naval guns in support of ground troops, landed from an LCA in the first wave of infantry with a driver and several radio operators. His account (97/7/1) is on file at the Imperial War Museum and describes the landing in torrential rain that had turned the city into a sea of mud and made everything exceedingly slippery:

So far there were no signs of the Japanese, and word came through that they had evacuated the city. Everything seemed too easy until news came that one of the landing craft [LCT 1238] had struck a mine in the Rangoon River and sunk, but no details were available. The next day came the worst possible news. The craft had been carrying the rest of our party. Elliot [Captain Knight's driver] had been below decks and the explosion of the mine had thrown him up smashing his head on the steel deck above, killing him. My radio operator was thrown up in the air and landed on top of a lorry. The canvas cover took most of the fall, but the steel framework had broken one arm, several ribs, and he was badly shaken. A landing craft alongside had managed to get all the dead and wounded off

*before the LCT sank, but all the vehicles including all our worldly possessions
had gone to the bottom. **

In the meantime, Knight and the rest of his party found themselves in Rangoon
tired, wet, filthy and in a very subdued frame of mind. Determined to make the
best of the situation, the Captain took action:

*I felt that the first essential was to get some fresh clothes for the party and on
making enquiries I learned that there was a Quartermaster's store of the
Japanese collaborators' Indian National Army not far away. We naturally looked
upon them as traitors and the Indian troops treated them with the utmost
disdain. There we found a clerk and I told him our requirements, two sets of
everything for us. He said he could not supply us because we had no authority. I
then committed an act of which I am not very proud. I put a magazine on my
Sten and pointed it at him, saying, 'Do I get the goods or do I pull the trigger?'
One of the RIN radio operators interpreted in case he didn't get the idea, but the
result was instantaneous. He darted over to the shelves and brought out shirts,
socks, slacks, shorts, in fact all we could wish for.*

Captain Knight needed to have no scruples about his actions, for as soon as he
and other members of the Allied forces entered Rangoon it was obvious that
wholesale destruction and looting had been going on ever since the Japanese had
pulled out. In the port, there was plenty of evidence of an attempt to destroy the
installations, although only a part of a bridge was down, probably due to lack of
explosives. Stockpiles of enemy stores, weapons and ammunition had been
broken into and the contents spirited away. The buildings occupied by officers
had been entered and everything removed from furniture and radios to lamps,
bath taps and even wall switches. Boxes of cigarettes and crates of alcohol
evidently intended for the troops had been ripped open by the looters and
gleefully emptied.

The city streets lay empty and deserted, clogged with mud, rubbish and
excrement. Manhole covers had been removed and every parked vehicle
stripped of its mechanics. Many of the shops were wrecked and pockmarked
with bomb damage, their empty windows and shelves lying open to the
elements. Inside many office buildings were all the signs of a hasty departure in
the chaos of broken furniture and scattered documents. In the business quarter,

---

* It would not be known until some time later that the mine had killed a total of twenty men.

some of the roads were even littered with millions of the now worthless Japanese occupation rupee notes. Everywhere, it was clear, there was no electricity, no water supply or even basic sanitation. To the men who now walked the city streets as the new occupiers, it seemed there was not a single item of any value left in the once grand place beyond the remarkably unscathed and still glowing golden pagoda of Shwe Dagon.

There was one other grisly reminder of the Japanese occupation, which not many people saw, but which seems, in hindsight, an apt finale to the operation named after a vampire. A collection of 37 large wooden chests was found on a boat lying at anchor in Rangoon harbour. It was apparently being made ready for the journey back to Tokyo as the Allied assault struck. When, several days later, the vessel was boarded and its contents inspected, the Allied officer in charge made a startling discovery. Inside the chests were almost 40,000 little boxes. On each was a name and rank.

They were the ashes of the Japanese soldiers killed on the Arakan.

EPILOGUE

Just a handful of missions remained for the Banzai Hunters to carry out before their job in Burma was finished. From 12 May, the 13th, 14th and 59th Fairmile Flotillas of the Arakan Coastal Forces, with back up from the Burma Navy's 146th Flotilla of 'tireless and reliable' 10 knot Harbour Defence Motor Launches (HDML), were assigned operations to cut any Japanese escape routes east of the Irrawaddy by patrolling the rivers from the coast as far as the Gulf of Moattama. The purpose of these missions was two-fold: to destroy any remaining enemy soldiers and at the same time impress the local people and help in the re-establishment of civil government. In the following month, eleven small Japanese craft were sunk and about 100 soldiers killed. A further ten were captured and 30 surrendered, the first substantial number to be made prisoners throughout the entire Arakan war.

Another small piece of history was created during these operations when a pair of Fairmiles shared the unique distinction of being the only boats to have been hit by both Japanese and German guns. Captain L.A. Hunt's ML 904 of the 13th Flotilla and ML 269 of the 14th Flotilla skippered by Lieutenant Peter Royal had both been in action in the English Channel and shelled by German defences before being transported to Burma. During operations off the Arakan, the pair had been hit again by Japanese 20mm armour piercing shells, ML 904 suffering a fatality and two injured ratings. A third Fairmile, Lieutenant R.R. Gallichan's ML 303 of the 13th Flotilla subsequently joined the pair as the only other boat to have fired *on* both German and Japanese targets during its tours of duty on the opposite sides of the world.

A further notable operation was 'The Battle of Kokkawa' that took place on the Bawle River, north of Rangoon, on 18 May. Referred to as 'the last ship-to-ship naval battle in Burma' it occurred at a locality that was known to be used as an escape route by Japanese troops trying to reach the Pegu Yomas. Ken Joyce, a nineteen-year-old Australian Able seaman on ML 269, has told the story in the *Burma Star Association Journal* (December 1985) in which he describes how three

Fairmiles of the 13th Flotilla ambushed a convoy of three Japanese boats, each carrying a dozen or so soldiers, and set on fire or beached them all off the village of Kokkawa. But the 'battle' did not end there, however, as Ken Joyce's account relates:

> *Two hours later, three more Jap craft came around the bend in the river. We had, of course, heard their engines and we were all closed up and ready for them. Seeing only our ML the Japs, instead of escaping, altered course to attack us. My memory is only of confused firing and streams of tracers from our Oerlikons and pom pom; the blast of our six pounder; a blazing Jap landing craft trying to ram us with her gunners still firing from among the flames. ML 904 and ML 303 raced up to join the battle and soon all the Jap boats either blew up with a terrible noise in the narrow river or were beached on the muddy bank. The final outcome was that whilst we had one man killed and three wounded, at least 55 Japanese were killed.*

Records of the Burma campaign indicate that a few skirmishes occurred in the weeks until 17 June when the weather finally brought a halt to any more operations. The monsoon was now in full fury on the Arakan and the banks of the *chaungs* and many of the smaller rivers had disappeared beneath particularly heavy floodwaters: waters that might just have frustrated the work of the Banzai Hunters and enabled the Japanese to retrench if they had hung on for a little longer and not been so wrong in their estimation of when the rains were due. Curiously, a variety of fast-growing, floating water hyacinth with pretty orchid-like flowers (*Eichhornia speciosa*) began chocking the rivers in great chains and clusters at this time and it has been observed by more than one historian that it was perhaps the final irony of the Burma campaign that the last amphibious operations were 'frustrated by hyacinths'.

The conflict had, of course, made heroes of Mountbatten and Slim, but many of their men – especially those who had featured in the Battle for the Arakan – were destined to be labelled the 'Forgotten Army', their achievements overshadowed by the triumphs closer to home in Europe. Yet the war in Burma had gone on for three years and eight months and was unquestionably the longest fought campaign in any one theatre of war during the Second World War. It had brought about 106,144 Japanese casualties of whom 46,711 had been killed or were missing; and 74,909 British and Commonwealth troops with 14,236 killed or missing. Significant among all the statistics were those of the Coastal Forces whose casualties, considering all the dangers they had faced on land and sea, had been less than two-dozen with the loss of just a handful of vessels.

The end of the war deprived Blondie Hasler of the opportunity to put into operation another plan he had been nurturing for more than a year for attacking the coastal shipping that was supplying the Japanese front line. He envisaged using specially trained small units to sink these ships outright, or alternatively, to capture them, inspecting the cargo and taking prisoners, before scuttling the vessels in deep waters. Hasler outlined the idea in a document suitably entitled *Suggested Additional Role for SOG* – doubtless to make clear where his operational preferences lay:

The bulk of the coastal traffic is carried in vessels of between 50 to 500 tons, many of them wooden ships and a high proportion of these are junks or other country craft manned by Burmese, Siamese or Malays, but always with Japanese supervisors on board. Some of them will be armed and normally only move at night, lying up in rivers or chaungs *under camouflage by day. Ships should be attacked either in harbour by day or at sea by night. In either case, attackers must lie in wait for periods of up to ten days.*

The methods Hasler envisaged for carrying out these assaults included boarding with smoke and/or covering fire; a shoot-up from the shore with Bazookas, mortars and flame throwers, and [my italics] *swimmers – preferably underwater – placing charges by stealth*. The 'Cockleshell Hero' advocated putting groups of the men into an advance base where they would conceal their boats during the day and operate against targets as they appeared. The best methods of assault, he thought, would be attaching small floating mines, limpets, or bottom charges to boats while they were at anchor or just underway . . . whenever the opportunity arose. His amphibious force might also undertake internal sabotage, scuttling or 'cutting out' individual vessels from larger convoys.

Despite Hasler's track record and the undeniable success of his four SOG units, his *Additional Role* got no further than the discussion stage. There is evidence that other officers in the Royal Marines and Navy looked at the report, but scepticism about the use of frogmen in the crystal clear waters of Bay of Bengal and the mishaps that had occurred to divers using self-contained oxygen breathing apparatus in confined spaces like narrow rivers or waterways, saw it gather dust in

* There was, however, one operation carried out in the Far East by a pair of 'Chariots', or human torpedoes, based in Ceylon, against Phuket Harbour on 28 October 1944. The two-man teams of Sub-Lieutenant A. Eldrige and Petty Officer S. Woolcott, and Petty Officer W.S. Smith and Seaman A. Brown, used an improved version of the 'Chariot' capable of a 30-mile range at 4½ knots. The two teams were released from the submarine, *Trenchant,* 6 miles from Phuket and the frogmen successfully targeted their 1,100lb bombs at two Japanese merchant ships, the *Sumatra* and the *Volpi,* causing the loss of 4,859 tons of enemy shipping.

a pending tray until the need for such action was no longer required.*

If, however, these British officers had known anything about a Japanese secret operation they might have had cause to rue their complacency. For the evidence suggests that *if* the plan had been brought into operation before the fall of Burma, it might just have changed the course of the war. It could certainly have had a devastating effect on the Banzai Hunters and all those who fought on the Arakan. Indeed, in what amounts to an extraordinary example of synchronicity, the Japanese plans for *Fukuryus,* or 'Crouching Dragons' – specially trained frogmen equipped to repel landing craft – were uncannily similar to those of Blondie Hasler: with one additional, terrifying element. The Japanese project had also long gone past the 'suggested' stage when the critical phase of the 'Third Arakan' was reached in the autumn of 1944.

The 'Fukuryus Plan' – as it was designated – had been evolved by the Japanese Naval Ministry who had been experimenting with the use of frogmen since 1941. As a result of the country's alliance with Hitler, they had received German underwater prototypes from Bremerhaven and used these to secretly develop even more advanced diving suits and breathing equipment of their own in the deep water tanks and remote coves at the Yokosuka naval base in Tokyo Bay.

Masterminding the operation was an Imperial Navy officer, Captain Toshiaki Shintani, an Olympic standard swimmer, experienced diver and – like Hasler – a passionate advocate of amphibious operations. He had been given the green light to form bands of 'Crouching Dragons' and was immediately inundated with volunteers when notices were circulated throughout the navy. Four thousand recruits, it was said, were sent to Yokosuka where 1,200 were fully trained and ready for action by the autumn of 1944. Bruce Wright, the Canadian leader of the Sea Reconnaissance Unit, who carried out an investigation into the *Fukuryus* in the immediate aftermath of war, later wrote about them in his book, *The Frogmen of Burma,* with an air of undisguised astonishment:

> *They could stay underwater for about ten hours and they carried liquid food. They were armed with a 10-kilogram charge with a contact fuse. Their job was to swim under an approaching landing craft and ram the charge into its bottom. They would go up with it in the same manner as the Kamikaze pilots who had caused 80 per cent of the damage to ships in Okinawa. Also in the planning stage were concrete underwater foxholes and pillboxes where the Fukuryus could wait out the preliminary bombardment before striking.*

Captain Shintani believed that any enemy force contemplating a landing would be in a constant state of fear that his frogmen were waiting beneath the surface to sabotage the boatloads of infantrymen heading for the shore. It would have been impossible to defend against these suicide squads, he told his Imperial Navy masters, and in any Allied attempt to invade Japan itself, the enemy would be met by his eager and fully prepared 'invisible human bombs'. Only the dropping of the first atom bomb on Hiroshima on 6 August 1945 prevented the world from ever finding out whether Shintani's boast was true.

BIBLIOGRAPHY

Allen, Louis *Burma: The Longest War 1941–1945* (JM Dent, 1984).

Beaton, Cecil *Far East* (Batsford, 1945).

Bidwell, Shelford *The Chindit War* (Hodder & Stoughton, 1979).

Brett-James, A. *Report My Signals* (Hennel Locke, 1948).

—— *Ball of Fire* (Gale & Polden, 1951).

Bush, Captan Eric *Bless Our Ship* (Allen & Unwin, 1958).

Callahan, Raymond *Burma 1942–1945* (Davis-Poynter, 1978).

Calvert, Michael *Fighting Mad* (Jarrolds, 1964).

Carew, Tim *The Longest Retreat* (Constable, 1969).

Ehrman, John *Grand Strategy* (HMSO, 1956).

Evans, Geoffrey *Slim As Military commander* (Batsford, 1969).

Fergusson, Bernard *The Watery Maze* (Collins, 1961).

—— *The Trumpet in the Hall* (Collins, 1970).

Granville, Wilfred & Helly, Rabin A. *Inshore Heroes* (W.H. Allen, 1961).

Hampshire, A Cecil *On Hazardous Service* (William Kimber, 1974).

Hanley, Gerald *Monsoon Victory* (Collins, 1946).

Hickey, Michael *The Unforgettable Army* (Spellmount, 1992).

Irwin, Anthony *Burmese Outpost* (Collins, 1945).

Jeffrey, W.F. *Sunbeams Like Swords* (Hodder & Stoughton, 1951).

Kirby, Major General S.W. *The War Against Japan* (HMSO, 1965).

Ladd, James *Commandos and Rangers of World War II* (Macdonald & Janes, 1978).

Latimer, Jon *Burma – The Forgotten War* (John Murray, 2004).

Lewin, Ronald *Slim: The Standard Bearer* (Leo Cooper, 1976).

Lockhart, Robert B. *The Marines Were There* (W.H. Allen, 1950).

Lodwick, John *Raiders From the Sea* (Lionel Leventhal, 1990).

Lowry, Michael *Fighting Through to Kohima* (Leo Cooper, 2003).

Lunt, James *A Hell of a Licking: The Retreat from Burma 1941–2* (Collins, 1986).

Lyall, Grant *Burma: The Turning Point* (Zampi Press, 1993).

Mackenzie, Compton *Eastern Epic* (Chatto & Windus, 1951).

Mackenzie, Tony *Achnacarry to the Arakan* (Donovan Publishing, 1996).

Mason, Philip *A Matter of Honour: An Account of the Indian Army* (Cape, 1974).

Madan, N.N. *Arakan Operations 1942–45* (Combined Inter-services History, 1954).

Mains, Lt. Col. Tony *The Retreat From Burma* (Foulsham, 1973).

Masters, John *The Road Past Mandalay* (Michael Joseph, 1963).

McKelvie, Roy *The War in Burma* (Methuen, 1948).

Neville, Ralph *Survey by Starlight* (Hodder, 1949).

Parker, John *SBS: The Story of the Special Boat Service* (Headline, 1997).

Perret, Bryan *Tank Tracks to Rangoon* (Robert Hale, 1978).

Phillips, C.E. Lucas *The Cockleshell Heroes* (Heinemann, 1957).

–––––– *The Raiders of the Arakan* (Heinemann, 1971).

Prasad, B. *Arakan Operations 1942–1945* (Longmans, 1954).

Roskill, Captain S.W. *The War at Sea 1939–1945* (HMSO, 1960).

Shipster, John *Mist on the Rice-Fields* (Leo Cooper, 2000).

Slim, Field Marshal Sir William *Defeat into Victory* (Cassell, 1966).

Smith, D.E. *Battle for Burma* (Batsford, 1979).

Smurthwaite, David *The Forgotten War* (National Army Museum, 1992).

Southby-Tailyour, Ewen *Blondie* (Leo Cooper, 1998).

Swinson, Arthur *Kohima* (Cassell, 1966).

Thompson, Julian *War Behind Enemy Lines* (Sidgwick & Jackson, 1998).

–––––– *War in Burma 1942–1945* (Sidgwick & Jackson, 2002).

Vian, Admiral Sir Pilip *Action This Day* (Muller, 1960).

Welham, Michael *Combat Frogmen* (Patrick Stephenson, 1989).

Winton, John *The Forgotten Fleet* (Michael Joseph, 1969).

Woodburn, Kirby *The War Against Japan* (4 Volumes, HMSO, 1959–1965).

Wright, Bruce S. *The Frogmen of Burma* (William Kimber, 1968).

Young, Peter *Storm from the Sea* (William Kimber, 1956).

–––––– *Commando* (Macdonald, 1970).

Ziegler, Philip *Mountbatten: The Official Biography* (Collins, 1985).

ACKNOWLEDGEMENTS

I am sad to have to record that Les Gunn who was so influential and helpful in the writing of this book died after the manuscript was complete and before it could be published. He lived long enough to see an initial design for the cover which, I believe, gave him the satisfaction of knowing that the idea he had supported from its inception would finally become a reality. I hope the members of his family will enjoy the finished product. In expressing my gratitude for Les' contribution to the telling of the story of *The Banzai Hunters*, I must also acknowledge my debt to Richard Morris, my 'Man in Burma', my late friend Bill Lofts whose notes and photographs have proved invaluable and another friend, Chris Scott, who designed the map of Burma and was responsible for copying the photographs in the illustrated section. The pictures are all either from the Lofts Archive, my own resources including the now defunct *War Illustrated* and from Les Gunn's own collection.

My thanks are also extended to Commander D.J. Hastings, Lieutenant Commander Bruce Wright, Lieutenant H.D. Rowe, Louis Allen, O.A. Goulden, James Ladd, C.E. Lucas Philips, John Winton, Ewen Southby-Tailyour and Wilfred Helion. Among the many organisations that aided my search for information about the war in Burma, I must mention my local libraries in Hadleigh, Sudbury and Colchester, the British Museum, The British Newspaper Library at Colindale, The Imperial War Museum and the National Archives at Kew. I also received assistance from the Burma Star Association, the Royal Marines Record Office, Royal New Zealand Air Force Information Centre, the Royal Indian Navy, the US Division of Naval Intelligence and the Arakan Coastal Forces Committee.

The sources of my quotes are indicated in the text and I would like to thank the following newspapers and publishers for permission to quote from their publications: *The Times*, The *Daily Telegraph* and the *Times of India*, Leo Cooper/Pen & Sword Books Ltd, William Kimber, Gale & Polden, Random House Publishing Group, Michael Joseph, Cassell, Macdonald & Janes, William Heinemann Ltd,

Penguin Books, Sidgwick & Jackson, John Murray, Phoenix Press, Thomas Reed Publications, Greenhill Books and Her Majesty's Stationery Office. Finally, thanks to my publisher, Jeremy Robson, my editor, Barbara Phelan, Kate Burkhalter for copy-editing the manuscript and Clive Hebard for proofreading the pages. *The Banzai Hunters* has proved another fascinating episode of history deserving to be recorded for posterity.

INDEX